Beginning Amazon Web Services with Node.js

T0215443

Adam Shackelford

Apress®

Beginning Amazon Web Services with Node.js

ISBN-13 (pbk): 978-1-4842-0654-6

ISBN-13 (electronic): 978-1-4842-0653-9

Managing Director: Welmoed Spahr
Lead Editor: Louise Corrigan
Technical Reviewer: Jose Dieguez Castro
Editorial Board: Steve Anglin, Mark Beckner, Ewan Buckingham, Gary Cornell, Louise Corrigan,
    Jim DeWolf, Jonathan Gennick, Robert Hutchinson, Michelle Lowman, James Markham,
    Matthew Moodie, Jeff Olson, Jeffrey Pepper, Douglas Pundick, Ben Renow-Clarke,
    Dominic Shakeshaft, Gwenan Spearing, Matt Wade, Steve Weiss
Coordinating Editor: Christine Ricketts
Copy Editor: Michael G. Laraque
Compositor: SPi Global
Indexer: SPi Global
Artist: SPi Global

Distributed to the book trade worldwide by Springer Science+Business Media New York, 233 Spring Street, 6th Floor, New York, NY 10013. Phone 1-800-SPRINGER, fax (201) 348-4505, e-mail orders-ny@springer-sbm.com, or visit www.springeronline.com. Apress Media, LLC is a California LLC and the sole member (owner) is Springer Science+Business Media Finance Inc (SSBM Finance Inc). SSBM Finance Inc is a Delaware corporation.

For information on translations, please e-mail rights@apress.com, or visit www.apress.com.

Apress and friends of ED books may be purchased in bulk for academic, corporate, or promotional use. eBook versions and licenses are also available for most titles. For more information, reference our Special Bulk Sales–eBook Licensing web page at www.apress.com/bulk-sales.

Any source code or other supplementary material referenced by the author in this text is available to readers at www.apress.com. For detailed information about how to locate your book's source code, go to www.apress.com/source-code/.

For the Roarks.

Contents at a Glance

v

Contents

About the Author

Adam Shackelford is an AWS certified solutions architect who has been architecting and developing web and mobile applications for the past ten years. He is currently the chief technology officer and lead developer at Caravan Interactive, a technology company that he cofounded in Brooklyn in 2009. Prior to his tenure at Caravan, Adam worked for several agencies in New York City, developing web sites and web applications. He currently resides in the Hudson Valley area of New York.

About the Technical Reviewer

Jose Dieguez Castro is a senior system administrator currently employed as a freelance consultant. He has worked on a wide range of projects—from small to large infrastructures, from private to public sectors. When asked about his specialty, he replies, "Get the job done." Jose thinks of himself as a developer as well, who cares too much about software libre. Photography, sports, music, and reading are his ways of freeing his mind from work. He can be reached at jose@jdcastro.eu.

Acknowledgments

This is the hardest part of the book to write, because there are so many people who played such a big role in helping me complete this book. First, I'd like to thank Frank McDermott and Nicole Duquette for challenging me every day to do my best work.

I'd like to thank Joseph Silver, my longtime mentor and friend, who helped me start my career. Thanks to my family, friends, and colleagues whose support was indispensable, including Brendan Enright, Becky Laughner, Junior Tidal, John Salvato, and Lushi Li.

And, of course, I'd like to thank the excellent editorial team at Apress, especially Chris Nelson and Christine Ricketts.

Preface

As I began to write this book, I found myself uncertain as to what type of book it would turn out to be. Is it a programming book? Is it a software architecture book? Or is it a guide to managing a scalable infrastructure? In the end, it turned out to be all three of these things, in some part.

The role of developer is changing as we move our computing power to the cloud. Prior to working with services such as AWS, I was a developer, rather than a systems administrator, and this meant there was a steep learning curve as I architected and built my first applications in the cloud.

Without question, I have benefited from the wisdom and openness of the larger developer community. But there are so many disparate themes and problems to solve on this topic that I felt I could make a contribution by untangling its many threads and organizing them into a coherent lesson plan. With this book, I hope to help other developers find their footing, as they gear up for their own projects in the cloud.

Preface

CHAPTER 1

■ ■ ■

Getting Started with Amazon Web Services

Welcome to *Beginning Amazon Web Services with Node.js*! Over the course of this book, you will learn how to optimize your Node.js applications for deployment on Amazon Web Services (AWS). By using AWS to host your application, you take advantage of a series of features that are commonly known as "the cloud." You will learn about some of the core features of AWS, understand how to design your application stack, and integrate your application into the AWS environment. Though you could easily upload your code to a server and call it a day, learning how to incorporate the various features of AWS into your project will allow you to make full use of the benefits of the cloud. But what are these benefits?

Understanding the Cloud

First and foremost is *scalability*, or the ability to rapidly deploy additional resources to support your application. Prior to the proliferation of cloud-hosting providers such as AWS, if demand for your application outstripped your hardware resources, deploying additional servers was an expensive and laborious task and often out of the capabilities of startups and small or medium-sized businesses. With your application hosted on AWS, you can allocate resources on demand, launching new servers and keeping your application online. According to the AWS white paper "Architecting for the Cloud: Best Practices,"[1]

> *Traditionally, applications have been built for fixed, rigid, and pre-provisioned infrastructure. Companies never had the need to provision and install servers on [a] daily basis. As a result, most software architectures do not address the rapid deployment or reduction of hardware. Since the provisioning time and upfront investment for acquiring new resources was too high, software architects never invested time and resources in optimizing for hardware utilization. It was acceptable if the hardware on which the application is running was under-utilized. The notion of "elasticity" within an architecture was overlooked because the idea of having new resources in minutes was not possible.*

The ability to respond to demand for your application is known as *elasticity*. Being able to replace one server with 100 is useless if it's not a strategic action. When additional servers had to be manually booted and configured for deployment in response to demand, the cost of doing so led many

---

[1]Amazon Web Services, "Architecting for the Cloud: Best Practices," http://aws.amazon.com/es/whitepapers/architecting-for-the-aws-cloud-best-practices/, May 21, 2010.

businesses/institutions to instead over-allocate resources. Instead of spinning up additional servers for a spike in traffic, the extra servers would just be left running at all times and required concomitant maintenance. With the elasticity of AWS, spikes in traffic can be detected, and additional resources can be automatically deployed. When the demand returns to normal, the application can be scaled down automatically to a normal state. Use what you need, and pay for what you use—a simple concept that revolutionizes web application development. This saves time, money, energy, and reduces the barrier to entry for enterprise-level software.

As you can see, scalability and elasticity are great attributes to have in your application. These benefits also mean thinking differently about your role as software developer and architect. Shifting from developing in a fixed-hardware environment to a cloud-computing environment means that we are now cloud architects, in addition to software developers. This constitutes a major change in the way developers must think about web applications. For many of us, there will no longer be a system administrator or database administrator maintaining the infrastructure. (They work at Amazon, IBM, Google, Rackspace, etc., now.) Instead, virtual hardware management/cloud architecture is now in our domain. Not only do we think about our application in terms of best coding practices and organization, we have to think about how to leverage the vast resources available to us as developers. This means we have to become familiar with the features of AWS and understand how to design, configure, and maintain a virtual-hosting environment.

As you learn how to be a cloud architect, you will learn about a lot of great features specific to AWS, as well as the general philosophies of elasticity and scalability. The many features of AWS are organized into a series of overlapping services. Many of them have redundant features, allowing for some creativity in the decisions we make as we architect our system. All of these services run in virtualized-hardware environments located in Amazon's many data centers around the globe. We will explore some of these services in the chapters that follow.

You will be familiarizing yourself with the fundamentals of Amazon Web Services. I have discussed some of the general principles and advantages of using AWS. Later on, I will discuss some of the core services in greater detail and the different ways we can interact with them. Before we dive in, it is important to start on the same page.

The Approach in This Book

This book assumes that you are already at least a beginner Node.js developer, looking to expand your skill set to include architecting and developing a Node.js application with scalability and elasticity in mind. You should have a basic understanding of the main concepts in web-application development. You should know what a RESTful web service is, know your way around Git or SVN, and have a code editor handy.

Designing and developing the application is a creative process. This means that a number of highly subjective decisions have to be made. First and foremost, we will be using Amazon RDS (Relational Database Service) to host a MySQL database on AWS. Many Node.js developers prefer MongoDB to MySQL. That is perfectly fine! However, the sample application and subsequent instructions focus on MySQL, which suits the needs of our application. If you want to use this book to deploy an app using MongoDB, you will have to be capable of rewriting the database connections and queries accordingly. In either case, you will need elementary knowledge of the database language in question. This is just one of many creative decisions to be made along the way. You may disagree with some or require a different approach in your next project, but you will end up being better equipped to make these decisions in your next project, and you will be prepared to work with AWS services as a developer and architect.

To gain the benefits of cloud computing in our application, you will be learning about a variety of AWS services that can be integrated into our application. This integration will be carried out through two means: via configuration and customization of multiple services in the AWS Console and programmatically in our application code base with the AWS SDK. In this case, we will be using the JavaScript AWS SDK, which is intended for use in Node.js applications. However, there are SDKs for a variety of server-side languages, and many of the lessons of the book could even be useful to developers using different languages. Integrating AWS services into a PHP application with similar functionality would not be that different.

Virtually every task you can carry out in the AWS Management Console (AWS Console) could also be carried out programmatically, and vice versa. The AWS Console adds a lot of clarity to the process by providing access to hints and documentation and by providing visual reference for the otherwise abstract concepts. It can help a lot to use the console while you wrap your head around everything AWS can do. You might ask, "How do I know when to use the console and when to use the SDK?" Learning curve aside, this is a highly subjective topic. You may, in time, decide what rules are best for your workflow, but we can follow a few ground rules.

■ **Note**   There is also a third approach for interacting with AWS services: the AWS command-line interface (CLI). We will not use the CLI until the final chapter.

First, routine tasks should definitely be carried out in the SDK. If your app needs to store a daily log or report in an S3 bucket for storage, you probably want to accomplish that programmatically. Routine tasks involving file transfers are especially good candidates for the SDK. In the case of our application, images uploaded by the user will be stored in an S3 bucket for use in the application. When you learn how to do this, I will illustrate clearly why using the AWS Console would be a bad idea. For now, know that the SDK is a tremendous time-saving tool in this use case. The same goes for event-driven tasks, except where CloudWatch can detect them (such as a server going offline). For example, if your app has to generate e-mails when a user registers for your application, you want your code to trigger it instantly when it happens. We will explore these types of events in greater detail in Chapters 6 and 7.

There are many one-time tasks, however, that we will carry out on the AWS Console, for clarity's sake. It will be a lot easier to diagnose errors or avoid them altogether with the AWS Console's GUI than it would be to debug code that you only need to run once. For instance, while we could programmatically create an alarm to notify us when our app is slow to respond to requests, for clarity's sake, we will do so in the AWS Console instead. When you're learning, you can find yourself causing comically absurd bugs with the AWS SDK. *Oops, I didn't mean to create server instances on an infinite loop.* If you were feeling ambitious after finishing the lessons, you could probably script many of the AWS Console tasks in the book. I'll call that extra credit.

Before you are introduced to the AWS products we will be using, it is important to reiterate that there is more than one way to achieve the same goal with AWS. The scope of this book is limited to a set of products that work well together for achieving our goal of application scalability and elasticity with the feature set we need and a reasonable budget. However, many AWS services have some redundancy. For example, we will be using OpsWorks to manage our application stack, but it is not the only service for doing so. Many AWS developers prefer to use Elastic Beanstalk over OpsWorks, for the simplicity it offers, among other reasons. As time passes, AWS services have become more and more cohesive, so I hope learning how to use a handful of products will put you on the path to learn more, and with greater ease.

The use of EC2 instances is common to many AWS products. EC2, or Elastic Compute Cloud, is the brick and mortar of AWS. An *instance* is actually a virtual server running your choice of operating system and hosted in one of Amazon's many data centers. The instance is not fixed to a single piece of hardware; it is a software process that runs on one machine; and if that machine were to crash or break, the process would resume on another. In the worst-case scenario, the failure of hardware in an AWS data center will disrupt your application, but the redundancy built into the cloud will prevent your data from being lost. If your application is unresponsive, you can check the status of all AWS services at http://status.aws.amazon.com/.

When you create and run an EC2 instance, you are renting computing resources in one or more AWS data centers, which are organized by geographic region. The price of these resources is based on the power and number of hours of use. EC2 uses a tiered pricing structure, whereby EC2 hardware specs (clock speed, RAM, etc.) are named according to their relative size. When you create an instance, the resources are allocated to your instance, and your billing begins. It doesn't matter how much you actually use the resources you've rented. You are charged for your price tier. You could spend a lot of money reserving the largest instances available, but that would be a waste, just like the traditional deployment method described earlier. Instead, we will use other AWS services to scale our EC2 instances up and down, according to our needs, getting the most bang for the buck. Since we're now also cloud architects as well as developers, we're going to do our best to be stingy. Pay for what you use; use what you pay for.

While you could manually create and configure EC2 instances by hand, using a management tool such as OpsWorks streamlines the process significantly and can drastically reduce the risk of human error when setting up a complex system. We will be using OpsWorks to manage our application layers, deployment, and many other vital facets of the application. OpsWorks will be your main interface for configuring our project, and the first thing you will need to master. In Chapter 2, you will be introduced to the core features of OpsWorks and configure your application for deployment to EC2 instances. By the end of the chapter, your application will be deployed via OpsWorks to an EC2 instance.

In Chapter 3, you will be adding a scalable MySQL database to your application with Amazon RDS. You will also learn how to add additional server instances to your app and set up a load balancer to manage traffic. In Chapters 4 and 5, you will learn how to set up a CDN in CloudFront, as well as how to work with file transfers and caching. You will also learn about DNS configuration with Route 53. You will learn how to send e-mail with SES (Simple Email Service) from your application, in Chapter 6, and in Chapter 7, you will learn how to use CloudWatch to monitor your application. Finally, in Chapter 8, you will secure your application for your users by restricting critical API endpoints to HTTPS connections.

Though the application we're building is relatively simple, using cloud computing is not. In addition to knowledge of Node.js, there are a number of tools and services you will require to complete this book.

Requirements

You will, of course, need all the tools for Node.js and MySQL development: an IDE, local MySQL database, and Git or SVNclient (unless you prefer the command line). Additionally, you will need accounts with a domain registrar, SSL certificate provider, and, of course, AWS.

AWS Account

The first thing you will need is your own AWS account. You can create one by going to http://aws.amazon.com/ and clicking the **Sign Up** button. You will need to provide billing information to complete the registration process. You should complete this process now; there is no charge for an account with no services activated. As you proceed through the lessons and activate more services, you will start to accrue some expenditure. Once you have registered, you can review your expenditure at any time here: https://console.aws.amazon.com/billing/home (see Figure 1-1).

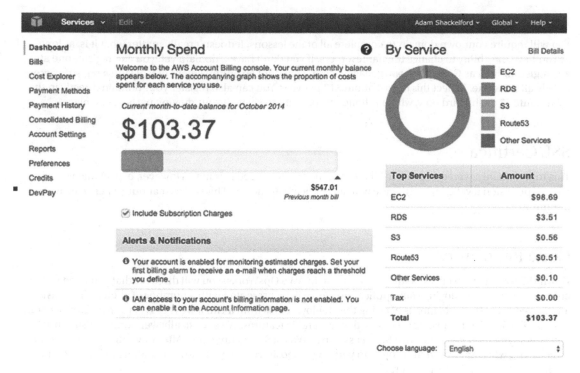

Figure 1-1. *The Billing and Cost Management dashboard*

In the preceding figure, you can see the main Billing and Cost Management dashboard (note that the entire screen is visible in this figure, which will not always be the case). Your current monthly bill is highlighted in a big, bold font, below which is a progress bar with a range of zero to your previous month's bill. This is to give you an informed projection of your monthly costs, though they will likely fluctuate, based on changes in usage. Don't let my bill scare you, though, there's a lot more than the sample app running on my account.

There is also a callout to enable Alerts & Notifications. You can configure AWS to alert you when certain cost metrics have been reached. The utility of this is self-explanatory. If only the electric company offered this feature!

To the right is a circle chart and breakdown of your bill by service. As you can see, EC2 is likely to be your biggest expense, followed by RDS or whatever database service you use. You can expect your database service bill to scale up with the volume of queries your application makes and, hence, with the size of your user base.

You only pay for what you use, but if you go overboard with power, you will feel it in your bank account. To complete the lessons in this book, you will undoubtedly incur a small cost. The exact cost will depend on how quickly you complete the book and whether you leave your application running 24/7 or not. There are a number of other reports and billing-related tools and options in here that are outside the scope of these lessons. We will return to the AWS Console later in the chapter, to begin configuring the account for use as a production environment.

■ **Tip** To save money, you can shut down many of your resources when you aren't working on the lessons.

Domain Registration

You will require your own domain to complete all of the lessons. It doesn't really matter what it is, as long as you have the ability to change the nameservers. If you don't have a domain yet, you can register one at any registrar, such as GoDaddy (`www.godaddy.com`). That's not an endorsement of GoDaddy; registrars are mostly all the same. Expect this to cost about $13 per year. You can also register your domain directly in the AWS Route 53 dashboard now, which is handy if you want to keep all your moving parts in one place.

SSL Certificate

This topic will be covered in detail in Chapter 8, so you don't need this now. However, expect that you will have to provision a valid SSL certificate with a Certificate Authority. This will cost about $9 per year, at a minimum.

Code Repository

Down the road, when you are setting up your app in AWS OpsWorks, you will discover that you need to choose a means of deploying your application. You will be presented with a number of choices. The easiest and arguably most secure means of doing this deployment is from a GitHub (`https://github.com`) account, or another Git account-hosting service with comparable features. We specifically want one that supports auto-deployment or can otherwise be accessed by AWS via SSH connection. After downloading the sample project, you will want to add the project to your own repository, in which you can alter it as you see fit and configure your own deployment process.

Download the Sample Project

You will not begin the coding lessons by duplicating lengthy, step-by-step code samples. Instead, you can begin by downloading the sample project here: (`www.apress.com/9781484206546`). We will then review the prepackaged code and make iterative changes throughout the lessons that follow. Before you do this, make sure you have the latest version of Node.js installed (or at least version 0.10.26). Download a zip of the sample project, or pull the branch to your machine, and open the directory in a code editor.

Local Environment

You should already have Node.js installed locally on your machine and be capable of running it in the command-line interface. In the beginning, you will also need a local MySQL database. The easiest way to set one up is with MAMP (`www.mamp.info/en/`) or XAMPP (`www.apachefriends.org/index.html`). I will just assume that you can get this installed on your own without step-by-step instructions (hint: go to the web site and click **Download**). Unlike PHP, you won't need MAMP/XAMPP to run your app, but it's the easiest way to get a local MySQL database set up and accessible. You will also want to have MySQL Workbench (`www.mysql.com/products/workbench/`) installed, but I will discuss this in further detail down the road.

The front end of our application is a RESTful JSON API, intended for consumption by a web or mobile client. We will be interacting with the API throughout the lessons, but we won't have a client yet. Because we will be making both `GET` and `POST` HTTP requests to the API, you will need more than just a web browser to properly test the application during development. Fortunately, there are many REST clients available on all operating systems, making it easier to interface with an API such as ours. There is an excellent Google Chrome extension called Advanced Rest Client, which should do the job nicely. You can find it at `https://chrome.google.com/webstore/detail/advanced-rest-client/hgmloofddffdnphfgcellkdfbfbjeloo`.

ExpressJS

You will want to be familiar with ExpressJS, a popular (perhaps *the* most popular) web application framework for Node.js. Using ExpressJS will do a lot of the heavy lifting of routing and parsing HTTP requests and simplify the process of sending a response via templating engine, raw text/HTML, or JSON. Additionally, ExpressJS accepts a few handy global configurations and allows you to create or install middleware. This allows you to pass all HTTP requests made to your server through common functions, which makes it easy to integrate such features as authentication, field validation, and error handling.

The sample project is optimized for Express 4, the latest major release. If you are more familiar with Express 2 or Express 3, there are significant changes in this version. You should review `http://expressjs.com/guide/migrating-4.html` to get up to speed.

Now let's get you familiarized with the sample project. Some basic functionality for a simple RESTful web service has already been created for you. Keep in mind that the goal of this book is not to teach you how to code, nor is the functionality intended to be groundbreaking. By learning with a simple app, you will, I hope, develop a vision of how to integrate AWS into your own work.

Sample Project

Though this is not technically a Node.js guide, we will use a sample project to contextualize the lessons in this book. The sample project will provide a real-world app to develop, while we work with AWS. In the beginning, we will be starting with a bare-bones application—it needs a lot of work before it's ready for use in the field. We'll be doing some of that work throughout the book.

Overview

The sample project is the code base for a very simple photo-based social media app. The functionality is minimal: users can register for an account and log in. They can create album objects, which consist of a title and a collection of photo objects. Users can upload photos with captions to the albums, one at a time (but we aren't storing and serving the files yet). Users can see a list of all other users and get all albums for specific users. Users interact with the app through a JSON-formatted RESTful API, and records are stored in a MySQL database.

As we progress through the lessons, we will be adding more functionality to the app. It will use a proper secure user-authentication scheme. Users will receive welcome e-mails when they register their account. We will store image files in a CDN, for easy and fast storage. Application logs will be generated and stored in AWS, and it will make use of a range of AWS services.

The use cases for an application such as this are many. Countless platforms, from social networks to newsreader apps, possess similar functionality at their core. With a little work, you could add the notion of *friending* or *following,* by creating a relationship among users, and the means for the user to create and delete them. You could add tagging, geolocation data, and comments to the photos.

Our application output is in JSON, but web templates could easily be generated by the application as well. Keep in mind that, although the app is simple at this point, it will become more complicated very quickly. The purpose of the sample project is not to dazzle you with Node.js coding skills but to provide a simple, clear code base that's easy to follow and could be expanded into a more sophisticated application.

■ **Note**   Much of the organization of the project was created using the `express` command, which auto-generates your project. If you start your own project after the lessons, it will be easy to re-create the project's organization.

Source Code Organization

Let's start by opening the project in a code editor and taking a look at the contents. You should see the following in the project directory:

```
/lib
/public
/routes
/setup
/views
server.js
package.json
```

Open `package.json` in your code editor. You will see some information and config options for the project, in JSON format. You will see the *dependencies* property, which looks something like this:

```
"dependencies": {
    "express": "~4.8.6",
    "body-parser": "~1.6.6",
    "cookie-parser": "~1.3.2",
    "morgan": "~1.2.3",
    "serve-favicon": "~2.0.1",
    "debug": "~1.0.4",
    "jade": "~1.5.0",
    ... // additional dependencies truncated
}
```

These are the other npm modules required to run the app. Many of them are automatically added to the list of dependencies when you use the ExpressJS app generator command. You will have to install these locally to run the app locally. Open your command-line interface (e.g., Terminal in OS X), and navigate to this directory. Type the following on the command line:

npm install

This command will look for a `package.json` file in the same directory and attempt to install all the modules in the dependencies attribute. You should see all the packages download and install over the course of a few minutes.

Let's run through a few of the other files and directories in the project. Overall, this project is structured to follow the Model View Controller (MVC) design pattern. If you don't know what this is, it's simply a way of organizing your code base into a logical separation between three types of classes. In MVC, the three types are the *model*, or object definition and manipulation; the *view*, or output of the app; and the *controller*, which contains all the logic determining what information is sent to/retrieved from the model, based on input to the application. This is, of course, a simplification of the concept, but it should give you an idea of how it all works as we walk through it.

First, we'll explore the `lib` directory, which contains `globals.js` and `/model`. True to what was described previously, the `model` directory contains all the class definitions for the various objects we'll be working with. Because the application output will primarily be JSON, or templates populated by that JSON, the models themselves will be much more abstract than if you were working with PHP, for example, where you might design a class that you use to instantiate objects with properties retrieved from a database.

The files in the `model` directory primarily receive commands to interact with the database from the controllers and send abstract objects back to the controllers in response. As such, the properties of the objects in the sample application are created on the fly. With an application of this nature, the life span of objects is so short that using a flexible data model often makes sense. If you wanted, you could create your own classes, instantiate them, and populate them, instead of following the approach in the sample project. You would not be wrong to do so, if it helps you to maintain your code base more efficiently.

The controllers for the MVC pattern are in the /routes directory. Each file corresponds to a directory path in a user's request (e.g., /**photos**/1 or /**users**/adam) and processes all requests to URLs within that path. It will retrieve whatever data it needs from the corresponding model and send a response.

So where is the view? In cases where the response is JSON, the view is the JSON data itself. However, as an ExpressJS4 app, the *jade* templating engine (http://jade-lang.com/) is natively supported. If you were to develop web templates, those files would be located in the /views directory. When thinking about MVC, in this case, the view is not always going to be accessible in a template file. The view is always going to be an HTTP response, whether the content type is text/html or application/json.

Moving on, the public directory stores all the static assets, such as style sheets, images, and JavaScript files used by the front-end templates. This directory was auto-generated by ExpressJS. In Chapter 4, you will learn how to more efficiently serve these files to the users, with AWS CloudFront.

You have already learned about server.js. If you look in this file, you will see how the request routes are mapped to files in the /routes directory. You will also see a bunch of middleware and ExpressJS configuration in here. For now, these aren't too important.

You should also be aware of /lib/globals.js. This file is simply a convenient place to store global configurations and commonly used values for easy reference, without polluting the global namespace. Developers have a variety of different ideas about how to approach this type of feature in their code, so this is merely one approach of many.

The sample project also includes a file called /setup/photoalbums.sql. This is the database schema that you can import to your local MySQL database. You will want to import it into a local database called *photoalbums*, if you intend to test the sample app in your local environment. You will also need to import this file into your Amazon RDS database at a later point.

Configuration and Startup

You can start the app in one of two ways:

- Typing **node app.js** on the command line

- Typing **npm start** on the command line

If the app compiled successfully, you should be able to view the welcome page at http://localhost:8081 (assuming you used port 8081). If not, you should see an error on the command-line interface. If so, most likely, one of your dependencies didn't install correctly. If that's the case, try running npm install again.

Another possible error is that port 8081 is not available on your machine. When we deploy our app to the cloud, we will be using port 80. If you have to change this, open /lib/globals and change the applicationPort property to a different value, such as 8081. If your app is trying to open a port that is not available, the error will look something like this:

```
events.js:72
        throw er; // Unhandled 'error' event
           ^
Error: listen EACCES
    at errnoException (net.js:904:11)
    at Server._listen2 (net.js:1023:19)
    at listen (net.js:1064:10)
    at Server.listen (net.js:1138:5)
```

If none of these suggestions resolves your issue, you will have to read the error in your command-line interface and attempt to resolve it on your own. Just a reminder: Anytime you make changes in your code, you will have to recompile your app. If you're used to working in PHP or front-end JavaScript and refreshing your browser to test a fix, it can take some time to get into the habit of recompiling your app routinely.

Working with the Sample App

Congratulations on getting the sample app to run properly. You shouldn't need to do any further configuration on your machine, aside from installing a few more npm packages. From here on out, the sample project source code is yours! You should check it into a repository now, so you have a good snapshot to return to if you get lost.

Throughout the rest of the lessons, we will be jumping back and forth between the source code, the command-line interface, and the AWS Console in your browser. Let's dive further into the sample code, to get a better idea of how it works. First, let's look at server.js. At the beginning of the file, you'll see all the included npm modules. Beginning at line 8, you will see all the source files we've added to the project:

```
var routes = require('./routes/index');
var users = require('./routes/users');
var photos = require('./routes/photos');
var albums = require('./routes/albums');
var globals = require('./lib/globals');
```

Farther down, around line 27, you'll see where these are used:

```
app.use('/', routes);
app.use('/users', users);
app.use('/photos', photos);
app.use('/album', albums);
```

We will now explore the functionality in each of the different routes we have registered in the application.

Home Route

The first line directs HTTP requests to the root path of our application to the file at /routes/index.js. We can make a quick stop here, as this route is only used to show a welcome page, so you know the app is running properly. At the top of the file you will see

```
var express = require('express');
var router = express.Router();
```

The way we are structuring our app, we need to include express and express.Router() in each controller (route), in order to interact with HTTP requests sent to said controller. This means that each of these router files will have variables named express and router instantiated at the top.

■ **Note**   It's entirely possible to organize your code in a way that your controllers don't have to require express, but we are following the ExpressJS template on this one.

There is only one route registered in `index.js`:

```
/* GET home page. */
router.get('/', function(req, res) {
  res.render('index', { title: 'Photoalbums' });
});
```

As you can see, we aren't doing anything with the request but sending a response. There is no reading of parameters, no interaction with the model, etc. We simply respond with the index template from the `views` folder, and the title 'Photoalbums'. The rest of our app is responding with JSON, but for this landing page, we're using an HTML response generated with a jade template. I won't cover this in much detail. The important thing to know is that you can send all sorts of different response types with an ExpressJS response object. More information is available here: `http://expressjs.com/4x/api.html#response`.

Requests to `/users/` are routed to `/routes/users.js`, and so forth. All routes, or controller files, have to be registered in `server.js` in order to be implemented in our application. All of the controllers are designed the same way, so we'll start with users as a good example of how everything works together. In `server.js`, we look at the line

```
app.use('/users', users);
```

and know to follow the request to `/routes/users.js` to see what happens.

Users Route

For now, we only have skeleton functionality. The app has just enough features for basic interaction. As we progress through the lessons, users will become more robust than they are currently. The out-of-the-box functionality for users includes

- Register account (`POST /users/register`)
  - params: `username`, `email`, `password`
- Login to account (`POST /users/login`)
  - params: `username`, `password`
- Logout of account (`POST /users/logout`)
- View all users (`GET /users/`)
- View all photo albums by user (`GET /users/user/:user`)
  - params: `user`

Once again, this sample code is only intended to get you started. With a little effort, you could add as much functionality to user accounts as you want. You could add additional fields to the user database table, such as a profile image, bio, or user web site. Then, you could add an update method, allowing the user to first register an account and then submit an update to complete his/her profile. You could require users to confirm their names after they register. You could allow them to reset their usernames or passwords. With that in mind, let's take a look at the code. At the top of the file, you'll see a different set of included files, as follows:

```
var express = require('express');
var router = express.Router();
var model = require('./../lib/model/model-users');
```

11

Because we're in the users controller, we know we will want to access the users model frequently. We will go ahead and include the users model file here. In fact, you can expect every controller to include its model at the top. However, some routes will require more than one model class to be included, especially as the functionality becomes more robust. For the sake of consistency, we can name the default model variable model, and any additional models modelPhoto or modelAlbum, etc. What if we only have to access another model once? We will determine the variable scope for any additional models on a case-by-case basis.

Let's take a look at a typical router method in the users controller.

```
/* GET users listing. */
router.get('/', function(req, res) {
  model.getAllUsers(function(err, obj){
    if(err){
      res.status(500).send({error: 'An unknown server error has occurred!'});
    } else {
      res.send(obj);
    }
  });
});
```

The preceding code is the typical way we will route and process HTTP requests in an ExpressJS controller class. You can see from the first line that GET requests to the /users/ path will be processed here. If there were any parameters to validate, we would do so at the beginning of the method. However, this is simply a means of retrieving a list of all users; there is no user input. As the app user base grows, we might want to allow users to pass parameters with this request, to support a paginated list of all users. For now, we can keep it simple and ignore any user input.

We immediately retrieve the data from the model with model.getAllUsers(). There are no parameters being passed to the model in this case. When we receive a message back from the model object, we check whether it is an error object or data that we want to use.

In some cases, we will want to send the model object's error back to the user. This would look something like the following:

```
model.getAllUsers(function(err, obj){
  if(err){
    res.send(err);
  }
});
```

However, we are going to refrain from doing that most of the time. Some of the errors returned from the model are probably going to be MySQL database query errors. It would not be a good security practice to expose information about the database tables to the user, nor is MySQL error information likely to be very useful to any of our end users. It would be more appropriate for the controller to check the error received from the model and send a suitable message to the client making the request to our API. Next, let's take a look at the model to see what getAllUsers does.

As with the routes file, let's start at the top.

```
var mysql = require('mysql');
var globals = require('./../globals');
var connection = mysql.createConnection(globals.database);
```

The mysql module is, of course, required in all model classes. We will use this module for connecting to the database and executing all queries.

■ **Note**   Full documentation for the `mysql` module is available at `https://github.com/felixge/node-mysql`.

As mentioned previously, `globals` is an object that stores common variables without polluting the global namespace and is used here for convenience. The MySQL database connection is initialized as `connection`, using the database configuration stored in `globals`. Let's look at the first method, which we already know about, `getAllUsers()`.

```
function getAllUsers(callback){
  connection.query('SELECT username, userID FROM users', function(err, rows, fields){
    if(err){
      callback(err);
    } else {
      callback(null, rows);
    }
  });
}
```

This method is about as simple as a model-getter function can get. There are no parameters to validate, no user input to escape, nor any other intermediary functions. We simply retrieve all users from the database and return them to the callback function in `routes/user`. For a moment, let's scroll to the very bottom of the file and note exports assignments.

```
exports.getAllUsers = getAllUsers;
exports.getUser = getUser;
exports.createUser = createUser;
exports.loginUser = loginUser;
exports.logoutUser = logoutUser;
```

These lines are very important, as they are the means by which you make a method in this file public; otherwise, all methods are private or inaccessible to other objects. If you build additional functionality with this sample application, it's easy to forget this step.

Review—The Order of Things

Returning to `/routes/user` for a moment, you should see now how a request is handled. Here's a quick recap of how a client would retrieve a list of users from our app:

1.   `server.js` is listening for all HTTP requests at the designated port.

2.   The client makes an HTTP GET request to `/users/`.

3.   `Server.js` forwards the request to the controller at `/routes/users`.

4.   The controller at `/routes/users` notes that the request is for "/" relative to "/users" and passes the request to the corresponding listener method.

5.   The GET "/" listener in the controller calls `model.getAllUsers()`.

6. The model method getAllUsers() queries the database, processes the results, and returns the data set to the controller.

7. The controller populates the response object with data.

8. server.js sends an HTTP response with the data requested by the user.

Does that all make sense? If you're already familiar with ExpressJS, it probably didn't tell you anything new. If you're learning about this for the first time, don't worry; we will be spending a lot of time with these concepts in further lessons. And the best way to learn is to try writing your own routes and seeing what it takes to make them function. Never underestimate the power of trial and error!

Example—Working with Parameters

Let's return to /routes/users to look at another concept. So far, we've looked at handling a basic request without any parameters or client input. When you have no variables involved, there is a very small likelihood of failure. Once we start accepting specific requests from the client, the points of failure start to add up quickly. We can look at the /users/login route as an example.

```
/* POST user login. */
router.post('/login', function(req, res) {
  if(req.param('username') && req.param('password') ){
    var params = {
      username: req.param('username').toLowerCase(),
      password: req.param('password')
    };

    model.loginUser(params, function(err, obj){
      if(err){
        res.status(400).send({error: 'Invalid login'});
      } else {
        res.send(obj);
      }
    });
  } else {
    res.status(400).send({error: 'Invalid login'});
  }
});
```

This route accepts HTTP POST requests and expects that the client has sent both a username and password. However, we cannot assume that both parameters were included. As such, we have to check that the parameters exist before we try to use them. If the parameters have been included, we proceed. If not, an *invalid login* error is sent in response to the request.

We can use the controller both to validate input and to format parameters to pass to the model. In this case, before we send the user's login credentials to the model, we also want to enforce one rule: usernames should be case insensitive. The params object is instantiated with the request parameters, and the username is converted to lowercase when params.username is set. We can then look at the model, to see what happens next.

```
function loginUser(params, callback){
  connection.query('SELECT username, password, userID FROM users WHERE username=' +
connection.escape(params.username), function(err, rows, fields) {
    if(err){
      callback(err);
    } else if(rows.length > 0){
        var response = {
          username: rows[0].username,
          userID: rows[0].userID
        }
        callback(null, response);
      } else {
        var error = new Error("Invalid login");
        callback(error);
      }
  });
}
```

For now, we're selecting the user from the database, if the username is valid. In the future, we will be decrypting the user's password to authenticate the user. Currently, we are automatically returning a success response, which includes the username and user ID of the authenticated user. The important lesson here is that the controller is used to sanitize and validate client input before sending it to the model. It is a good idea to separate concerns and encapsulate functionality in this way. The model will expect an object with the necessary properties to be sent to its methods, and the controller is responsible for constructing that object or rejecting malformed requests. If you follow this pattern, you will be able to safely reuse the public methods in your model classes in different scenarios, and your app will be much easier to maintain and debug in the long run.

Try It Out

It's time to fire up the app and see it in action. If the app isn't running, open your command-line interface, navigate to the app directory, and type node server.js. Open your REST client, and enter the following URL:

http://localhost:8081/users/register

If you're running the app on a different port, remember to replace 8081. Set your HTTP method to POST. Add POST parameters named username, password, and email. You can enter whatever values you want into those parameters. Send the request!

You should receive the following success message:

```
{
  "message": "Registration successful!"
}
```

Next, you should be able to log in with the username you just registered. Remove the email parameter and change the URL to

http://localhost:8081/users/login

You should receive the following username and user ID in response:

```
{
  "username": "adam",
  "userID": 1
}
```

You can now make a GET request in the browser to `http://localhost:8081/users/`. You should see the user you created in the response. You can create additional users, and they will appear in this response as well. From here, you can use the user ID from the login response to create albums and photos for your user. I will discuss these in more detail soon. For now, let's make a quick GET request to the user detail API endpoint at `/users/user/:user`, replacing `:user` with the username you just registered. You should see something similar to the following response:

```
{
  "username":"adam",
  "userID":1,
  "albums":[]
}
```

For now, there's not much new information here. But once you start creating albums for this user, you will get information about them here. Let's take a look at albums next.

Albums

Each user can have an unlimited number of albums. The album object is very simple, consisting of a title and user ID. Any number of photos can also be associated with the album.

Albums have the following functionality:

- Create a new album (`POST /albums/upload`)
  - params: `userID`, `title`
- Gets an album by ID, including all photos included in it (`GET /albums/id/:albumID`)
  - params: `albumID`
- Delete an album (`POST /albums/delete`)
  - params: `albumID`

Let's open `/routes/albums.js` and take a closer look. The variables declared at the top should already be familiar. In this case, you can see that the `model` variable is set to `/lib/model/model-albums.js`. The first route will allow us to create an album. Using the user ID you received when you registered, point your RESTful client to `http://localhost:8081/albums/upload`, set the method to `POST`, and add fields for the user ID and title. You can put whatever name you want in the title. We'll go with "Hello World" for now. You should receive the following response:

```
{
"id":7,
"title":"Hello World"
}
```

In /routes/albums.js, find the route:

```
/* POST create album. */
router.post('/upload', function(req, res) {
  if(req.param('title') && req.param('userID')){
    var params = {
      userID : req.param('userID'),
      title : req.param('title')
    }
    model.createAlbum(params, function(err, obj){
      if(err){
        res.status(400).send({error: 'Invalid album data'});
      } else {
        res.send(obj);
      }
    });
  } else {
    res.status(400).send({error: 'Invalid album data'});
  }
});
```

First, the required parameters are validated, and an object named params is constructed with the parameters we passed to it. While you could pass the request parameters directly to the model, using an intermediary variable is a good habit, largely for readability. Let's go to the model file at /lib/model/model-albums.js to see what happens in createAlbum().

```
function createAlbum(params, callback){
  var query = 'INSERT INTO albums SET ? ';
  connection.query(query, params, function(err, rows, fields){
    if(err){
      callback(err);
    } else {
      var response = {
        id : rows.insertId,
        title : params.title
      };
      callback(null, response);
    }
  });
}
```

All the parameters we passed here are inserted into a new row in the albums table. We then create a response object with the auto-incremented ID and the title. Note that the ID is accessible as rows.insertId. When creating a row in the MySQL database, the rows parameter is a single object. You'll find slightly different behavior for SELECT queries.

The next route allows you to get an album by ID.

```
/* GET album by ID */
router.get('/id/:albumID', function(req, res) {
  if(req.param('albumID')){
    var params = {
      albumID : req.param('albumID')
    }
```

17

```
    model.getAlbumByID(params, function(err, obj){
      if(err){
        res.status(400).send({error: 'Invalid album ID'});
      } else {
        res.send(obj);
      }
    });
  } else {
    res.status(400).send({error: 'Invalid album ID'});
  }
});
```

This is pretty straightforward. If the album ID is included in the request, the controller will retrieve the album from the model and send the album data as a response. You can use the album ID from the album you just created. Now, head over to /lib/model/model-albums.js and find the getAlbumByID() method.

```
function getAlbumByID(params, callback){
  var query = 'SELECT * FROM albums WHERE albumID=' + connection.escape(params.albumID);
  connection.query(query, function(err, rows, fields){
    if(rows.length > 0){
      getPhotosForAlbum(rows[0], function(err, obj){
        if(err){
          callback(err);
        } else {
          callback(null, obj);
        }
      });
    } else {
      callback(null, []);
    }
  });
}
```

First, the album and all its fields are retrieved from the database. In all database queries, rows is an object populated from the database query. In the case of a SELECT query, rows is always an array. If you found what you were looking for, rows will have a length of 1 or more. In this case, we're selecting a single row by its unique identifier, albumID. But this time, we don't stop here and return the data we found. Instead, we call getPhotosForAlbum() and pass our results to it, then finally send the data back to the controller. Scroll down to getPhotosForAlbum() to see what happens there.

```
function getPhotosForAlbum(album, callback){
  var modelPhotos = require('./model-photos');
  modelPhotos.getPhotosByAlbumID(album, function(err, obj){
    if(err){
      callback(err);
    } else {
      album.photos = obj;
      callback(null, album);
    }
  });
}
```

If we're sending a single album by ID, it seems reasonable for the end user to expect that we would provide all of the data associated with that album. In this case, we need to get all the photos associated with the album.

■ **Note** We know the client has the user's information, because that's how he/she retrieved the album ID. In a more full-featured application, you might want to include some user information in this response as well.

First, we instantiate a reference to the *photos* model at /lib/model/model-photos.js. We give the album a photos property, set to the array of photos (even if it's empty) we retrieved from the *photos* model. Navigate to /lib/model/model-photos.js and find getPhotosByAlbumID() to finish the route.

```
function getPhotosByAlbumID(params, callback){
  var query = 'SELECT * FROM photos WHERE published=1 AND albumID=' + connection.
escape(params.albumID);
  connection.query(query, function(err, rows, fields){
    if(err){
      callback(err);
    } else {
      if(rows.length > 0){
        callback(null, rows);
      } else {
        callback(null, []);
      }
    }
  });
}
```

This method simply retrieves all photos with the album ID we passed to it. Note that the photos must have the value published set to 1. For both albums and photos, we will use published=1 to mean the object is available for public consumption and published=0 to mean the object is hidden. This allows us to provide delete functionality without actually destroying the data in our database. We can look at deletion next, starting in /routes/album.js.

```
/* POST delete album. */
router.post('/delete', function(req, res) {
  if(req.param('albumID')){
    var params = {
      albumID : req.param('albumID')
    }
    model.deleteAlbum(params, function(err, obj){
      if(err){
        res.status(400).send({error: 'Album not found'});
      } else {
        res.send(obj);
      }
    });
  } else {
    res.status(400).send({error: 'Invalid album ID'});
  }
});
```

By now, you've seen this pattern many times. So, we will advance to `model.deleteAlbum()` immediately.

```
function deleteAlbum(params, callback){
  var query = 'UPDATE albums SET published=0 WHERE albumID=' +
  connection.escape(params.albumID);
  connection.query(query, function(err, rows, fields){
    if(err){
      callback(err);
    } else {
      callback(null, {message: 'Album deleted successfully'});
    }
  });
}
```

As you can see, we are not actually deleting the album. We are unpublishing it, which means it's invisible to all users. This is a good way to prevent permanent accidental deletion by users, and it reduces the risk of malicious use of our application. If someone's password was stolen or cracked and all his content deleted, we could restore it without too much trouble. Note also that our callback does not return any data, simply a message confirming that the deletion was successful. Our app is very simple, and there's currently no expectation as to what the user sees after he's deleted something. This is OK for now, but in your own app, you might consider what sort of response your users will expect. Lastly, we will review photos.

Photos

Photos are the objects for individual photo/image uploads. Currently, the photo objects used in the app do not include actual files. A photo object is little more than an ID and a caption at this point. File uploads and URL generation are features we will be tailoring specifically to AWS. We will be building this functionality in later lessons.

Photos have the following functionality:

- Create a new photo (`POST /photos/upload`)
  - params: `albumID`, `caption`, `userID`
- Get a photo by ID (`GET /photos/id/:id`)
  - params: `id`
- Delete a photo (`POST /photos/delete`)
  - params: `id`

You'll notice that these methods are virtually identical to those of albums. Let's review a few points about photos, starting by uploading a "photo." You should have an album ID and user ID from the previous API queries you've made. (We'll assume both are equal to 1.) Let's go ahead and create a new photo object, using those IDs as parameters. In your REST client, make a `POST` request to `http://localhost:8081/photos/upload` with the following params:

```
userID: 1
albumID: 1
caption: "My First Photo"
```

The response simply contains the ID of the photo you just created.

```
{
  "id": 5
}
```

Take a look at the method you just queried, in /routes/photos.

```
/* POST create photo. */
router.post('/upload', function(req, res) {
  if(req.param('albumID') && req.param('userID')){
    var params = {
      userID  : req.param('userID'),
      albumID : req.param('albumID')
    }
    if(req.param('caption')){
      params.caption = req.param('caption');
    }

    model.createPhoto(params, function(err, obj){
      if(err){
          res.status(400).send({error: 'Invalid photo data'});
      } else {
        res.send(obj);
      }
    });
  } else {
    res.status(400).send({error: 'Invalid photo data'});
  }
});
```

One difference worth noting is that the caption parameter is optional. If the caption is present, we're including it in the parameter object that gets passed to model.createPhoto(). This shows the value of constructing an intermediary object and not just passing request parameters directly to the model. If an optional field is omitted from the request, we simply let the database apply the default value. Go ahead and make another request to /photos/upload and remove the caption parameter. You should receive the same response from the API.

Now let's take a moment to check our album, to make sure our photos are there. Make a GET request to http://localhost:8081/albums/id/1. Note that the photo without a caption has an empty string for a caption. The response should look something like this:

```
{
  "albumID":1,
  "userID":1,
  "title":"Hello World",
  "photos":[
    {
      "photoID":4,
      "userID":1,
      "albumID":1,
      "caption":"My First Photo"
    },{
```

```
        "photoID":5,
        "userID":1,
        "albumID":1,
        "caption":""
    }
  ]
}
```

Take another moment to browse through the rest of the code for the photos route and model. There shouldn't be any surprises.

Developing with the Sample App

You've seen by now that the sample app has only basic functionality. If you're an experienced MySQL developer, you will have noticed by now that there are no association tables, which constrains our ability to make many-to-many relationships between objects. For the sake of providing simple examples, this functionality has been omitted. Other more essential features—uploading files, authentication, etc.—are incomplete. You will be fleshing out these features as you learn more about working with AWS. As you work through the lessons with the sample app, keep in mind that our goal is to develop an app that utilizes AWS services. There are plenty of other books that teach the finer points of RESTful web services, Node.js, and MySQL. With that in mind, let's begin!

The next step is going to be our first task in AWS. You should have already registered for an AWS account while following the previous steps. The first thing we will do in the AWS Console is learn how to use IAM (Identity and Access Management) to manage permissions and security within the application infrastructure. IAM is Amazon's solution to the problem of needing to manage a variety of permissions. When managing permissions, we aren't just talking about giving other users access to our AWS infrastructure, but access among AWS services as well. For example, you may have an EC2 instance that you want to be able to connect to your RDS database, but you don't want it to have permission to access send commands to OpsWorks.

It would be bad practice to be too generous with security credentials. Imagine for a moment that you were administrating a news web site. You would want to provide different rights for different types of users. Readers would only be allowed to read articles and post comments. Editors would be allowed to post and edit articles and delete user comments. Administrators would be able to ban users, create new editors, and perform site-level administrative tasks. You would not want to give all of your users admin privileges and trust that they behave accordingly. Even just making your editors administrators, you could wake up one day and find that your own admin powers have been taken away.

We will manage our AWS infrastructure with the same caution. Users in the AWS Console should only have the rights that they require to do their job. Similarly, every server instance has a role to play and should be limited to that role only. When you have a good grasp on IAM, you can deploy your application without having to store passwords in configuration files waiting to be hacked.

Identity and Access Management

There are a lot of challenges to managing rights and credentials in an application of this type.

First, we only want a select group of users to have administrative access to our infrastructure. Only certain team members should be able to reboot a server, for example. Perhaps a different set of users should have administrative access to the mail server, and a different set of users should have access to the database administration.

Then there is the issue of managing security for each individual server. Organizing and restricting access to the security keys for a series of servers is an art in itself. Typically, we would also have to include database access credentials in the source code for our application. Not only would we have to worry about restricting access to the source code where credentials are stored, we would also have to make certain that development environment credentials didn't accidentally get deployed to production, and vice versa.

On top of all of these concerns, we have the problem of staff turnover. Engineers and administrators quit their jobs or are fired, and we have to review all of our security, to make sure they don't have access to anything sensitive. If someone with lots of security access quits unexpectedly, we are left scrambling to lock down all of our credentials. Security breaches, though they may be brief, are guaranteed. Every time we have to reset credentials, all the risks of misconfiguring something are reintroduced into the system. It should be clear by now that even with an application as simple as ours, there are many points of failure and great risks of human error in controlling internal security.

AWS solves these problems by unifying all user security, database and server security, and API access into a single system called Identity and Access Management (IAM). For now, we're going to assume that there are no other AWS users whom we need to be concerned about. However, we do want to be certain that the EC2 instances we create in OpsWorks will be able to interact with other AWS services properly.

The IAM Dashboard

Let's log in to the AWS Console and navigate to IAM. When you log in successfully to AWS, you are presented with a three-column list of AWS products. You'll find IAM listed under the *Deployment and Management* header in the second column. Click it, and you should see something like Figure 1-2 (some user interface elements have been cropped out for clarity).

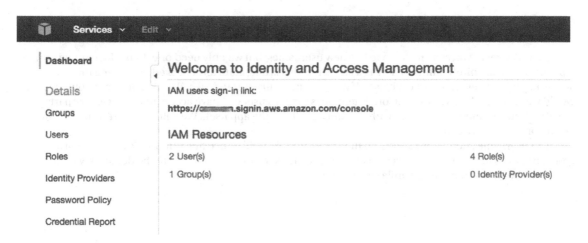

Figure 1-2. *IAM dashboard*

On the left-hand side of the IAM dashboard, you will find the navigation for IAM (this is a standard interface paradigm for the AWS Console). On the right side, you will see a list of all IAM resources you have already created. There are a number of other tutorial and advisory UI elements on the page. Feel free to explore these at your leisure, to familiarize yourself with the dashboard. As your first official task in AWS, you'll have to create a user in IAM.

IAM Users

User is an administrative account, which has a login (username/password) as well as other security credentials, if needed. For now, let's create a single user account to administrate our application. Select the **Users** link in the navigation, and you should see an empty table view. Click the **Create New Users** button at the top of the page. This will take you to the screen shown in Figure 1-3.

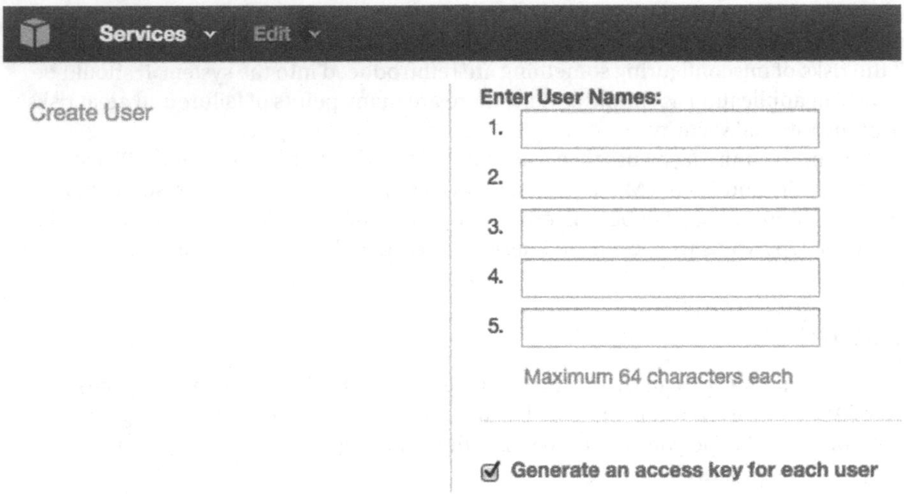

Figure 1-3. Create up to five IAM Users

On this screen, you can create up to five new usernames, but we only need one. In the first input field, type the username **photoadmin**. There is a check box that is automatically checked, indicating that an access key will be generated for each user. If we were using this user to make AWS API queries in our app, we would want an access key. However, our intention is that this user will have access to the necessary parts of the AWS Console and nothing to do with the functionality of the app itself. We will, therefore, uncheck the box before clicking **Create**.

The username should now appear in the users table. You will notice that our user is not a part of any group, nor does the user have an access key. Clicking the user's row will bring us to the detail view for the user. You should see something similar to Figure 1-4.

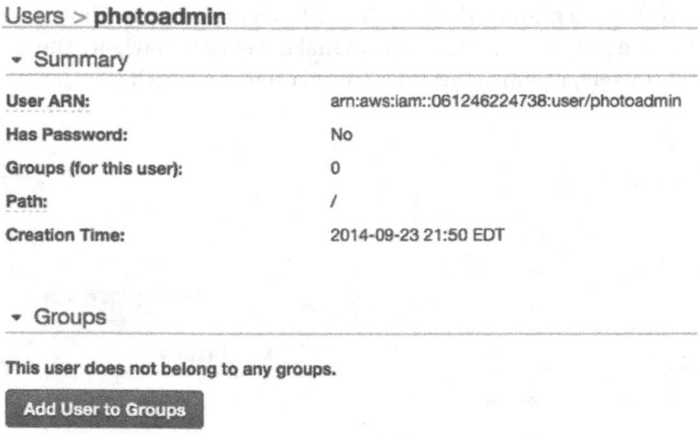

Users > **photoadmin**

▾ Summary

User ARN:	arn:aws:iam::061246224738:user/photoadmin
Has Password:	No
Groups (for this user):	0
Path:	/
Creation Time:	2014-09-23 21:50 EDT

▾ Groups

This user does not belong to any groups.

Add User to Groups

Figure 1-4. *The user detail view*

There's a lot of information on this page. First, is the User ARN, or Amazon Resource Name. An ARN is essentially a global identifier for all AWS resources of any kind. Anytime any resource, such as a user, an EC2 instance, a database instance, etc., is created, an ARN is automatically generated. You may find them useful at a later point, but we don't need to do anything with this ARN right now. You'll notice bold text under both the Groups and Permissions headers. Our user has no groups and no policies!

Policies are perhaps the most important concept in IAM. A policy is essentially a declaration of one or more permissions for a user, group, role, or other resource. In short, they are the universal system for configuring permissions for all entities in AWS. A policy can contain remarkably granular permissions, or a sweeping "Allow" for all attributes within an AWS product. In contrast, you also can explicitly deny access to services or resources. For our purposes, we want the user to have full permissions to manage all the AWS products our application uses. This user is our superadmin.

IAM Groups

The temptation here will be to start adding new policies to this user. Wait! Are we certain that this is such a good idea? Do we know for a fact that this is the only user who will ever possess all this power? In the long run, there will probably be more than one superadmin on the project. Perhaps it would make more sense to create a *Group* and manage our policies there instead.

Select **Groups** in the navigation, and you will be brought to a screen similar to the users table we saw earlier. Click **Create New Group**. What should we call this group? We know that we want these administrators to have access to all products used by our app. We're giving enormous power to this group, because right now, we are only creating a user for ourselves. Let's call the group **PhotoAdmins**. Click **Next Step**, and you will be brought to the Attach Policy view.

IAM Managed Policies

If you've used AWS before, you may notice that the IAM policy generation tools have changed. There are now two types of IAM policies: *managed* policies and *inline* policies. A managed policy is one or more permissions grouped in a policy curated by AWS. For instance, the *AmazonEC2FullAccess* policy includes full access to EC2 services, as well as related services like Elastic Load Balancing and CloudWatch. Inline policies are custom permissions that you can create when you have specific policy needs, which we will discuss shortly.

When you create a group, you're prompted to attach a managed policy. The Attach Policy view, shown in Figure 1-5, will soon become a dear friend. The sole purpose of this tool is to make it easy to navigate the complexity of selecting correct permissions for your users, groups, and roles (more on these later).

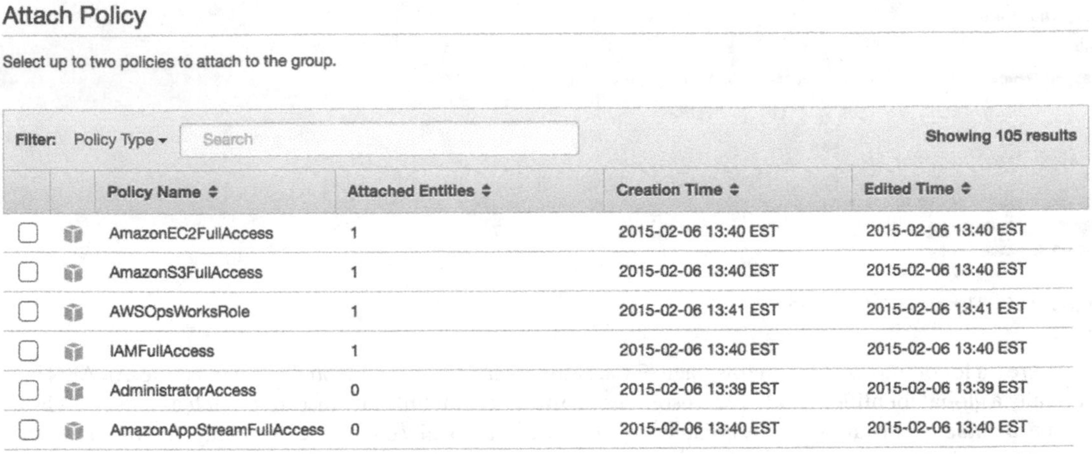

Attach Policy

Select up to two policies to attach to the group.

		Policy Name ⬦	Attached Entities ⬦	Creation Time ⬦	Edited Time ⬦
☐	🗐	AmazonEC2FullAccess	1	2015-02-06 13:40 EST	2015-02-06 13:40 EST
☐	🗐	AmazonS3FullAccess	1	2015-02-06 13:40 EST	2015-02-06 13:40 EST
☐	🗐	AWSOpsWorksRole	1	2015-02-06 13:41 EST	2015-02-06 13:41 EST
☐	🗐	IAMFullAccess	1	2015-02-06 13:40 EST	2015-02-06 13:40 EST
☐	🗐	AdministratorAccess	0	2015-02-06 13:39 EST	2015-02-06 13:39 EST
☐	🗐	AmazonAppStreamFullAccess	0	2015-02-06 13:40 EST	2015-02-06 13:40 EST

Filter: Policy Type ▾   Search   Showing 105 results

Figure 1-5. *Selecting a managed IAM policy in the Attach Policy view*

While we could just choose one of the managed policies and call it a day, that wouldn't be any fun would it? Instead, let's create the group and then manually add inline policies to it. Click **Next Step** to proceed to the Review view, shown in Figure 1-6, where you will see your group name and policies again. Click **Create Group** to finish.

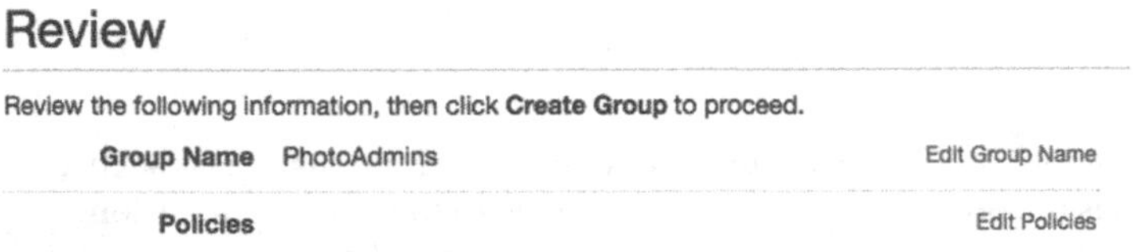

Review

Review the following information, then click **Create Group** to proceed.

Group Name PhotoAdmins   Edit Group Name

Policies   Edit Policies

Figure 1-6. *Review Group*

You will be returned to the Group list view. Select the **PhotoAdmins** group and expand the **Inline Policies** panel. Click the link to create a new inline policy. In the next view, you can choose from the following options:

- **Policy Generator**: This option will launch a wizard, which allows you to add a series of individual policy statements to the group. This is a handy way to configure a group that requires access to some, but not all, services.

- **Custom Policy**: This is the path of greatest resistance. All policies are read and written in JSON format. The custom policy selection allows you to input by hand the JSON for your policy. If, for instance, you want to configure a policy to give permissions to specific AWS resources, you can use the ARNs in your policy JSON here. At some point, you can count on working directly with IAM policy statement JSON. Amazon also provides a stand-alone JSON generator here: http://awspolicygen.s3.amazonaws.com/policygen.html.

Let's go ahead and make sure our PhotoAdmins group has all the power it needs (and no more!) and choose the **Policy Generator** option. Click **Select**.

IAM Permissions Editor

The next screen is the Permissions editor. Here, we will add each individual permission that our users will need. We're going to give them the power to complete the rest of the lessons, with the exception of returning to IAM to create additional policies. See Figure 1-7.

Figure 1-7. *Generating individual IAM policy statements*

Our first option in configuring permissions is Effect. While we could choose Deny to forbid access to specific services, because our group currently has no permissions, this would be working backward. We will leave **Allow** selected, as we will be allowing access to a specific service.

Select an AWS Service from the drop-down. To start, we want to select **AWS OpsWorks**. Next, we could choose only specific *Actions* for which the group has permission. This drop-down is populated with all possible actions that could be performed in this AWS Service. Each selection in the AWS Service drop-down will repopulate the Actions list. There are hundreds, if not thousands, of Actions in total across AWS. For now, select **All Actions**. If we wanted to grant permission only to a specific resource, we could enter its ARN in the *Amazon Resource Name (ARN)* input. Let's leave it as *, or *all*, for now. Click **Add Statement**. You should immediately see your permissions statement appear on this screen, as shown in Figure 1-8.

Edit Permissions

Figure 1-8. *Permissions statement listing*

Let's add the rest of the permissions we need. For each of the services below, create a statement that allows all actions for the service.

- Amazon CloudFront

- Amazon CloudWatch

- Amazon CloudWatch Logs

- Amazon EC2

- Amazon RDS

- Amazon Route53

- Amazon Route53 Domains

- Amazon S3

- Amazon SES

You should see all of these permissions appear on the page. Then click **Next Step**. You will see an auto-generated policy name. You can leave this as it is unless you want a specific name for your own ease of use. And behold! Your policy JSON appears in the Policy Document text area. Click **Apply Policy**, and your inline policy will be added to the group, as shown in Figure 1-9.

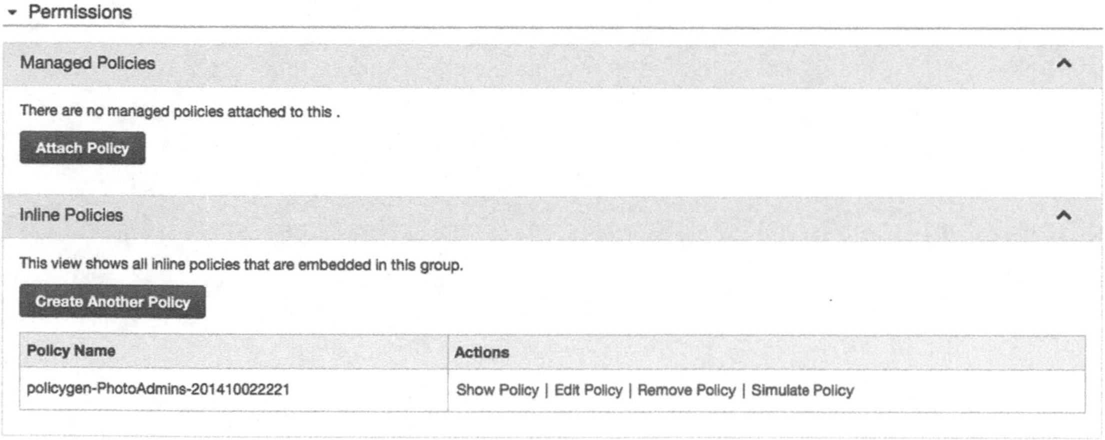

▼ Permissions

Managed Policies ︿

There are no managed policies attached to this .

Attach Policy

Inline Policies ︿

This view shows all inline policies that are embedded in this group.

Create Another Policy

Policy Name	Actions
policygen-PhotoAdmins-201410022221	Show Policy | Edit Policy | Remove Policy | Simulate Policy

Figure 1-9. IAM Group Inline Policies view

Next, we want to add our user to the group. Navigate to the Users tab and select **photoadmin** from the table. Under the Groups heading, click **Add User to Groups**. Check the box next to our **PhotoAdmins** group and click **Add to Groups**. You will see that the group now appears on the Users detail view. Soon the user will be able to sign in and start working.

Scroll down a bit, and you'll see that the user doesn't have a password yet. Let's give him a default password. Click **Manage Password** at the bottom right. On the Manage Password page, let's assign him a custom password for now. Select the radio button next to **Assign a custom password** and, in the boxes, type the word **photo**. Just below these fields is a check box to require the user to change his password when he signs in. Obviously, photo is not a secure password. Let's check the box and click **Apply**.

If you don't trust your users to choose secure passwords on their own, you can navigate to the Password Policy tab and select a number of rules to enforce when users set a password, such as minimum length or requires one number.

Head back to the IAM dashboard. At the top of the page, you should see the text "IAM users sign-in link." This is the URL your users will employ to sign in to their account. Let's test our progress.

Copy the URL to your clipboard and sign out of the AWS Console by clicking your name in the top-right corner of the browser window and choosing **Sign Out**. Paste the URL back in your address bar, and you'll see a typical login screen. Enter the username **photoalbum** and the password **photo**. If you forced the user to reset her password on login, you will be asked to do this now. Then proceed to the AWS Console. You should still see all AWS services on the dashboard, but you will not be able to perform any actions that you're now restricted from taking.

Summary

You've now set up your local environment and walked through the sample project. You should now have a clear idea of what the application is intended to do and be ready to take the next steps in developing the app. You've taken your first steps in working with AWS, by creating users, groups, and policies in Identity and Access Management, and learned about Amazon Resource Names, the global identifiers for AWS. You're now ready to start architecting your app. In the next chapter, you'll learn about AWS OpsWorks and begin setting up the application on AWS for the first time!

CHAPTER 2

■ ■ ■

Working with AWS OpsWorks

Having completed the first chapter, you should now have a good grasp on the application we're building. You should have also registered your AWS account and set up your administrative users in IAM. If you skipped the introductory chapter, the tutorial on Identity and Access Management (IAM) is important. You will have to be familiar with the main concepts of IAM to do almost anything with AWS.

Next, we will begin the process of deploying our basic application to AWS, using the OpsWorks application deployment service. In this chapter, you will create an instance of your app in OpsWorks and deploy it to the Web for the first time. We won't be adding any functionality to the code base in this chapter. Regardless, we're taking the first step to actually hosting our application in the cloud!

Understanding OpsWorks

Interestingly, AWS OpsWorks was not built from the ground up by AWS. In 2012, Amazon acquired a company called Peritor that provided a third-party enterprise-deployment service with similar functionality. The technological underpinning of both products is called Chef (`www.chef.io/`), a framework for configuring, automating, and streamlining server deployments programmatically. While there are preset configurations for every EC2 instance that you launch, with Chef, you can easily make your own changes to the environment with very little coding. One advantage of using Chef is that you don't have to learn about all the nuances of the AWS virtual server packages. Instead, Chef gives you an API for configuring common server-side software, such as nginx, Apache, PHP, even Node.js. Later in the book, you will work directly with Chef to see how easy it is.

OpsWorks is designed to make it easier to customize and manage your application environment, providing a graphical user interface (as well as an API) for different types of resources in your application stack. I will review these resources in greater detail shortly. Anyone who has tried to manually configure and deploy an app the way OpsWorks does can tell you it's a huge time-saver and drastically reduces the risk of errors. And the average software developer who hasn't dabbled in system administration will find that he/she now possess superhuman abilities as a cloud architect.

The benefits of using OpsWorks should be self-evident as we continue through the lesson and discuss specific features of the service. That being said, with ease of use there is always a price to be paid in customization. In a February 2013 blog post (`www.allthingsdistributed.com/2013/02/awt-opsworks.html`) about the launch of AWS OpsWorks, Amazon chief technology officer Werner Vogels provided the handy diagram shown in Figure 2-1, as is the style of AWS.

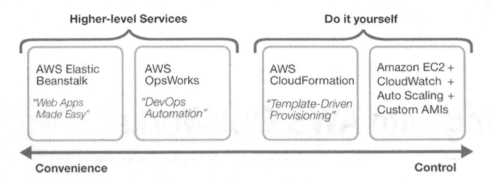

Figure 2-1. *The plane of Convenience vs. Control in AWS application deployment*

This diagram depicts a one-dimensional plane of Convenience vs. Control, showing OpsWorks's relative position to other application deployment options. As you can see, OpsWorks rests between the DIY method of managing an application stack and the easier and less customizable Elastic Beanstalk. If this makes you pause and re-evaluate whether OpsWorks is really the best idea for you, don't worry. Some people regard OpsWorks as the next-gen counterpart to Elastic Beanstalk. The longer you work with AWS, the more you will see them roll out new features and better synergies between services. At times, the pace of these improvements can be overwhelming: you will receive an announcement e-mail every few weeks from AWS with a half-dozen new features that you may be able to use in your application. As such, don't worry too much about the chart. Two years is a very long time in the AWS world, and the important takeaway is that with the services AWS provides, there is a broad spectrum of abstraction that creates a range of features and limitations, depending on how the service was designed.

Furthermore, while we are deploying our application with OpsWorks, we are using many other AWS services in our application. The end product will truly be a sum of its parts. By the end of the lessons, you will likely be able to figure out how to swap out OpsWorks for Elastic Beanstalk or CloudFormation, with some effort. Figure 2-1 merely illustrates that when you are wearing your cloud architect hat, there is a cost-benefit analysis to be done.

In a moment, we will begin exploring the OpsWorks control panel. We will review a variety of its features and, in doing so, learn about a variety of other AWS services that are fundamental to OpsWorks. We will also get a glimpse of how the foundational technology Chef is still relevant to AWS users like us. As you allocate resources in OpsWorks, you will begin incurring usage charges on your AWS account. Keep this in mind when asking yourself whether you need ten m3.2xlarge EC2 instances to host the Photoalbums application. But before we start allocating resources in OpsWorks, we should learn a little more about these resources.

Allocating Resources

When you allocate EC2 instances, RDS (Rational Database Service) database instances, and many other resources, the most important decisions you make are *what* and *where*. The *what* is self-explanatory. AWS has its own pricing tiers for these resources, which you can find in the official documentation. The relationship between usage and pricing varies by service, and they are documented individually.

For example, EC2 instances are reserved based on power (memory, CPU clock speed, and physical processor) × hourly rate × hours used. To review the specs of EC2 instance types, a breakdown is provided here: `http://aws.amazon.com/ec2/instance-types/`. When determining an instance type, you would use your judgment, comparing your technical needs to your financial resources, cross-referencing the instance types with the pricing here: `http://aws.amazon.com/ec2/pricing/`. While traditional hosting (and, again, some cloud-hosting platforms) will charge you a monthly rate for the resources you've reserved, the hourly rate is what makes AWS so useful. Once again, *pay for what you use*. So that's what the resources are; the *where* is a separate issue, and a new concept if you're moving from traditional hosting.

■ **Caution** Once you've provided your billing information, AWS will let you provision expensive resources as you need. If you're new to AWS, be careful about requesting excessive resources. A rate of $1.50 per hour doesn't sound like much, until you accidentally leave an instance online for three months.

Regions and Availability Zones

A lot of people think of the cloud as some nebulous, location-less global entity. Of course, there are still actual servers and data centers—the data isn't literally floating in the troposphere. AWS runs data centers all around the globe, usually geographically proximate to major population centers. In most cases, there are several data centers serving the same geographic areas, or *regions*. These regions have names like US East (N. Virginia), US West (Oregon), and Asia Pacific (Tokyo). While the name of the region typically describes a continental area such as Western Europe, the location in parentheses describes a more specific area in which the data centers are located (see Figure 2-2). Keep in mind that AWS maintains additional supporting infrastructure in other parts of a region, and not all services are available in all regions. You can find more detailed information at http://aws.amazon.com/about-aws/global-infrastructure/regional-product-services/.

Geography is important in architecting a web application. No matter how fast your code is, or how many servers you're running, your data still has to get to and from users via the Web. Along with the technology, user expectations have evolved significantly since the dial-up days. Your best bet is to host your application in the region(s) closest to your expected user base.

■ **Note** I will discuss other ways to distribute your content globally with S3 and CloudFront in Chapters 4 and 5.

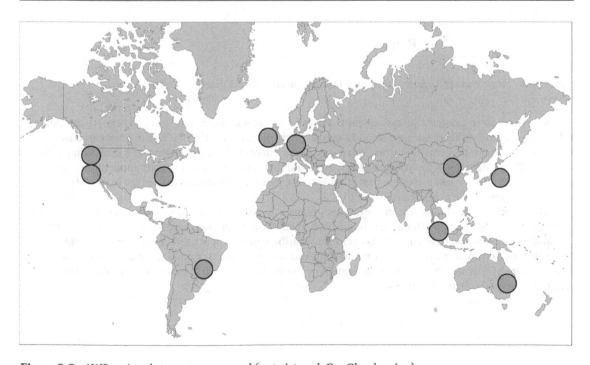

Figure 2-2. *AWS region data centers mapped (not pictured: GovCloud region)*

As discussed earlier, many regions have more than one physical data center. If some sort of service outage temporarily disables a data center, other data centers keep the region online. These data centers are abstracted in AWS services as *availability zones*. Within each availability zone are the EC2 instances and other resources we provision. You can think of an availability zone as a data center containing the hardware on which AWS services run. This concept is illustrated in Figure 2-3.

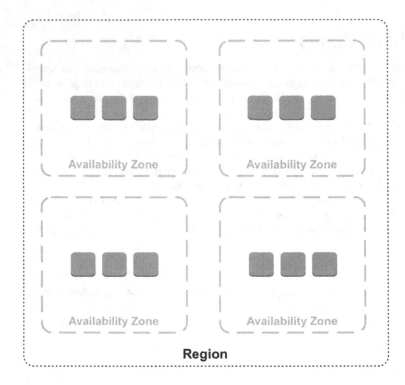

Figure 2-3. *Illustration of a region containing four distinct availability zones*

Now that you're familiar with the concept of regions and availability zones, you can begin to ponder different scenarios. At heart, we are still working with physical servers in the real world. They can crash; they can lose power; they can have a random part fail, etc. There are countless points of failure What if all of your EC2 instances are in a single availability zone and that zone loses power? Your application is going to go offline. In fact, it's safe to assume that at some point, there will be an isolated outage in one of your availability zones, so we're going to plan for that.

One could write a whole book on contingency plans with cloud architecture. For the scope of this book, we're going to keep it simple. Our application will be hosted in a single region with instances in multiple availability zones. We will use other AWS services to distribute our content more quickly in other regions. If we wanted additional redundancy, we could clone our app to different regions as well. As long as our databases are in sync across all regions, we should be free to duplicate our app at will. I'll discuss these sorts of optimizations throughout the book.

Additional IAM Roles

Before we head over to the OpsWorks dashboard, we are going to create a new role in Identity and Access Management. In the first chapter, you created an administration-level user in the PhotoAdmins IAM Group who should have the ability to perform any tasks in OpsWorks. I also discussed the security risks of storing credentials in our code, in the event that a developer leaves the project or a machine with a local copy of the app is stolen or goes missing.

To avoid these risks, we will instead use IAM roles to manage authentication with other services. We actually need two new IAM roles: one for the EC2 instances hosting our application and one that allows the entire application stack to act on our behalf. By creating a role for our instances, generally referred to as an *instance role*, we can programmatically access other AWS services via the AWS API, without storing security credentials in our source code. We will create this role first.

Instance Role

Return to the IAM dashboard, and click **Roles** in the left-hand navigation. Find the **Create New Role** button toward the top of the page and click it. On the next screen, you will be prompted to enter a name for your role, as in Figure 2-4.

Figure 2-4. Set Role Name

We want a logical name for our role, so we'll use **aws-opsworks-photoalbums-ec2-role**, the role for EC2 instances in the Photoalbums app, which are initialized by AWS OpsWorks. You can use whatever conventions make sense, but we're using the format [service]-[app]-[role]. Click **Next Step** to proceed. Once again, we have many options to choose from when creating our IAM policy for this role. For now, we will create a basic role with no policies. As we proceed through the rest of the book, we will add more policies to this role. You will first be prompted to select a Role Type. In the Service Roles option box, you will see Amazon EC2 at the top of the list. Click the **Select** button to advance.

We will once again have the ability to select a policy (see Figure 2-5). We will attach a policy later, so click **Next Step** to proceed to the Review view.

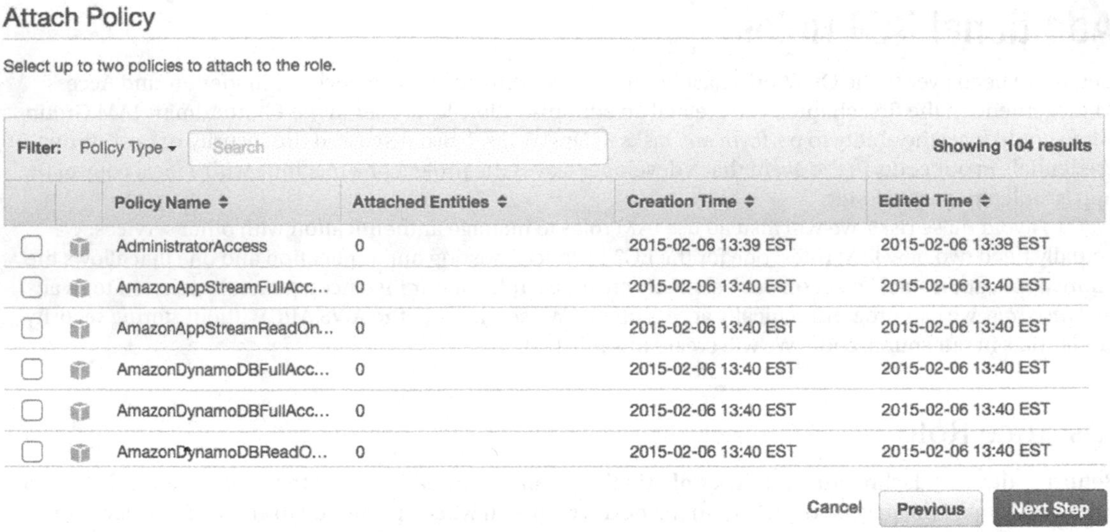

Attach Policy

Select up to two policies to attach to the role.

Filter: Policy Type ▾	Search			Showing 104 results
	Policy Name ⬍	Attached Entities ⬍	Creation Time ⬍	Edited Time ⬍
☐ 📦	AdministratorAccess	0	2015-02-06 13:39 EST	2015-02-06 13:39 EST
☐ 📦	AmazonAppStreamFullAcc...	0	2015-02-06 13:40 EST	2015-02-06 13:40 EST
☐ 📦	AmazonAppStreamReadOn...	0	2015-02-06 13:40 EST	2015-02-06 13:40 EST
☐ 📦	AmazonDynamoDBFullAcc...	0	2015-02-06 13:40 EST	2015-02-06 13:40 EST
☐ 📦	AmazonDynamoDBFullAcc...	0	2015-02-06 13:40 EST	2015-02-06 13:40 EST
☐ 📦	AmazonDynamoDBReadO...	0	2015-02-06 13:40 EST	2015-02-06 13:40 EST

Cancel   Previous   Next Step

Figure 2-5. *Selecting no policies for the aws-opsworks-photoalbums-ec2-role*

In the next view, you have a chance to review your role before creating it. If everything looks good, click **Create Role**. We now have a role that we can assign to the EC2 instances running our application. However, we still need a role for the entire application stack itself.

Service Role

As an OpsWorks application, our stack will need permission to carry out routine tasks, such as rebooting instances, reporting metrics to the AWS Console, etc. As a user, you have the power to click around the OpsWorks dashboard and manually perform various tasks. We want to make sure the application we create is able to perform these actions on its own. We will ensure this by creating a role for the entire application stack. This role is referred to generally as a *service* role. Once this role is created, we can finally proceed to the OpsWorks dashboard to create our application.

Return to the Roles tab in the IAM dashboard and again click **Create New Role**. Once again, we need a name for our new role. Following our previous naming conventions, we'll call this one **aws-opsworks-photoalbums-service-role**. The naming convention again is [service]-[app]-[role]. Proceeding to the next step will take you to the Select Role Type view, where AWS Service Roles is already opened and listed before you. Scroll down this list to the end, where you will find AWS OpsWorks, and click **Select**. In the Attach Policy view, there will be only one possible policy to select: AWSOpsWorksRole. This is the default managed policy that AWS provides for OpsWorks service roles. Select the box and click **Next Step**. Review the policy one more time, and finish the process by clicking **Create Role**.

You will be taken back to the Roles view, where you will see your new role has been created. Select your new role to proceed to the Role detail view. Under the Permissions header, you will see the AWSOpsWorksRole as the only policy (see Figure 2-6). Click on **Show Policy**, and a modal view will appear.

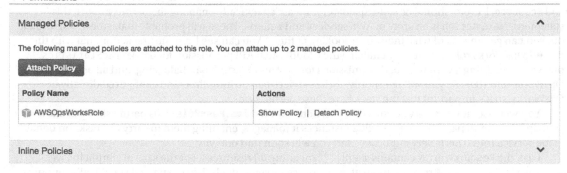

Figure 2-6. *Policies attached to the aws-opsworks-photoalbums-service-role*

In the modal view, you will have the opportunity to view the raw JSON of your policy document. The JSON should look something like Listing 2-1, following:

Listing 2-1. The OpsWorks Service Role Policy

```
{
  "Version": "2012-10-17",
  "Statement": [
  {
    "Effect": "Allow",
    "Action": [
      "cloudwatch:GetMetricStatistics",
      "ec2:DescribeAccountAttributes",
      "ec2:DescribeAvailabilityZones",
      "ec2:DescribeInstances",
      "ec2:DescribeKeyPairs",
      "ec2:DescribeSecurityGroups",
      "ec2:DescribeSubnets",
      "ec2:DescribeVpcs",
      "elasticloadbalancing:DescribeInstanceHealth",
      "elasticloadbalancing:DescribeLoadBalancers",
      "iam:GetRolePolicy",
      "iam:ListInstanceProfiles",
      "iam:ListRoles",
      "iam:ListUsers",
      "iam:PassRole",
      "opsworks:*",
      "rds:*"
    ],
    "Resource": [
      "*"
    ]
  }
  ]
}
```

You will notice a single JSON object in the Statement array, which has the properties Effect, Action, and Resource. Effect should be self-explanatory: we are specifically enabling the permissions in this statement. Next, Action is an array of AWS services and actions. These will probably make more sense later, but you can get an idea of what they are by looking at them. You can see from the first action that with the default OpsWorks role, we are only enabling the CloudWatch API permission for GetMetricStatistics, but we are enabling a variety of read permissions for EC2 and Elastic Load Balancing, and all actions for OpsWorks and RDS. As you will see shortly, these services can be initialized and configured directly in OpsWorks, so it's important that the stack have these permissions.

You will also notice a very important action here, entitled **iam:PassRole**. This permission will allow your application to pass its role to the EC2 instances it manages, enabling them to carry out tasks on behalf of the service role. This is very important, and you will soon find out why.

Last, the Resource array contains simply "*", meaning *all* resources. For the sake of simplicity, we are provisioning our IAM roles for use with all resources, even though they are named specifically for our application. In the future, you could return to the policy documents for these roles and restrict them to the resources for your application. You will learn that the ability to target specific resources in your policy documents is a powerful feature.

Unfortunately, the default OpsWorks service role is not going to be powerful enough for our purposes. As noted previously, we have only read permissions for EC2. However, we are going to want to be able to create resources in OpsWorks, so we need to attach an additional policy. From the detail view for the aws-opsworks-photoalbums-service-role, click on **Attach Policy** to add another managed policy. Select **AmazonEC2FullAccess** from the policy list, and click **Attach Policy**. You will be returned to the role detail view, and should see that there are now two managed policies attached to this role.

To follow best practices, Amazon recommends that root account access keys be revoked and multifactor authentication be enabled for root accounts. Follow these guidelines at your discretion, but you should at least learn how to manage your architecture via a user account rather than the root account. However, when creating our first application stack in OpsWorks, we must have *IAM Administrator Access*, which we did not give to our PhotoAdmins group in Chapter 1. As such, creating our application stack will be our last action as the root user. While you may have root access to the AWS account for now, it's best to get into the habit of working as a user on any AWS account, i.e., your employer's or client's account.

You've done a lot of work in IAM so far and learned a lot about technologies that we haven't yet begun to work with directly. It might be a little confusing, as we've moved quickly with some very abstract concepts. To recap, this is what you've accomplished with IAM and OpsWorks so far:

- You are signed into AWS with your root account, which you used in IAM and will use to create your first application stack next.

- You have created a PhotoAdmins group and defined its policy, giving the group permissions to administrate a large number of AWS services that we will use later.

- You added a user to the PhotoAdmins group, which you can use in the future to log in and work with your app in the AWS Console.

- You have created an *instance role* for the EC2 instances in your application stack.

- You have created a *service role* for your application stack itself.

Before we proceed to the OpsWorks dashboard, there is one other step we will make to learn about SSH keys. Please note that this step is completely optional. You won't need this lesson for the sample application, but it might be handy to learn. Skip the following section if you don't care about learning this right now.

QUICK DETOUR: SSH KEYS

We learned earlier that one of the benefits of running Amazon Linux instances is the strict default security settings. Out of the box, your instances can only be connected to via SSH—FTP, SFTP, and other common methods of connecting are disabled. To enable them, you would have to open the correct port in AWS and install the software on the command line, which is a separate tutorial in itself. To set up these methods, you would first need the capability to connect to your instance via SSH. Fortunately, Amazon makes it easy to generate keys for your instances.

Wouldn't it be annoying if we had to store a separate SSH key for each instance in our application? Aside from the risk of losing and confusing the keys, adding and removing instances to your stack would be a more labor-intensive process. Amazon has made this easy, by allowing us to create an SSH key in the AWS Console and set it as the default key for all instances in a stack. You could theoretically use one master key for all stacks, but one key per stack seems to make a lot more sense. Let's go ahead and create our keys now. First, we must head over to the EC2 dashboard. You can do this by clicking the orange box icon in the top-left corner, or by opening the Services menu next to it, and finding EC2 in the Compute & Networking section, as shown in the following image. Sometimes it's easier to go back to the AWS Console if you aren't sure in which category you will find the service you need.

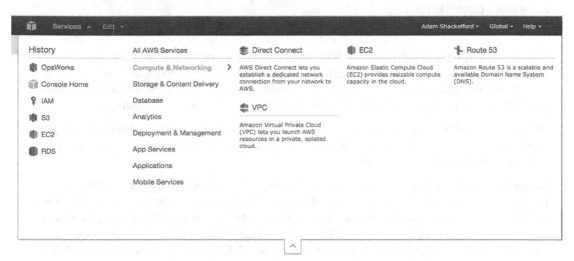

There is a whole lot going on in the EC2 dashboard, more than I need review in detail right now. We will be spending more time here later. In the left-hand navigation you should see a series of collapsible sections, which are expanded by default. Under Network & Security, click **Key Pairs**, as seen in the following image:

☐ NETWORK & SECURITY

   Security Groups

   Elastic IPs

   Placement Groups

   Load Balancers

   Key Pairs

   Network Interfaces

Here you will see a list of all the SSH keys you have generated for your EC2 instances. The encryption on these keys is 1024-bit SSH-2 RSA. There is a limit of 5,000 keys per region, but it seems unlikely that most users would ever approach this cap. Aside from creating your key pairs in the console, you can also generate them yourself and import them into AWS; however, this is outside of the scope of the book.

■ **Note**   If you delete a key pair, it will not affect the instances already using them. You will still be able to connect to your instances if you have a copy of the private key. However, you will not be able to provision new instances with a deleted key pair.

By now, some of the UI design choices in AWS should start to feel familiar. Similar to IAM, the **Create Key Pair** button is at the top-left corner of the main content area. Rather than start a multistep process, this just opens a modal window where you name your key pair. Let's name it **aws-opsworks-photoalbums-key**, following a similar naming convention to the IAM roles we created earlier.

When you click **Create**, the key will be generated, and a file named **aws-opsworks-photoalbums-key.pem** should automatically download to your machine. The extension .pem is short for "Privacy Enhanced Mail," and this file is known as the private key.

A corresponding public key will be generated and stored by AWS, forming a key pair. A copy of the public key will be saved to all instances provisioned with this key pair, and you will have to provide the matching private key to make secure connections to your instances, either on the command line or in the browser, using a Java plug-in provided by Amazon. We don't have any instances yet, so we won't be using the private key to connect to anything at the moment. Keep the key in a safe place, preferably backed up somewhere. (Hint: You could store a copy in a private S3 bucket, which we will be setting up later.)

The OpsWorks Environment

When we set up our first app in OpsWorks, it's important to understand what our tools are. Fortunately, Amazon has provided a great illustration of the OpsWorks environment, as it pertains to a PHP application. You can find it in Figure 2-7.

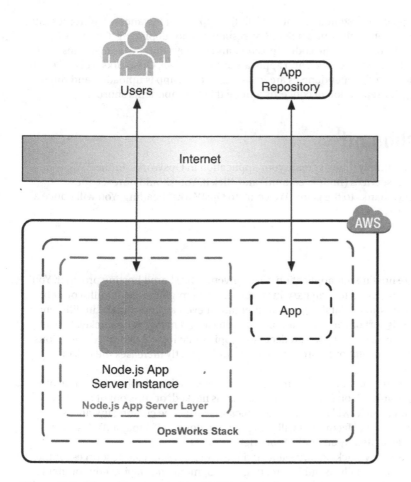

Figure 2-7. *The components of an OpsWorks stack*

As you can see, all of the components of our app that exist in AWS are grouped inside the OpsWorks stack. Stacks are the collection of all components making up your application deployment. You've probably heard of the term *application stack* before; I've been using it frequently. An OpsWorks stack is simply the application stack in the context of AWS. Unlike in the traditional hosting environment, the stack in OpsWorks organizes all the resources allocated to your application.

In Figure 2-7, you can see the PHP App Server Layer contained within the OpsWorks stack. Depending on its complexity, we could have many layers to our app. For a basic web application such as ours, there will only be a few layers: the application hosting servers (EC2 instances), the load balancer, and the database.

You will notice also that the app is represented distinctly from the app server instances. This represents the actual source code of our application, which the stack will be responsible for deploying. OpsWorks retrieves the source code (via the Internet) from the code repository and deploys the source to our instances. Based on the requirements defined at the stack, layer, and application source level, OpsWorks will make sure that the instances are properly configured, dependencies are installed, and the app is uploaded and run on your instances. I will be discussing the separation of concerns among these components shortly.

The OpsWorks Dashboard

We took some major detours, but it's finally time to create your application in OpsWorks. In the AWS Console, find OpsWorks in the list of services (middle column) and click it. You should now see the OpsWorks dashboard unmistakably, thanks to the giant "Welcome to OpsWorks" heading. You will notice a big blue button that reads **Add First Stack**.

Stacks

Imagine for a moment that we were hosting our application on a conventional shared hosting provider. You log in to the admin console for your account, to manage your resources. You might have a handful of web applications in one tab and then a handful of databases in another tab, or even all apps hosted in different tables of the same database. With this sort of paradigm, administration can get messy very quickly. You are at the mercy of yourself, your colleagues, and/or your predecessor, hoping that logical naming conventions were followed. Even some cloud-hosting platforms are still like this, and it greatly increases the risk of human error, in this author's opinion.

With each stack consisting of an independent set of resources, this means that problems affecting one application are limited to that application. If one of your apps crashes, is hacked, or runs out of resources and becomes unresponsive, the other stacks will be unaffected. Because we will be creating instances in multiple availability zones, the only external factor that will bring our app down is if a major AWS service breaks down. Sounds like a good way to deploy an application, right?

In OpsWorks, you can create as many stacks as you want, and it will organize all your resources for the project neatly into each stack. This is especially useful for creating development and staging environments, as there is a **clone** button on each stack! You can also start and stop *all* of your services with one button and run commands on all instances simultaneously. So simple and yet so powerful! Let's get our photoalbums stack online. Go ahead and click **Add First Stack.** There's a lot happening on the next page, as shown in Figure 2-8.

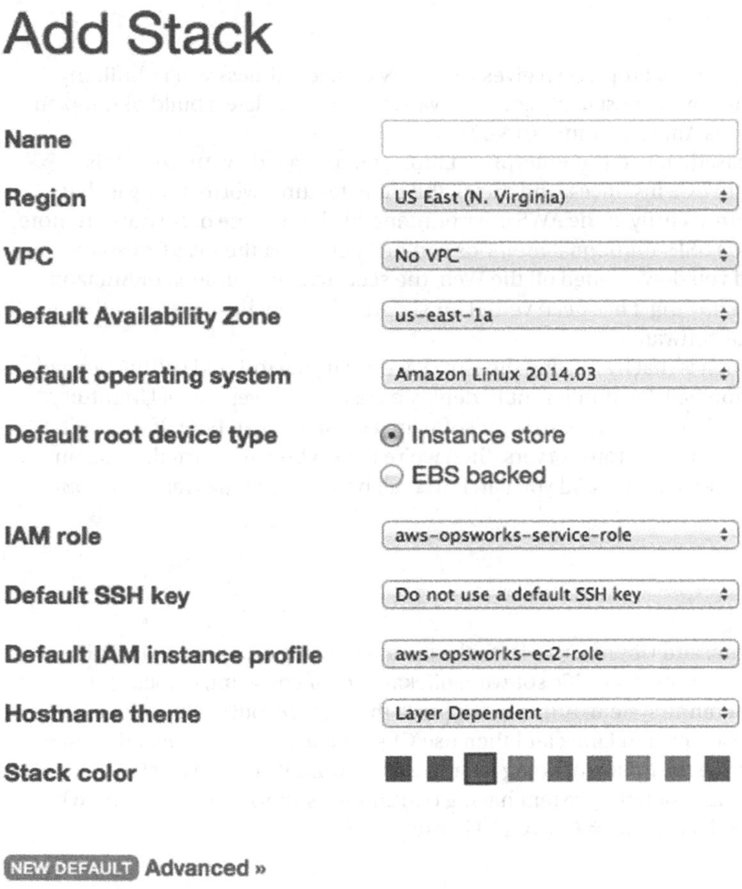

Add Stack

Name	[ ]
Region	US East (N. Virginia) ⬍
VPC	No VPC ⬍
Default Availability Zone	us-east-1a ⬍
Default operating system	Amazon Linux 2014.03 ⬍
Default root device type	⦿ Instance store ◯ EBS backed
IAM role	aws-opsworks-service-role ⬍
Default SSH key	Do not use a default SSH key ⬍
Default IAM instance profile	aws-opsworks-ec2-role ⬍
Hostname theme	Layer Dependent ⬍
Stack color	■ ■ ■ ■ ■ ■ ■ ■ ■

(NEW DEFAULT) Advanced »

Figure 2-8. *Creating an application stack in OpsWorks*

The first field is easy, enter **Photoalbums** and go to the next field. Now we must choose a region. Is it possible to discern the geography of your target audience? Amazon's main data center is in northern Virginia, so the region defaults to US East. Unless you have a reason to change this, we can leave it as is.

The next field asks you if you want to choose a VPC, or Virtual Private Cloud (http://aws.amazon.com/vpc/). If you wanted to deploy your application to a private network, you would assign your app to a VPC here. In our case, we're building an app for public consumption on the Web, so we will not be selecting a VPC. A VPC could contain both public and private subnets, but this might be a topic for a sequel!

■ **Note**　If you want to use a VPC, you must create it before creating your OpsWorks application.

I have already talked about availability zones, so you know that each instance you create will run in a specific availability zone. The *Default Availability Zone* is simply the preselected availability zone when you assign new instances. This is a field purely intended for convenience. If you are managing a lot of instances and know that you want them in a specific availability zone, selecting it here saves you the trouble of changing the zone on a bunch of instances later. However, you can certainly change the availability zone of your instances later. Let's leave the default value here.

43

Amazon Linux

You will see that the *Default operating system* drop-down gives you a few choices. Unless you're building an app that explicitly requires Ubuntu, you're most likely going to want to select the latest build of Amazon Linux. At the time of writing, the latest is Amazon Linux 2014.09.

Amazon Linux is a Linux build based on Red Hat Enterprise Linux and managed by Amazon. It is designed specifically for deployment to EC2 instances, and one of the main features worth noting is that Amazon Linux is tailored for maximum security in the AWS environment. By default, the only way to remote access an Amazon Linux instance is via SSH. Additional methods can be opened via the AWS Console. Compared to deploying a Linux build you downloaded off the Web, the security configuration of Amazon Linux gives you the peace of mind of knowing it has been vetted for security flaws by the experts, without being so restrictive that it impairs your software.

This brings up another point, which is that by utlizing the cloud, we are trying to avoid getting bogged down in operating system configuration hell. We don't want to deploy a customized version of Ubuntu; we want to start an instance and know that it's ready to run our software as fast as it can boot. If we can't trust the operating system running on our numerous servers, then we're back where we started. Amazon has written plenty more about their build of Linux, and you can find it all here: `http://aws.amazon.com/amazon-linux-ami/`.

Amazon Machine Images

You'll notice that besides Amazon Linux and Ubuntu, you have the option of using a custom AMI. This option allows you to create an instance running specific software packages or, if you want, to lock your instance to a specific version of an operating system. Amazon supports this feature, but seems reluctant. Its recommendation is that you should use Amazon Linux and then use Chef to customize your install, if need be. This is the best practice, but you have the option of doing whatever you want. If you use Chef instead of a custom AMI, you get the benefit of your operating system having continuous support from Amazon while allowing you customization options. Select **Amazon Linux** and continue.

Instance vs. EBS

Uh-oh! Another unfamiliar question. Should our *Default root device type* be Instance store or EBS backed? What does it all mean? Based on the discussion of EC2 instances thus far, you should realize now that these instances are ephemeral beings. When you stop an instance (whether by choice or not), all data stored on the instance is lost. As such, it is not a good idea to depend on an EC2 instance for data persistence. Even if EC2 instances provided permanent data persistence, would we want to use them? AWS is supposed to make infrastructure easier to manage, and managing unique data stored across instances could get complicated.

Amazon's solution to this provlem is called Elastic Block Storage. With EBS, you can provision a scalable disk drive for persistent data storage. You can only attach an EBS instance to one EC2 instance at a time, but you can take a snapshot of our EBS and use it to instantiate a new EBS.

Will this be useful in our application? Eventually, we will be accepting file uploads and storing them for access by users via the Web. You know for certain that you need persistent disk storage and that we want to run our app on multiple EC2 instances. Clearly, this is not the solution, because there is a risk of instances being out of date. It's good to know that this feature exists; it just doesn't work for our use case.

We know that we will need some persistent data storage, and we know that EBS won't work for multiple instances. So, we can select **Instance store** for now, with the knowledge that we can only store temp data on our EC2 instances. This means that file uploads, log files, etc., will have to be stored elsewhere, which we will be discussing in more detail soon.

Having selected **Instance store** as your Default root device type, you have to choose an IAM role. This is the stack-level service role that we created earlier. Select **aws-opsworks-photoalbums-service-role** from the drop-down. Next, we have the option of setting a Default SSH key. This is a convenient field to have if you will frequently have to connect to your instances on the command line. It simplifies key management by assuming that all EC2 instances in your stack should use the same key, which is a far better approach than generating a new key pair for each instance. We will not be needing this for our application, so you can choose not to select a Default SSH key. As a reminder, SSH keys were discussed in greater detail earlier in the chapter. If you followed those steps and created a key pair, go ahead and choose it from the drop-down now.

Next, we must select a Default IAM instance profile. You will recall that we previously created two IAM roles: one service role and one instance role. This is where we select our instance role, **aws-opsworks-photoalbums-ec2-role**. You'll notice that you have the option to create a new role on the fly while you're in this screen, which will cause OpsWorks to auto-generate one for you.

Speaking of naming conventions, the next option is perhaps confusingly titled *Hostname theme*. The drop-down is full of options such as "Baked Goods," "European Cities," "Wild Cats," etc. When you create EC2 instances in OpsWorks, you don't want them just to be named instance-1, instance-2, etc. The Hostname theme options are simply thematic names to use for your instances, such as "Photoalbums - london-1" or "Photoalbums - paris-2," etc. You can choose whatever makes you happy, but note the first option in the list, **Layer Dependent**. This will name the instances after the OpsWorks layer they are a part of, a concept we will review shortly. I tend to prefer this option, as it means your instances will be named "Photoalbums nodejs-app1," "Photoalbums nodejs-app2," etc. For the remainder of the lessons, we will be using the Layer Dependent theme, but feel free to choose another option if you think it would be fun to have servers named after cats.

Last is the *Stack color*, which has no technical significance whatsoever. This is a color scheme used for the stack in the OpsWorks dashboard and is purely a matter of preference. Let's select the red on the far right.

Stack Options—Summary

Now we're finally ready to click **Add Stack** at the bottom right. The options we've selected appear in Listing 2-2. Review your choices one more time and click the button.

Listing 2-2. Summary of Stack Creation Options

```
Name: Photoalbums
Region: US East
VPC: No VPC
Default Availability Zone: us-east-1a
Default operating system: Amazon Linux 2014.09
Default root device type: Instance store
IAM role: aws-opsworks-photoalbums-service-role
Default SSH key: aws-opsworks-photoalbums-key (optional)
Default IAM instance profile: aws-opsworks-photoalbums-ec2-role
Hostname theme: Layer Dependent
Stack color: red
```

Congratulations! You have created your first stack. We're now in the stack detail view, which should list the next four major steps in setting up our app:

- Add your first layer.

- Add your first instance.

- Add your first app.

- See your application online.

So, yes, we do still have a long way to go in this lesson. Remember that the goal for this chapter is to simply see "Hello World" on the Web via an OpsWorks deployment. The next step in getting there is to learn about layers.

Layers

Layers are the main software ingredients of your application, and the hardware that goes with it. Let's break that down a little bit. When you were setting up your local environment in the first chapter, you had to do two main tasks: get your Node.js environment running and get your database running. These are the two layers of our application. In OpsWorks, each layer will require resources allocated to it.

The first layer, our Node.js application, is useless without machines running the code—it's just words on a page! As such, our Node.js App layer will require EC2 instances assigned to it. The Layers view lets you tie together these moving parts: the source code, the environment, and the instances running both.

The second layer, the database layer, is a little different. We will be hosting our database using Amazon RDS, which we will set up in a later chapter. For now, it is sufficient to understand this way of looking at it.

Every stack must have at least one layer, of which there are two types: OpsWorks layers and service layers. An OpsWorks layer is simply the blueprint for EC2 instances assigned to it. OpsWorks provides you with a number of preset OpsWorks layer types, which are themselves categorized as either Load Balancer, App Server, DB, or Other. For some OpsWorks layer subtypes (especially App Server), you may want several instances based on the same blueprint. Other types, such as load balancers, are typically only used for a single instance.

In addition to OpsWorks layers, AWS also offers a second type, which we referred to as service layers. Service layers allow you to add other AWS services as layers in your OpsWorks stack. Currently, only one service layer type is supported: RDS. I would expect more services to be rolled out in the future.

Creating an OpsWorks Layer

It's time to create our first layer. Under the first heading on the Stack detail page, click **Add a layer**. Just like when we created our stack, we're presented with a number of options, as shown in Figure 2-9.

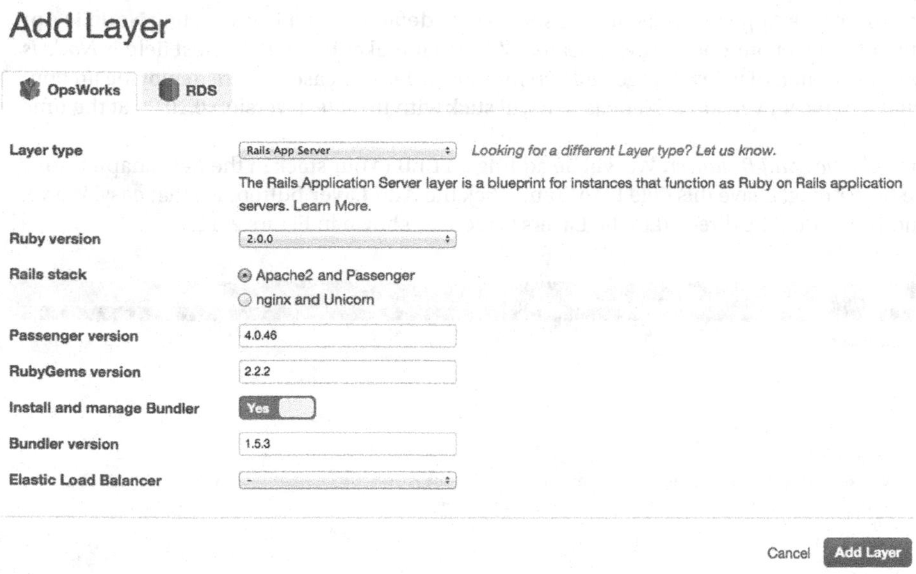

Add Layer

OpsWorks   **RDS**

Layer type	Rails App Server ▾	*Looking for a different Layer type? Let us know.*
	The Rails Application Server layer is a blueprint for instances that function as Ruby on Rails application servers. Learn More.	
Ruby version	2.0.0 ▾	
Rails stack	◉ Apache2 and Passenger	
	○ nginx and Unicorn	
Passenger version	4.0.46	
RubyGems version	2.2.2	
Install and manage Bundler	Yes ⬤	
Bundler version	1.5.3	
Elastic Load Balancer	- ▾	

Cancel   **Add Layer**

Figure 2-9. *Add Layer view*

You can see that the main layer types are distinguished by tabs at the top. We aren't ready to add an RDS (service) layer, so we'll stay in the OpsWorks tab. Our first option is *Layer type*. This is where different OpsWorks layer types are organized. Opening the drop-down should show you a list that looks something like that shown in Figure 2-10.

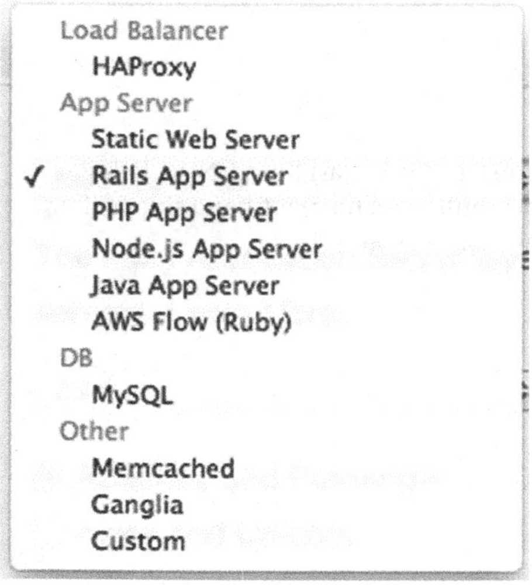

Load Balancer
    HAProxy
App Server
    Static Web Server
✓   **Rails App Server**
    PHP App Server
    Node.js App Server
    Java App Server
    AWS Flow (Ruby)
DB
    MySQL
Other
    Memcached
    Ganglia
    Custom

Figure 2-10. *OpsWorks layer types*

Rails App Server, under the App Server heading, is selected by default. We will be selecting **Node.js App Server** instead. Suddenly, a lot of our options disappeared. Well, that makes it easy! The next field is *Node.js version*. This gives you the option of using deprecated versions of Node.js, in case you are deploying an app that hasn't been tested in a recent version of Node.js. We will stick with the latest, version 0.10.29 at the time of this writing.

The last option is *Elastic Load Balancer*. We will be adding an ELB to our stack in the next chapter, so we'll skip this for the time being. Leave this field blank, and click the **Add Layer** button. It's that easy! We've got our first layer, and you should be directed to the Layers screen, as shown in Figure 2-11.

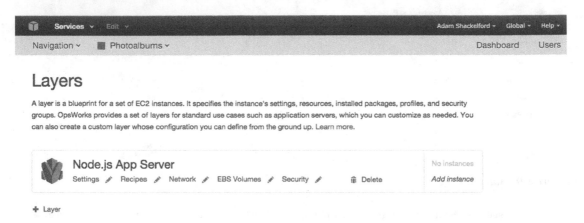

Figure 2-11. *Layers view*

There is a single layer in our stack now, which is the app server layer. All EC2 instances running our application will be a part of this layer. Take another look at Figure 2-7 if you need a refresher on how this works.

Instances

As you can see, there are already a lot of new places to explore in the OpsWorks dashboard. Next, let's go ahead and add our first instance to the layer. Click the **Add Instance** button on the right-hand side of the screen. The next view has some introductory text, as well as the interface in Figure 2-12.

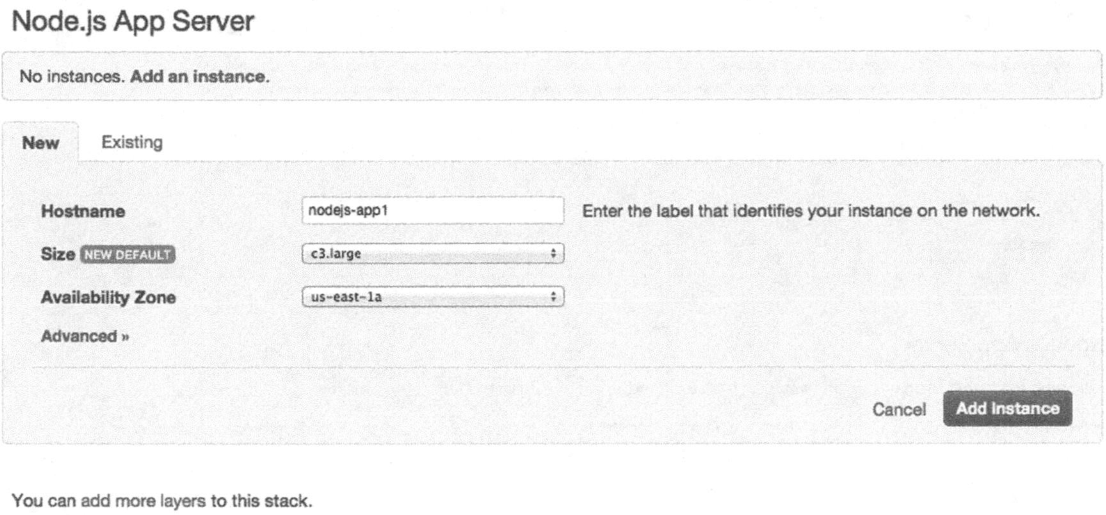

Node.js App Server

No instances. **Add an instance.**

New   Existing

Hostname	nodejs-app1	Enter the label that identifies your instance on the network.
Size NEW DEFAULT	c3.large ⬍	
Availability Zone	us-east-1a ⬍	
Advanced »		

Cancel   **Add Instance**

You can add more layers to this stack.

Figure 2-12. *Add an instance*

You will notice there are only a few settings to choose from. Most of the configuration is based on the defaults we chose when we were creating our stack. The *Hostname* field, for example, is pre-populated with a unique name based on the Hostname theme we chose earlier. You can leave this as **nodejs-app1**, unless you have your own naming conventions in mind.

Probably the biggest decision (no pun intended) is size. You will see a long list of options here, with sizes from the current generation as well as the previous generation and with various optimization options. Periodically, Amazon releases new generations of instances with different specs and price points than the previous generation. You can cross-reference this list here: http://aws.amazon.com/ec2/instance-types/#Instance_Types. In order to keep this page from getting too bloated, the previous generation specs are moved to a separate page here: http://aws.amazon.com/ec2/previous-generation/.

In the production environment, you're going to have to consider a lot of factors when creating the first instance(s) for your app server layer. I will discuss this more later. For now, it makes sense to choose the smallest and cheapest option on the list, **t1.micro**, all the way down at the very bottom.

Next, we choose the availability zone for this instance. Once again, the default that we choose when creating our stack is selected. You could change the availability zone, but let's leave it as **us-east-1a** for now. We will be creating instances in other zones later, so we want to keep at least one in the default zone. Go ahead and click **Advanced**, so you can see the additional options.

First is *Scaling Type*. This is a topic we will delve into later, but for now we want our instance to be online 24/7, so we'll leave that option selected. The other fields you will recognize from the stack creation process. Let's leave these default values alone, but it's good to know that they're here if you want to modify them at the instance level. Click **Add Instance** and you will be brought to the Instances detail view, a screen you will become quite familiar with (see Figure 2-13).

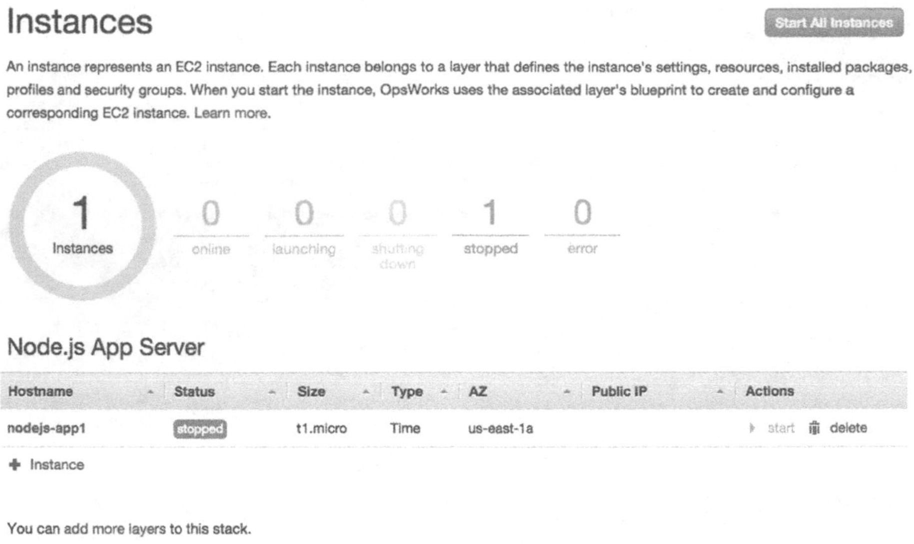

Instances

An instance represents an EC2 instance. Each instance belongs to a layer that defines the instance's settings, resources, installed packages, profiles and security groups. When you start the instance, OpsWorks uses the associated layer's blueprint to create and configure a corresponding EC2 instance. Learn more.

1	0	0	0	1	0
Instances	online	launching	shutting down	stopped	error

Node.js App Server

Hostname	Status	Size	Type	AZ	Public IP	Actions
nodejs-app1	stopped	t1.micro	Time	us-east-1a		▶ start 🗑 delete

➕ Instance

You can add more layers to this stack.

Figure 2-13. *Instances view*

In this view, you can see the status of all instances in your layer. At the top, a circle chart shows the number and percentage of instances in each state: online, launching, shutting down, stopped, or error. We currently have one instance, which is stopped, so there isn't much actionable information here. At the top right, you will notice a button that reads *Start All Instances*, which does exactly what it says. You can also start or stop instances individually, for example, if you wanted to manually scale up one of your instances. Alternatively, if you wanted to manually scale many of your instances, you could stop them one at a time, scale them, and reboot them, so your application does not experience any downtime. You can also add more instances to your layer on this screen.

Underneath the black AWS navigation bar at the top, you will notice that OpsWorks attaches a gray navigation bar. On the left side, you have Navigation for your current stack, and just next to it is a drop-down to navigate to a different stack entirely or create a new one. Click the **Navigation** button, and you should see a drop-down similar to that shown in Figure 2-14.

Figure 2-14. *OpsWorks stack navigation menu*

You will see a number of views that we have already visited, as well as some which are unfamiliar. Select **Apps**, where we will finally create our app in OpsWorks.

Apps

The introductory text at the top of the Apps view explains the concept as well as I could hope to:

> *An app represents code stored in a repository that you want to install on application server instances. When you deploy the app, OpsWorks downloads the code from the repository to the specified server instances.*

When we create our app, we are configuring OpsWorks to take a copy of the sample app and deploy it to every instance in the app server layer, and then start those instances. You should see a blue message box that informs you that you have no apps but can **Add an app**. Click this, and we can begin getting this app created.

First is the *Name* field, where you can enter the name **Photoalbums**. The next field is *Type*, which should default to Node.js, so we can leave that alone. The next section is titled *Data Sources*, where you can choose what sort of database you want to use. You could select RDS, which you recall is a service layer. You could choose OpsWorks, if you wanted to create a MySQL database layer in OpsWorks, or None, if you were hosting a static application. We will choose **RDS** and create an RDS instance at a later point (see Figure 2-15).

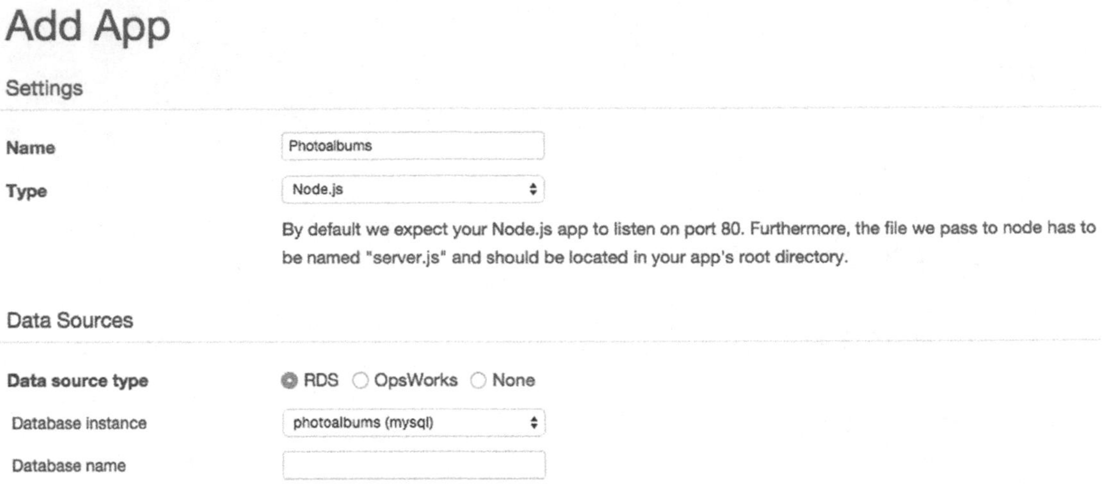

Add App

Settings

Name	Photoalbums
Type	Node.js ⧨

By default we expect your Node.js app to listen on port 80. Furthermore, the file we pass to node has to be named "server.js" and should be located in your app's root directory.

Data Sources

Data source type	⦿ RDS ○ OpsWorks ○ None
Database instance	photoalbums (mysql) ⧨
Database name	

Figure 2-15. *Add an app to your OpsWorks stack*

Application Source

We've come to an important decision point: how are we going to get our source code deployed to our servers? This is an important decision, not for the functioning of your app, but for your development team's workflow. We will review each of these options. You can choose the method which suits you best, and in future lessons, I will assume that you can manage the deployment on your own. Figure 2-16 shows a sample configuration.

Application Source

Repository type	Git ⧨
Repository URL	https://github.com/user/appsource.git
Repository SSH key	Optional
Branch/Revision	Optional

Figure 2-16. *Application Source configuration in OpsWorks app*

If you open the **Repository type** menu, you will see five types under three headings: Source Control, Bundle, and Other. If you deploy from Source Control, you provide a URL and credentials, which will allow OpsWorks to connect to your repository and download the source from the specified branch. If you choose Bundle, OpsWorks will retrieve a zip from the specified location, unzip it, and run the app. The last option is Other, which is for more advanced users. Instead of OpsWorks retrieving your code, you can use Chef recipes to handle the deployment process.

If you're familiar with GitHub, the easiest way to proceed is to deploy from your own GitHub repository. If you use another Git repository service that allows you to connect via SSH, the process is basically the same. I'll describe the different methods below, of which you can choose the one that suits you and continue on.

Deploying from Git

You will need to generate an SSH key, so that OpsWorks can connect to your repository. If you need help doing this, there's a handy guide here: https://help.github.com/articles/generating-ssh-keys/.

■ **Note** When generating your SSH key, do not set a password. OpsWorks does not support SSH keys with passwords, and you will be unable to use your key to deploy.

Once you've generated your key, we can fill out the fields. First is the Repository URL, which you can find at the right-hand side of the screen in GitHub (see Figure 2-17). If you use Beanstalk or another repository service, you'll find the SSH clone URL in a similar sidebar.

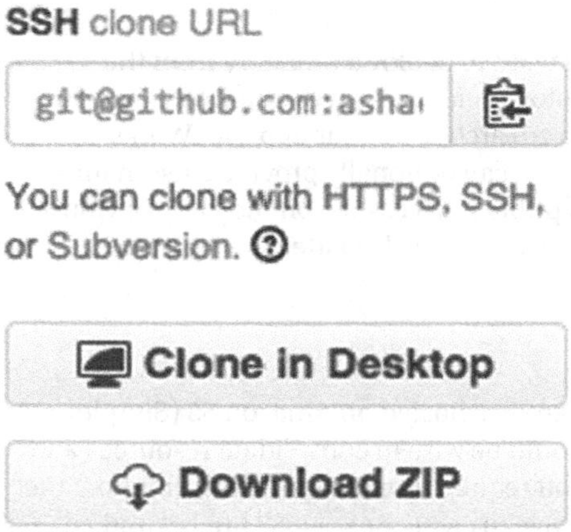

SSH clone URL

git@github.com:ashaı

You can clone with HTTPS, SSH, or Subversion. ⓘ

🖥 **Clone in Desktop**

☁ **Download ZIP**

Figure 2-17. *SSH clone URL in GitHub*

Copy the SSH clone URL to your clipboard and paste it into the Repository URL field in OpsWorks. Next, we need the private key you generated. It should be named something such as "github_rsa" and be located in `./ssh` on your computer. Open the file in a plain-text editor. It should look something like the following:

```
-----BEGIN RSA PRIVATE KEY-----
Proc-Type: 4,ENCRYPTED
DEK-Info: AES-128-CBC,3048941ED91AFBCE12E396E516EC35D4

OgkTkCilHDYOgommrpNVlmZjtKxrD4smsFOVgvhweaNvoG8aTMQcjYb461TqwdsJ
{{A BUNCH OF RANDOM CHARACTERS}}
iLOdRv+4XFKhN3ZKyJ9VwVOyxrV6hSROFOwFzGtXAD8OJctMcyAwGctJJmNQmRe2
-----END RSA PRIVATE KEY-----
```

Copy the file's contents onto your clipboard and paste it into the Repository SSH key field. Last, you can select a specific branch/revision to deploy. HEAD is used by default, so we'll leave that alone. If, for instance, you were creating a new stack to serve as your dev environment, you would enter your dev branch name here.

Deploying from Subversion

As with Git, you will provide credentials for OpsWorks to connect to your repository and download a copy of the source. With Subversion, you must connect via HTTP, providing your account username and password. As in the case of OpsWorks, you can specify a specific revision to deploy. However, note that you must include the full path to your code in the *Repository URL* this time. If you want to deploy from a specific branch, be sure to include the directory path in your *Repository URL*.

Deploying from HTTP Archive

If you aren't using a code repository, or for some reason you don't want to deploy a directory from the repo to OpsWorks, there are a few other options. First, you can deploy from an archive hosted anywhere on the Web. If you select HTTP Archive, you simply need the URL to a zip archive of your app. OpsWorks will download your archive, extract it, and deploy it to your instances. You can optionally provide a username and password, if your archive is password-protected. If your zip is publicly accessible on the Web, obviously this means your source code can be accessed by anyone, which may not be the best idea.

Deploying from S3 Archive

Just like deploying an HTTP archive, you can also deploy from an archive hosted on Amazon S3 (Simple Storage Service). To set this up, we have to make a detour, but it would be wise to consolidate resources and use S3 over HTTP, if you can. When you select S3, you'll see that you require three pieces of information: the URL for your archive, an access key, and a secret. This means we have to create both an S3 bucket and an IAM User to access the bucket. We'll run through these steps quickly and spend more time with S3 later in the book.

First, let's create our IAM User with permission to access S3 buckets. We could first create a group and then add the user, as we did before. However, the permissions are simple, and we can reuse this user if we have to, so let's keep it simple and just create a user. It would be best to make this detour in a new tab. Click (or right-click or Control-click, depending on your operating system) the orange box at the top-left corner, to return to the AWS home screen, and select IAM. Click **Users** in the left navigation, and then click **Create New Users** at the top of the Users page. We'll call this user *photoalbums-s3*. When you proceed to the next screen, be sure to click **Download Credentials**, to save a copy of the user's access key/secret. Then click **Close**.

You should now see your user in the Users list. Click the name to proceed to the User detail view. You've been here before! Next, we have to generate a policy for the user that will allow it to have full access to S3. Under the Permissions header, click **Attach User Policy**. Once again, we're in the Policy generator. Under the Select Policy Template header, scroll down and select **Amazon S3 Full Access**. You will have the chance to review your policy before generating it (see Figure 2-18).

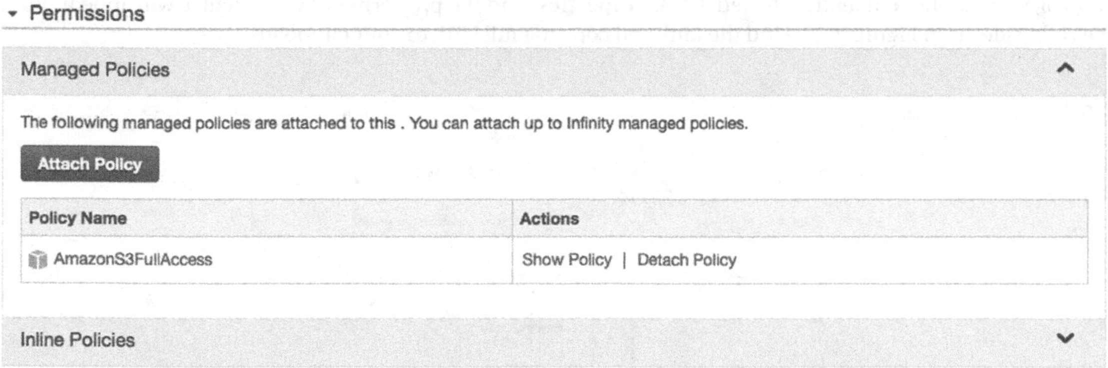

▾ Permissions

Managed Policies	▲

The following managed policies are attached to this . You can attach up to Infinity managed policies.

Attach Policy

Policy Name	Actions
📦 AmazonS3FullAccess	Show Policy | Detach Policy

Inline Policies	▾

Figure 2-18. *S3 Full Access Permissions policy*

Next, we have to create our S3 bucket. Head back to the AWS home screen and click **S3**. Click **Create Bucket** at the top left. A modal pop-up will appear, prompting you to name the bucket. Enter **photoalbums-source-[*your initials*]** as your bucket name and select **US Standard** for your region (see Figure 2-19).

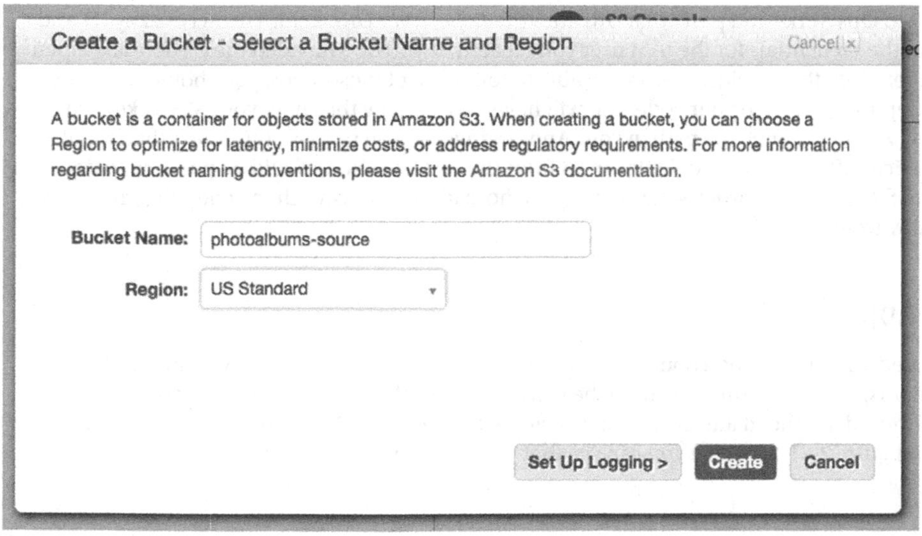

Create a Bucket - Select a Bucket Name and Region   Cancel x

A bucket is a container for objects stored in Amazon S3. When creating a bucket, you can choose a Region to optimize for latency, minimize costs, or address regulatory requirements. For more information regarding bucket naming conventions, please visit the Amazon S3 documentation.

Bucket Name: photoalbums-source

Region: US Standard   ▾

Set Up Logging >   Create   Cancel

Figure 2-19. *Creating an S3 bucket*

With the name and region selected, click **Create**. You will be returned to the main view for S3, and your bucket will appear on the left side. Click it, and you'll see the contents of your bucket, which is currently empty. Click **Upload** in the top-left corner of this view. Create an archive of your source code and drag it into the upload dialog. You don't need to set any of the other options here; just click **Start Upload**.

You will again be returned to the list of files, and the upload progress will appear on the right side of the screen. When it's finished, click your `.zip` in the list of files. In the top-right corner, you will see a segmented control, with "None" currently selected. Click **Properties**, and the properties of your archive will appear on the right side, as in Figure 2-20. Find the Link and copy the full URL to your clipboard.

Figure 2-20. *S3 object properties*

Head back over to OpsWorks and paste that URL into the *Repository URL* field. The Access key ID and Secret access key are the credentials for the IAM user you created. If you downloaded the credentials, open them up and copy them into these fields. If you were able to follow all of these steps, you should be set up to deploy from S3. To deploy updates to your code, you will have to overwrite the zip in your S3 bucket every time or upload a new zip and change the path in your App settings. As you can see, this is less than ideal. Some repository services also allow you to deploy to S3 from their servers, so it would be possible to deploy a zip from your repo to S3 as well. Regardless, this method is more labor-intensive than generating an SSH key and deploying directly from Git.

Creating your App

After you've configured your Application Source, you will see the following sections: Environmental Variables, Add Domains, and SSL Settings. You will be learning about these in subsequent lessons. If everything else looks good, go ahead and click **Add App** at the bottom right. You should be returned to the Apps view, shown in Figure 2-21, in which you can see that your app has been created.

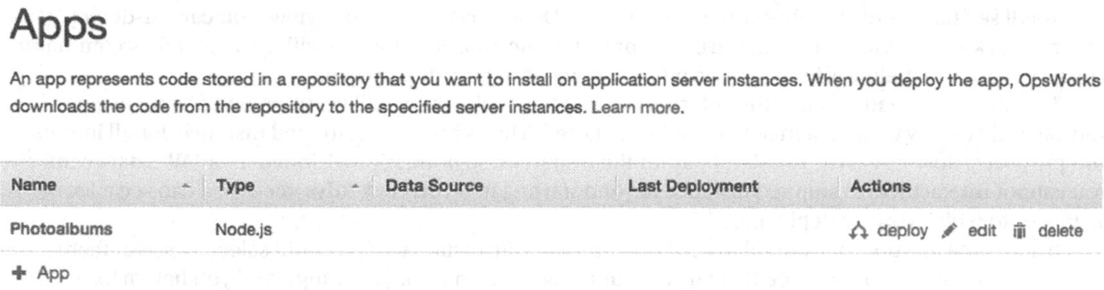

Apps

An app represents code stored in a repository that you want to install on application server instances. When you deploy the app, OpsWorks downloads the code from the repository to the specified server instances. Learn more.

Name	▲	Type	▲	Data Source	Last Deployment	Actions
Photoalbums		Node.js				⚙ deploy ✏ edit 🗑 delete

✚ App

Figure 2-21. *The Apps view*

Deploying Your App

Well, there's not much left to do besides deploy your app! Before we can do this, we have to start one of our instances. Click **Navigation** at the top left and select **Instances** to return to the Instances view. At the top right, click **Start All Instances**. You will see the *Status* field next to your instance change to *requested*, then *pending, booting, running_setup*, and, finally, *online*. The whole process should take a few minutes.

Now that we have an instance online, we can deploy. Under Navigation, select **Apps** to return to the Apps view. You'll see the deploy button in the Actions column on the right side of the Photoalbums row. Click it, and you should now find yourself in the Deploy App view, as shown in Figure 2-22.

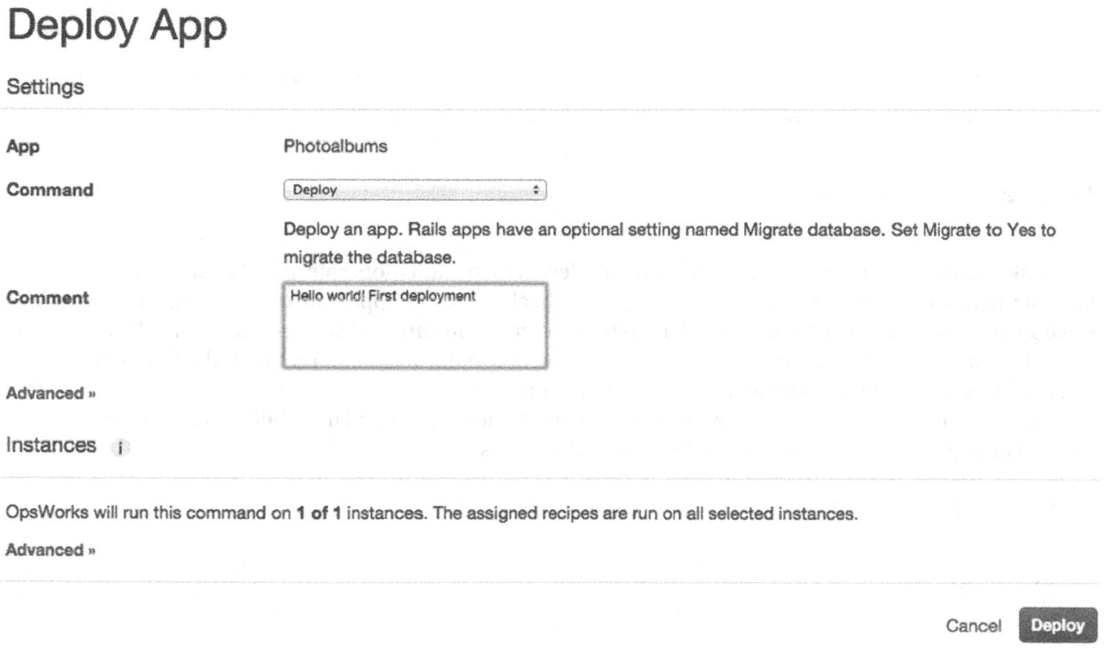

Deploy App

Settings

App	Photoalbums
Command	Deploy ⇕
	Deploy an app. Rails apps have an optional setting named Migrate database. Set Migrate to Yes to migrate the database.
Comment	Hello world! First deployment

Advanced »

Instances ⓘ

OpsWorks will run this command on **1 of 1** instances. The assigned recipes are run on all selected instances.

Advanced »

Cancel **Deploy**

Figure 2-22. *Deploy App view*

You'll see that there are other commands besides Deploy available in this view. You can un-deploy your app, roll back to a previous version, start, stop, or restart the app. For now, we will use the Deploy command. The *Comment* field below is for your own internal notes about the deployment.

The Instances header below this informs you that the deployment will occur on one of one instances. You can only deploy to an instance that has been started. This is because a stopped instance, for all intents and purposes, does not exist. You don't pay for the resources, so none is provisioned in an AWS data center. You cannot interact with a stopped instance beyond starting it. If you click **Advanced**, you can see a list of instances to which you are deploying.

If, for some reason, you wanted to deploy to only specific instances, you could select/deselect them here. One such scenario would be that one of your instances is in error (crashing), and you have a fix to deploy to resolve the issue. You deploy to the instances that are currently online, while you're trying to bring the problematic instance back online. Once it's online, you run the deployment again, but only on the instance that just recovered from an error. You may never encounter this use case, but it's nice to know that OpsWorks can handle it!

Click **Deploy** and you will be brought to the Deployment view, shown in Figure 2-23.

Figure 2-23. *Deployment view*

While the deployment is running, you will see a few activity indicators spinning. When it finishes, the Status at the top will change to *successful*, and a green check mark will appear next to your instance. You'll notice a few interesting features here. Under the SSH column, you can choose to connect via SSH directly to any of your running instances. You may never need to do this, but it's good to have it. In the Log column, you can click **Show** to see the deployment logs for your instance.

These logs may be a bit overwhelming at first; they are the output of all the Chef recipes that are executed to deploy your app. They should mostly look like this:

```
[2014-10-26T18:48:44+00:00] INFO: Chef-client pid: 3167
```

If you see any log types besides INFO and WARN, you may want to investigate further. If you're feeling adventurous, you can sort of follow the logs to get an understanding of what's happening under the hood. A few of the major events in broad strokes follow:

- The opsworks_custom_cookbooks::load and ::execute commands are run.

- A list of additional cookbooks based on the configuration and language of your app are executed.

- Your code is copied via SSH and validated.

- Your code is deployed to /srv/www/photoalbums, and the Node.js environment is configured.

- Your package.json file is detected, and node_modules is installed.

- Your app is started (or restarted).

This is a simplification, but it should give you an idea of what happens behind the scenes to make your code run in the cloud. Now it's time for the moment of truth. Open the OpsWorks Navigation menu and choose **Instances**. In the Public IP column, you should see the IP address of your single instance. Click it, and you should see our welcome screen, shown in Figure 2-24.

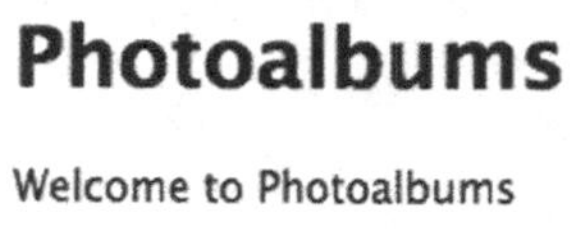

Photoalbums

Welcome to Photoalbums

Figure 2-24. *Welcome to Photoalbums!*

Can you believe it? We finally got our app up and running in the cloud! Because we haven't configured a load balancer or added a domain, we're just looking at the app on a single instance. This is not our intended use of OpsWorks—we do not want our users to directly access an EC2 instance. We will be remedying this soon.

Summary

Congratulations, you have an application residing on the Web, in the cloud! Sadly, it's still basically useless until we have configured our database at the very least. You've covered a lot in this chapter, from exploring the major concepts of AWS architecture to creating our application stack from the ground up and deploying our code. In the next chapter, we will use Amazon RDS to host our database, and our application will become usable for the first time. By learning how to use OpsWorks, you have also learned a lot about the paradigms and vernacular of AWS in general and a lot about Identity and Access Management and EC2 in particular. This was a big step on the way to architecting and developing for the cloud.

CHAPTER 3

■ ■ ■

OpsWorks Part II: Databases and Scaling

Now that we have a functioning application stack, we can start to really build out the functionality. First and foremost, we must connect the application to a database, so we can start storing and retrieving content. Second, we will add a load balancer to our stack. Last, we will set up some auto-scaling behavior for our application, so that the app can scale up to meet increases in demand automatically, possessing elasticity.

You will recall from the previous chapter that an OpsWorks stack contains one or more layers within it. In Chapter 2, we created a single layer: the App Server. We will be adding the additional layers in this chapter, which will round out the major tasks in setting up OpsWorks. We will create the database layer by provisioning and attaching a high-availability, managed MySQL database. We will also attach a load balancer to our stack, distributing web traffic among multiple EC2 instances. While we will return to the OpsWorks dashboard many times, we will be working with other AWS services to construct the core components of our application.

Relational Database Service (RDS)

RDS is one of the AWS database service offerings and our choice for this project. RDS supports MySQL, is cost-effective, and can be integrated into OpsWorks as a service layer. Similar to those of EC2, RDS instances can be scaled, cloned, and monitored for performance issues.

The keen observer will wonder why we can't just make a new OpsWorks layer and run MySQL on some EC2 instances. Wasn't there a MySQL layer type in OpsWorks? Yes, there was, and you could make this fairly easily. However, there is a lot more to RDS than raw computing power. RDS has some great features that we will explore a little more in this chapter.

If you create an EC2 instance in a MySQL layer in OpsWorks, you are merely installing the necessary software to run a MySQL database on that instance. It will still be up to you to perform all the administrative tasks—most important, backing up your data. It will also be up to you to install software updates as needed. If MySQL crashes, or the instance is in error, you will have to manually recover.

None of this sounds appealing, does it? Fortunately, there is RDS to automate all of these tasks for you! If we had to do this much maintenance, we wouldn't be making the most of the cloud or taking advantage of the benefits I've been talking about for the past two chapters. When you use an RDS instance instead, you don't have to worry about all of this maintenance. Most important to your application performance is the error recovery. When you create an RDS database, you are provisioning resources in the same way you would with EC2 instances. Your database is hosted in a particular availability zone within a specific region. If the database layer goes down and you're trying to recover manually, it could cause significant downtime for your entire app. Not only does RDS minimize this downtime, it allows you to keep a backup instance ready to go to work if your main instance is down, in a feature called Multi-AZ deployment.

Multi-AZ Deployment

When your app is dependent on a single RDS database instance, this naturally creates a point of failure in your application: if that availability zone (or instance) experiences an outage, it can cause a global outage for your stack. To mitigate this problem, you can use Multi-AZ deployment. When you enable Multi-AZ deployment, RDS automatically provisions a standby database in another availability zone (see Figure 3-1) and replicates the data to the standby instances through a synchronous process. Every time a write or commit operation is executed on your database, before the transaction is complete, the operation is carried out on your standby database also. The downside is that this causes a slight increase in latency compared to a single availability-zone deployment. If your application required thousands of database writes per second, this minor difference in latency could become noticeable. Keep in mind that this could constitute a tangible performance cost in your application. Multi-AZ deployments are also more expensive, as you're essentially doubling the resources you would be using otherwise.

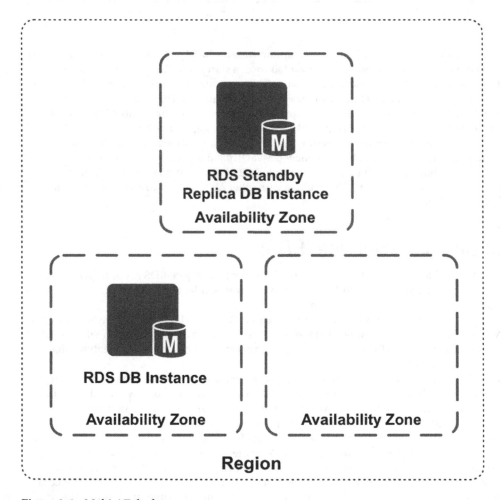

Figure 3-1. *Multi-AZ deployments*

Clearly there is a cost-benefit analysis to be done with Multi-AZ deployment. On the one hand, you don't have to worry about responding to an outage by manually booting up a backup copy of your database. Any engineer who's had to sign on to work at 11 p.m. on a Friday night knows the value of this. Having a completely up-to-date backup copy ready to run your application and available in minutes is a technological wonder for which the general population has no appreciation. On the other hand, we will lose a little bit of write speed with Multi-AZ, and it's more expensive. If Multi-AZ is not worth the cost, AWS is committed to 99.95% monthly uptime for RDS instances. If you choose to use a single instance, you will risk your application experiencing an outage.

However, in an application such as ours, we may not even notice the difference in latency. Our database schema is simple, and the queries are simple. Users are unlikely to perform a large number of write operations per user at a time, so in our case, this doesn't seem like a major concern. The truth is that while the benefits of Multi-AZ may be universal, the performance cost of Multi-AZ deployment is contingent on both the nature of the application and the projected user base size and behavior.

Read Replicas

As was just discussed, we're expecting our database operations to be read-heavy. If the sheer volume of read operations on our database (in MySQL terms, any SELECT query) is bottlenecking our database, it's going to have a ripple effect on the entire application. Fortunately, there is a way to offload some of this work to another database instance, a read replica. You can create an RDS instance of this type (up to five), designating a master database and selecting a region and availability for your read replica. As you may infer from the term *replica*, these instances should have the same resources as the original database.

In Figure 3-2 you can see how read replicas work. Database reads can be routed to the read replicas, which read from the master instance at a lower query volume. Any write operations bypass the read replicas and go to the master instance in the original availability zone of the application stack. Using a read replica can offload a significant amount of work from the master database instance to the replica(s). If the master database only has to handle a small number of reads and all of the writes, there could be a significant benefit.

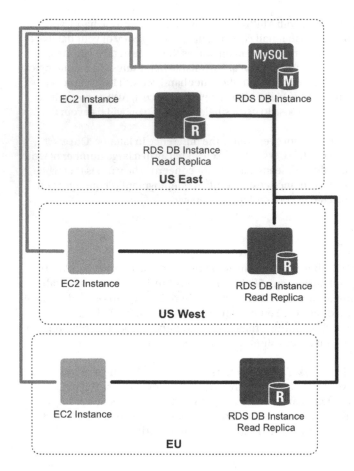

Figure 3-2. *Cross-Region Read Replica behavior. The green lines represent write operations, and the black lines represent read operations*

As you may have surmised from Figure 3-2, RDS does in fact support read replica creation in other regions, with a feature called Cross-Region Read Replicas. There is a benefit here in disaster-recovery scenarios. If for some reason an entire AWS region was experiencing an outage, you would have to quickly redeploy your entire stack in another region. To do this, you would clone your stack to a different region and promote one of your preexisting read replicas to be the new master database. It would otherwise be possible to recover from a regional outage, but this feature simply makes it easier.

Cross-Region Read Replicas are also useful in a non-disaster scenario, if you simply want to move your stack to a different region. Suppose our app was a flop in the United States but became huge in Germany. There would be a case to be made for moving the stack to a geographic region closer to our user base.

Since OpsWorks is designed to let you deploy your stack in a single region and use other services to improve your performance in other regions, we will not get much use out of Cross-Region Read Replicas, unless we were to plan for a regional disaster. You will soon be learning about other services that will help us to improve performance, but it's good to know about this feature regardless.

PRICING

With these extra features, you may be immediately suspicious of RDS's affordability. Indeed, it is a bit less straightforward than EC2 pricing, as you can see here: http://aws.amazon.com/rds/pricing/. The main difference is this: in addition to paying for the processor and memory, a.k.a. computing power of your instances, you also pay for both data storage and data transfer. Data storage refers to the raw volume of data stored in your instance, and data transfer is the input/output from our database to the app layer. Similar to other services, it's an on-demand, pay-as-you-go model, but there's a lot of room for deviation here.

Provisioned IOPS Storage

Though we've chosen our instance size, we have given Amazon no information about how many input/output operations we want to perform, and I/O speed and capacity are key metrics in measuring database performance. If our traffic surged from five users to five thousand users in the course of an hour, making about one database query per second, we would be relying on AWS to automatically provide additional I/O capacity on the fly.

It makes sense if you think about what happens when you query the database. When there is a sudden rush of requests exceeding the database I/O capacity, they are placed in a queue, while RDS attempts to keep up with the traffic. In the meantime, RDS attempts to scale up the I/O resources for your instance, which happens entirely behind the scenes in an AWS data center (a.k.a. *in the cloud*). But it will most likely take more than a split second to allocate additional capacity, and every second that requests remain in queue is an extra second that users have to wait for the data they requested. When traffic dies down, the resources are de-allocated, and you are charged for what you used.

This doesn't seem like the best idea in production, if we have performance expectations to manage. Fortunately, you can reserve I/O resources with Provisioned IOPS Storage (input/output operations per second). When you use Provisioned IOPS Storage, you reserve IOPS resources by storage volume and I/O operations per second. Though this is more expensive than pay as you go (if you don't use the resources you provisioned), reserving the resources ahead of time guarantees consistent speed and performance during periods of high traffic.

Let's imagine the same scenario as before, only with Provisioned IOPS Storage in use. This time, you have reserved 10,000 IOPS and 10GB of storage. Again, your traffic surges from five to five thousand users, making one database query each per second. In this case, we already have resources available to handle double the I/O as our traffic requires. Of course, if our traffic doubled, we would again be in trouble, but we can prepare for this eventuality as well.

DB Security Groups

Before we create our database, we must create a DB security group. If our database were in a Virtual Private Cloud, public access would be restricted. Because we're not using VPC, we want to restrict database access to the EC2 instances in our application stack. Because we will also want to work locally, we will allow access to the database from our IP address as well. While you will recognize the concepts from the work we've done in Identity and Access Management, we will actually provision our security group in RDS.

Begin by returning to your Sign-in URL and logging in as the photoadmin IAM user you created in Chapter 1. From the AWS Console home (or the menu), select **RDS**. You should see a view similar to that in Figure 3-3, which shows the two left-most columns of the RDS dashboard. As usual, there is a right-hand column with additional links and resources that are not shown here.

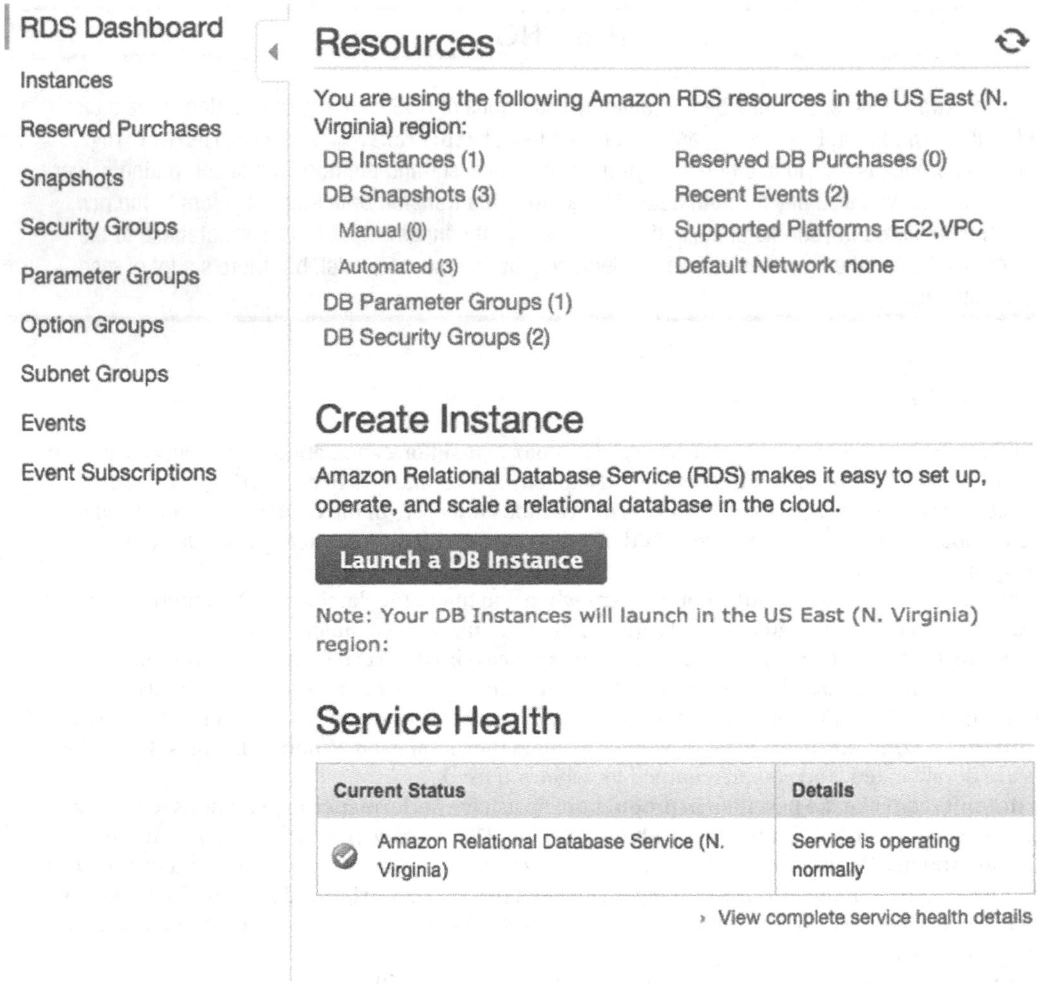

RDS Dashboard

Instances

Reserved Purchases

Snapshots

Security Groups

Parameter Groups

Option Groups

Subnet Groups

Events

Event Subscriptions

◄ # Resources ↺

You are using the following Amazon RDS resources in the US East (N. Virginia) region:

DB Instances (1)   Reserved DB Purchases (0)

DB Snapshots (3)   Recent Events (2)

  Manual (0)   Supported Platforms EC2,VPC

  Automated (3)   Default Network none

DB Parameter Groups (1)

DB Security Groups (2)

Create Instance

Amazon Relational Database Service (RDS) makes it easy to set up, operate, and scale a relational database in the cloud.

Launch a DB Instance

Note: Your DB Instances will launch in the US East (N. Virginia) region:

Service Health

Current Status	Details
✅ Amazon Relational Database Service (N. Virginia)	Service is operating normally

› View complete service health details

Figure 3-3. *The RDS dashboard*

In the left-hand column, click **Security Groups**. On the right side, you will see a large blue button that reads **Create DB Security Group**. The first view is simple. You provide a name and description for your security group (see Figure 3-4).

Figure 3-4. *Create DB Security Group view in the RDS dashboard*

You can name the group **photoalbums-rds-group**. The description can be anything that will be useful to you down the road. Then, click **Yes, Create**. You will be returned to the RDS Security Groups view, and you should see your group appear in the table, as in Figure 3-5.

Figure 3-5. *Your RDS security groups*

You will notice the red text in the Status column that reads "No Authorizations." This means that although this security group has been created and can be assigned to RDS instances, the group does not currently provide access to any instances. This is a handy warning that your work here is incomplete.

Select the table row for your security group, and you will be able to create a new connection type to authorize in your security group. The two types are CIDR/IP and EC2 Security Group. We will be creating one of each.

When you authorize a CIDR/IP, you are white listing a specific IP address to connect to your database. This is ideal for development, as we can white list our own IP address to connect to the RDS instance. By default, you will see your current IP address in the field. If you're using a proxy/firewall, you'll have to disable it, or if you're on a company network, work with the network admin. If you're not proxied or behind a firewall, leave the CIDR/IP address as is, and click **Authorize**. Otherwise, determine the correct IP and change the value accordingly. Keep in mind that if you have a dynamic IP, you will have to repeat this process every time your IP address refreshes.

You'll see an activity indicator next to your security group, and a new table will appear with the authorized connections for your security group (see Figure 3-6). Next, we'll create a new connection of the EC2 Security Group type. Just like RDS, EC2 has its own security groups. In fact, all the instances in our App Server layer are part of their own security group.

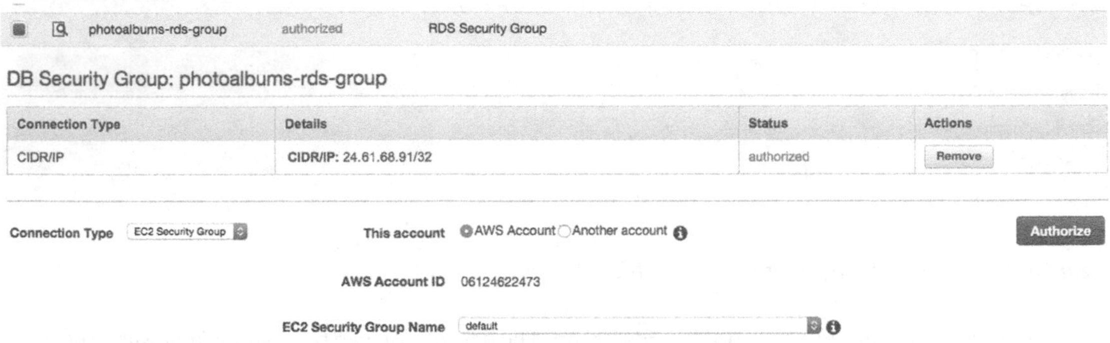

| | photoalbums-rds-group | authorized | RDS Security Group |

DB Security Group: photoalbums-rds-group

Connection Type	Details	Status	Actions
CIDR/IP	CIDR/IP: 24.61.68.91/32	authorized	Remove

Connection Type	EC2 Security Group	This account	● AWS Account ○ Another account ●		Authorize
		AWS Account ID	06124622473		
		EC2 Security Group Name	default		

Figure 3-6. *DB Security Group, authorizing connections*

Select **EC2 Security Group** from the Connection Type drop-down. You will notice that you have the option of choosing another AWS account besides your own. At the time of this writing, Amazon was rolling out cross-account connectivity, thus allowing EC2 instances on another AWS account to connect to your database. Leave this account selected and in the EC2 Security Group drop-down, choose **AWS-OpsWorks-nodejs-AppServer** and click **Authorize**. You should now see a second row in the table of connections for your security group.

Creating an RDS Database

You now have an RDS Security Group that will permit connections from your local machine, your App Server layer in OpsWorks, and nowhere else! Without further ado, let's go ahead and create our database layer. From the RDS home screen, you will see a large blue button inviting you to **Launch a DB Instance**. Clicking the button will take you to the multistep instance setup. Step 1, as shown in Figure 3-7, is choosing the database engine, which includes four options at the time of this writing: MySQL, PostgreSQL, Oracle, and SQL Server. This is a no-brainer, as I've already discussed using MySQL for our app. Click **Select** and continue.

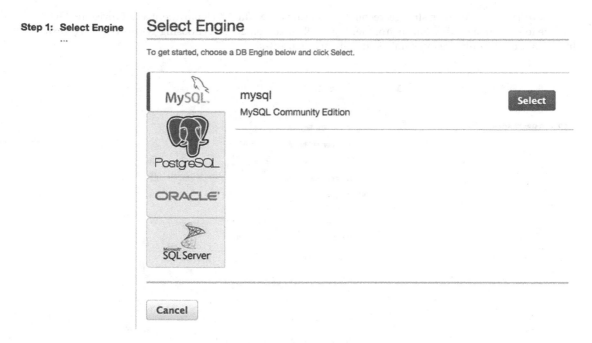

Figure 3-7. *RDS database engine selection*

Step 2 is interesting, as it's one of the rare scenarios in which AWS will make an explicit recommendation on how to configure a production vs. development environment. As you can see in Figure 3-8, Step 2's title is "Production?" In our case, the answer is yes!

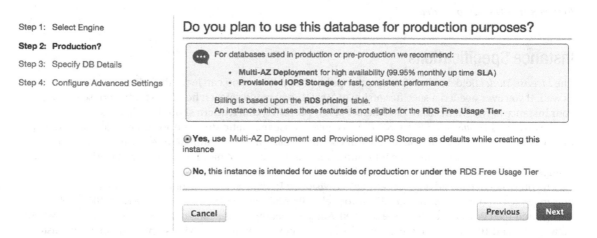

Figure 3-8. *Choosing to use an RDS instance in a production environment*

As you can see, Amazon strongly recommends using the Multi-AZ Deployment and Provisioned IOPS Storage features in a production environment. We will heed their advice, choosing **Yes** and clicking **Next**. In Step 3, we will configure our database details (see Figure 3-9).

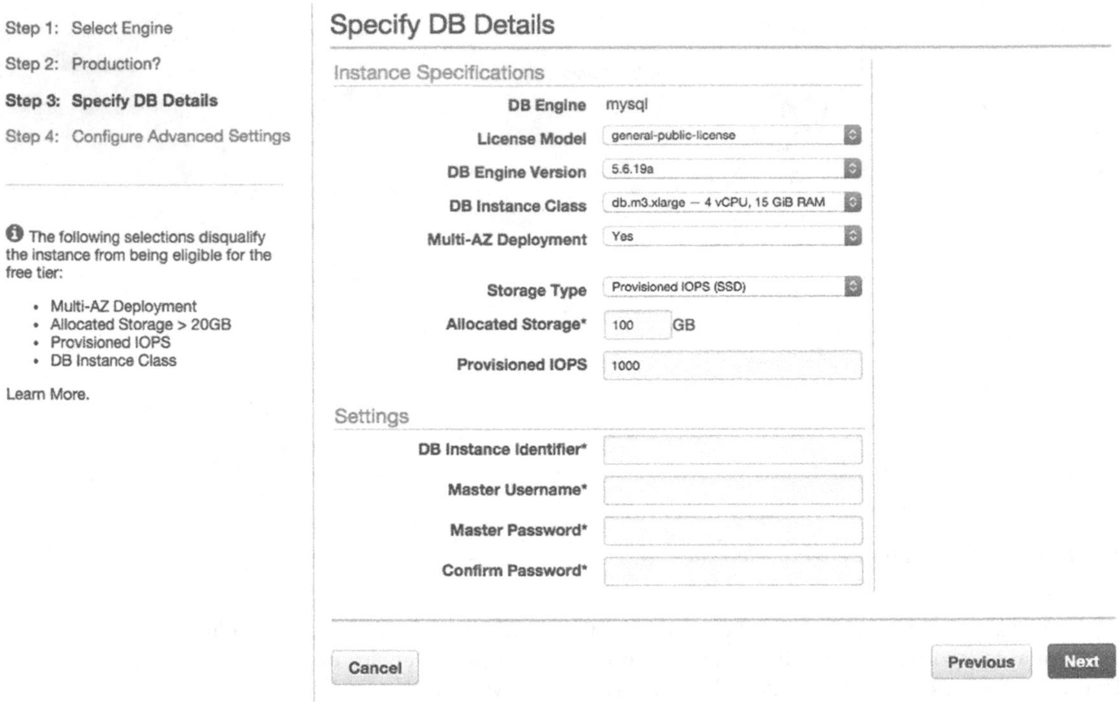

Step 1: Select Engine	**Specify DB Details**
Step 2: Production?	Instance Specifications
Step 3: Specify DB Details	
Step 4: Configure Advanced Settings	

Instance Specifications fields:

- **DB Engine**: mysql
- **License Model**: general-public-license
- **DB Engine Version**: 5.6.19a
- **DB Instance Class**: db.m3.xlarge — 4 vCPU, 15 GiB RAM
- **Multi-AZ Deployment**: Yes
- **Storage Type**: Provisioned IOPS (SSD)
- **Allocated Storage***: 100 GB
- **Provisioned IOPS**: 1000

ℹ The following selections disqualify the instance from being eligible for the free tier:

- Multi-AZ Deployment
- Allocated Storage > 20GB
- Provisioned IOPS
- DB Instance Class

Learn More.

Settings:

- **DB Instance Identifier***
- **Master Username***
- **Master Password***
- **Confirm Password***

Cancel   Previous   **Next**

Figure 3-9. *RDS database details*

Instance Specifications

The *License Model* field can be left as general-public-license, and you can leave the *DB Engine Version* alone as well. If you ever needed a specific version of MySQL, you could select it here. Next, you choose the size of your instance in the *DB Instance Class* field. For our purposes, **db.t1.micro** should work. Let's keep *Multi-AZ Deployment* and *Provisioned IOPS (SSD)*. You could choose magnetic storage now to save money and switch to Provisioned IOPS later, but converting will take an indeterminate amount of time. In this scenario, the AWS Console will display a message informing you that the Multi-AZ backup instance will work while your changes are being applied. I have learned the hard way that this is not always the case.

If you've heeded my advice and selected **Provisioned IOPS**, you have to choose how much storage and how many IOPS you wish to allocate. When you select **Provisioned IOPS** as your storage type, 100GB of storage and 1000 Provisioned IOPS are selected. Amazon recommends a ratio of IOPS to storage of somewhere between 3:1 and 10:1. We can leave this setting alone for now. Over time, we will establish an operating history for our app and scale these resources up or down based on our analysis of the metrics we collect.

■ **Note**   In real-world applications, it's a bit silly to use all these RDS features with the smallest instance AWS offers. We're just selecting **db.t1.micro** for cost-effective practice.

Settings

If you've ever set up a database before, these settings will be familiar. You will set a unique identifier, username, and password for your database. In the *DB Instance Identifier* enter **photoalbums**. For the sake of argument, we'll name our *Master Username*, **admin**. You can actually set whatever username and password you want, so long as you remember it! After you've set your credentials, click **Next**.

Advanced Settings

Step 4 takes us to the advanced settings, which you can see in Figure 3-10. In Network Security, you will not be able to choose a *VPC* or *Availability Zone*. Select **photoalbums-rds-group** as your *DB Security Group*. In Database Options, you can name your database **photoalbums**. Likewise, *Database Port, Parameter Group*, and *Option Group* do not have to be changed.

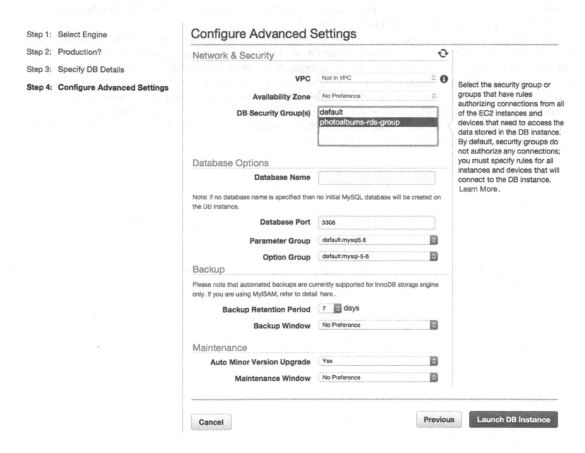

Figure 3-10. *RDS advanced settings*

The next subsection is titled Backup, from where you can select the automated backup schedule for your instance. RDS will take daily backups (snapshots) of your instance automatically, and you can specify a window during which these backups are taken and the length of time to keep the backups. First, you select a *Backup Retention Period*, which defaults to 7 days. This is the number of days which Amazon will keep backups, from 0 to 35. If you choose 35, you will be able to restore your instance to any of the daily snapshots taken for the past 35 days. It is convenient to have these backups in case of disaster. However, if you need more long-term backups, you will have to generate them manually (or programmatically with the AWS API).

You can also select a *Backup Window* for your database. You may want the backups created at a specific time, such as before or after an expected surge of traffic. If you have no preference, they will default to late at night, when traffic is anticipated to decrease. **No Preference** works just fine, and you can likewise leave the Maintenance settings set to their default values. Click **Launch DB Instance**, which will take you to an intermediary screen. Click through to return to the RDS dashboard, where you will see that your database first has a status of creating, then modifying, then backing up, and, finally, available.

Database Import

While our RDS instance is being created, let's get ready to import our local database schema to our RDS instance. In Chapter 1, you saw that there was a MySQL database packaged with the sample project, at /setup/photoalbums.sql. We're going to use MySQL Workbench to connect to our RDS instance and import this file into the database. If you prefer another interface for connecting to MySQL databases, that's fine. We're using MySQL Workbench simply because it's easy.

Just to jog your memory, we created an RDS security group, which grants access only to our designated EC2 instances and your personal IP address. (If you're working in multiple locations, you'll have to add more IPs to the security group.) We created an RDS instance in that security group, and we're about to make sure we can connect to the instance, at which point we'll know everything is working as planned. Open up MySQL Workbench, or whatever MySQL client you're using. In the top-left corner, you should see a + button, which you will click to create a new connection. You should see a window like the one in Figure 3-11. Name the connection **Photoalbums RDS**. The connection method can stay as TCP/IP. We will have to refer back to RDS to fill out the rest of the fields.

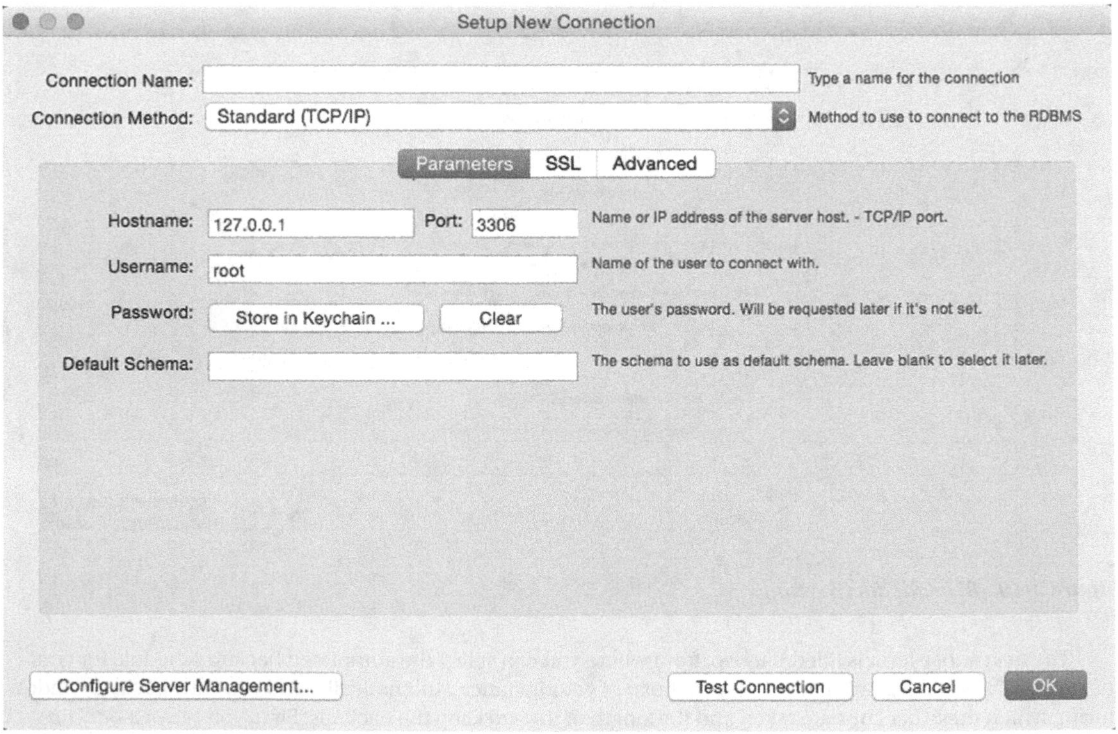

Figure 3-11. Setting up a new connection in MySQL Workbench

Your hostname is going to be generated by RDS when the instance has been created successfully. Let's head back to the console and find that. In the RDS dashboard, you should see your instance in the table view, with a status of **available** in green. Click the row to reveal details about the instance, as shown in Figure 3-12.

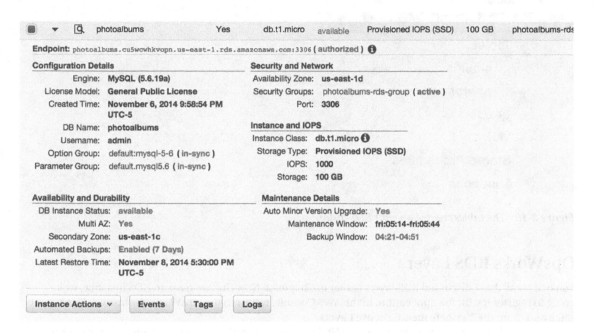

Figure 3-12. *RDS instance details*

Right at the top, you should see Endpoint. This is the URL at which you can connect to your instance, on port 3306. Only connections from your IP will be accepted. Copy this URL and paste it into the *Hostname* field in MySQL Workbench (remember to leave off :3306 when you paste). Input the username and password you chose earlier and click **OK**.

MySQL Workbench will automatically open a connection to the database. We're now ready to run the SQL export script from the sample project. Under the File menu, select **Run SQL Script** and navigate to the .sql file. A window will appear with the contents of the SQL script, giving you the option to change the Default Schema Name or Default Character Set. In the Default Schema Name drop-down, choose **photoalbums**. Leave the character set blank and click **Run**. The window should change its subtitle to *Output*, and the output should look something like this:

```
Preparing...
Importing photoalbums.sql...
Finished executing script
Operation completed successfully
```

Click the **Close** button, and find the photoalbums database under the SCHEMAS heading in the left-hand navigation. Control-click (or right-click, on a PC) **photoalbums**, and select **Refresh All**. In a moment, you should be able to expand *Tables* under photoalbums and see the tables you worked with locally already: albums, photos, and users (see Figure 3-13). We got that running rather quickly, didn't we? Now if only our app could connect to it as well!

SCHEMAS
Filter Objects
innodb
photoalbums
Tables
albums
photos
users
Views
Stored Procedures
Functions

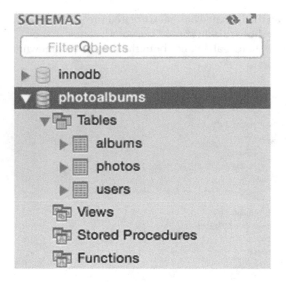

Figure 3-13. *The tables created on your RDS instance*

OpsWorks RDS Layer

You will recall that I discussed RDS layers earlier in Chapter 2. Now that we have an RDS instance, we're going to register it with the application. In the AWS Console, return to the OpsWorks dashboard. Select your stack and, from the Navigate menu, choose **Layers**.

You should only see one layer in the list: Node.js App Server. Below that, click the **+Layer** button. We're back to the Add Layer view, and this time, we have to click the **RDS** tab to create an RDS layer. The setup is somewhat different than that you saw for the App Server layer, as shown in Figure 3-14.

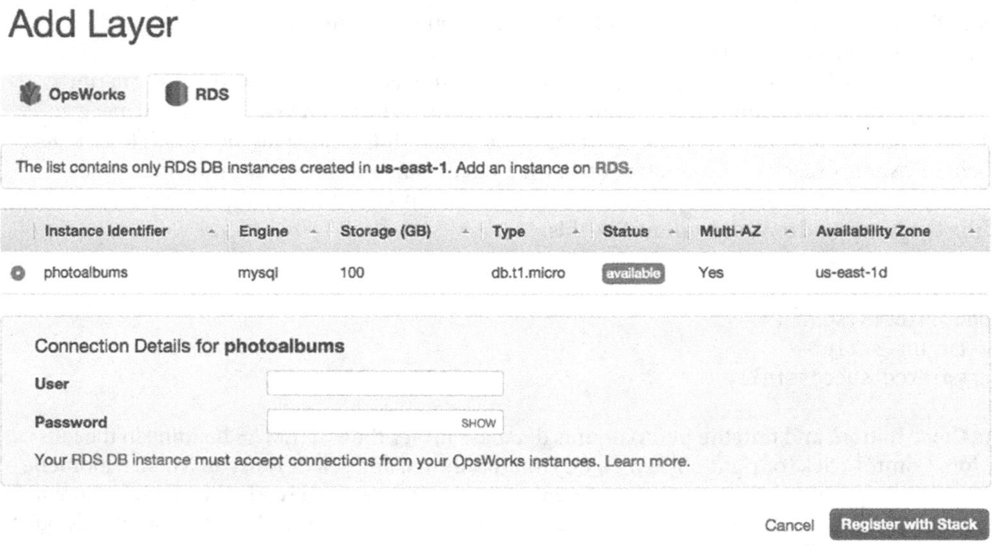

Add Layer
OpsWorks
RDS
The list contains only RDS DB instances created in us-east-1. Add an instance on RDS.
Instance Identifier
Engine
Storage (GB)
Type
Status
Multi-AZ
Availability Zone
photoalbums
mysql
100
db.t1.micro
available
Yes
us-east-1d
Connection Details for photoalbums
User
Password
SHOW
Your RDS DB instance must accept connections from your OpsWorks instances. Learn more.
Cancel
Register with Stack

Figure 3-14. *Adding the RDS layer*

The photoalbums instance was auto-detected, because it's in the same region. All you have to do is type in your username and password and click **Register with Stack**. You will be returned to the Layers view, and you will now see the RDS layer below the App Server layer, as shown in Figure 3-15. But it says no app is connected!

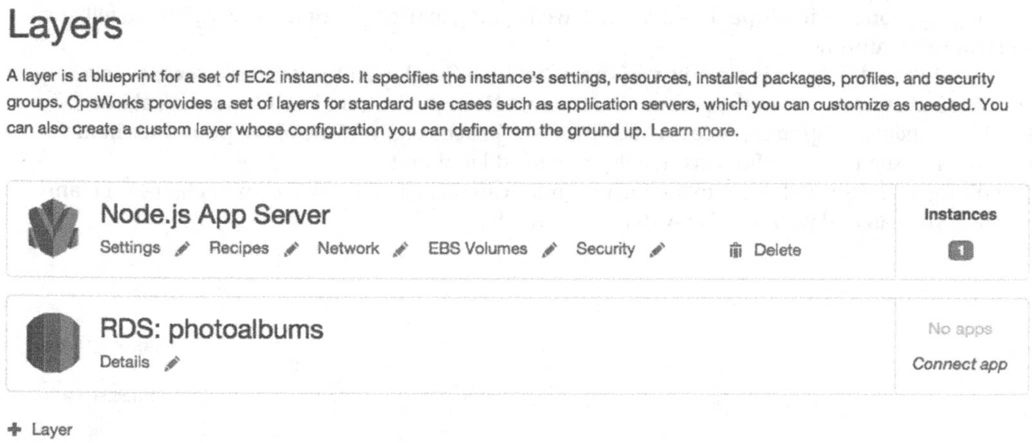

Layers

A layer is a blueprint for a set of EC2 instances. It specifies the instance's settings, resources, installed packages, profiles, and security groups. OpsWorks provides a set of layers for standard use cases such as application servers, which you can customize as needed. You can also create a custom layer whose configuration you can define from the ground up. Learn more.

Figure 3-15. *Layers in our stack, with RDS layer added*

For our app to be connected to the RDS layer, we have to set the database as the Data Source for the App Server. First, click **Connect app**, which will simply take you to the list of apps in your stack. In the Actions column for Photoalbums, click **edit**, which will allow you to edit a few of the settings for the app.

The second heading is titled Data Sources. You will notice that currently the Data source type is set to None. Click the radio button next to **RDS**; choose **photoalbums (mysql)** as your *Database instance*; and enter **photoalbums** as your *Database name*. It should look exactly like Figure 3-16. Don't leave this screen just yet; there's one more thing we have to do here.

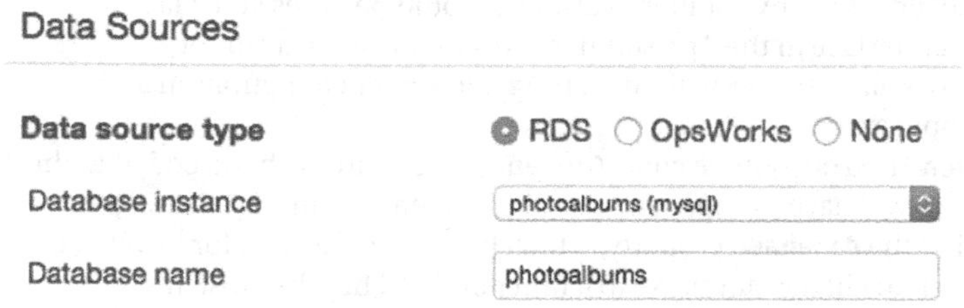

Figure 3-16. *RDS selected as data source for the app*

Environments and Environment Variables

As stated previously, one of our goals is to move our database credentials out of our source code. In Chapter 1, I discussed how storing these credentials in a source file could pose a security risk if a member of the team left or had his/her computer stolen. There's also another reason to consider, which is swapping out databases in our stack. You have seen by now how easy it is to create an RDS instance from scratch. In the future, you will be able to create new database instances from existing ones, and this will give you the ability to run a backup database in your stack in the event of a critical failure. It will also make it significantly easier to clone your entire stack and maintain separate stacks for production and development, a practice that is strongly recommended. By following these next steps, you will be able to maintain code that works under all of these scenarios, without having to deploy code changes or manage credentials.

Thus far, I've largely talked about two environments: local and production. The reality is that your workflow is likely to include writing and testing code in your local environment, then deploying and testing on a development stack, and, lastly, deploying to production. This involves three sets of credentials to manage! If we were to keep different credentials in different branches of our repository, it would be a pain to manage and highly prone to developer error. Instead, we're going to use Environment Variables to tell our application where it's running.

If you're well-versed in Node.js already, you know that there's a global object called **process.env** that stores some information about the user environment in Node.js. You can find information about this here: http://nodejs.org/api/process.html#process_process_env. None of the properties in the documentation may seem that useful. Fortunately, we can add to them!

While editing the app, scroll down to the Environment Variables header, as shown in Figure 3-17, and you will see that you can add your own key-value properties here.

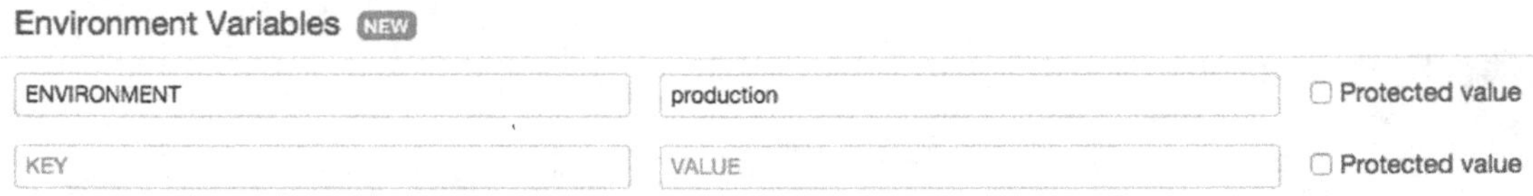

Environment Variables NEW

| ENVIRONMENT | | production | | ☐ Protected value |
| KEY | | VALUE | | ☐ Protected value |

Figure 3-17. *App Environment Variables*

Add a variable called **ENVIRONMENT**, and give it a value of **production**. If/when you create a dev stack, you'll change that value. Go ahead and click **Save**, at the bottom right. We've now set our app's data source and environment variable ENVIRONMENT.

What is the connection between this Environment Variable and process.env? This is one of the subtle ways that the underlying technology of Chef works behind the scenes to make things easier and is only available as of Chef 11.10. When your app is deployed to the instances in the App Server layer, the Environment Variables you have set (up to 20) are included in the deployment script for your instances. Because our app is Node.js, the Environment Variables are added to process.env during the deployment process. If we were instead running a PHP app, the Environment Variables would be accessible via getenv($variableName). Regardless, this interface in the App settings gives us an easy way to set environmental variables dynamically across all instances without getting into server configuration and without disrupting the elasticity of our application.

Next, after much delay, we have to return to our source code. Currently, the source is hard-coded to the local database. As described previously, we will have to support three different environments. First, open your code editor to /lib/globals.js. Find the **database** property, which has the credentials for localhost. Instead of returning a static object, we want to change database to a function (and hey, because it's JavaScript, it's not that hard!). Because there's nothing else in this file yet, you will want to replace the entire file with Listing 3-1, but keep your local credentials handy, as we will not be discarding them entirely.

Listing 3-1. /lib/globals.js

```
module.exports = {
  applicationPort  : 80,
  database : function(){
    if(process.env.ENVIRONMENT){
      var opsworks = require('./../opsworks');
      var opsWorksDB = opsworks.db;
      var rdsConnection = {
        host : opsWorksDB.host,
        port : opsWorksDB.port,
```

```
        database : opsWorksDB.database,
        user : opsWorksDB.username,
        password : opsWorksDB.password
      };
      return rdsConnection;
    } else {
      var local = require('./../config/local');
      var localConnection = local.db;
      return localConnection;
    }
  }
}
```

OK, there's a lot happening here, so let's break it down. First, instead of returning the static object, we're checking to see if process.env.ENVIRONMENT exists. If it does, we don't care what it is, and we will try to load database credentials from OpsWorks, hence the line var opsworks = require('./../opsworks');.

You'll notice that we have no such file in our project. The **Configure** stack command, which runs during deployment, dynamically compiles an opsworks.js file in the root directory of our project. When we connected the RDS layer to the Photoalbums app, it automatically started storing credentials for the database in that file. This means that even if we change the database instance that's used by the layer, we can update the credentials by running the Configure command on our stack, which we will return to in a moment. In the opsworks.js file, the database credentials are stored in a public variable named db. In fact, the whole file looks something like Listing 3-2.

Listing 3-2. Sample opsworks.js file

```
exports.db = {"adapter":"mysql",
              "database":"ops_db",
              "password":"AsdFGh3k",
              "port":3306,
              "reconnect":true,
              "username":"opsuser",
              "data_source_provider":"rds",
              "host":"opsinstance.ccdvt3hwog1a.us-east-1.rds.amazonaws.com"
             }

exports.memcached = {"port":11211,
                     "host":null}
```

In the ideal world, the syntax of the db variable would match the syntax we need in the mysql Node.js module. Sadly, the two are slightly different. For this reason, we instantiate a variable named **rdsConnection** and re-map the values to it. Then, the rdsConnection variable is returned.

In the event that process.env.ENVIRONMENT is not set, we want to preserve our local database credentials. In your project, create a directory named config and an empty file named local.js. Using your local database credentials, paste the following into it:

```
module.exports = {
  db : {
    host : 'localhost',
    port : 8889,
    database : 'photoalbums',
    user : 'root',
    password : 'root'j
  }
}
```

I hope that made sense. We moved our local credentials to a separate file, which we will read from in globals.js only if process.env.ENVIRONMENT is not found. Now, because we changed globals.database into globals.database(), we will have to fix that in a few places. In server.js, navigate to the bottom of the file and make the change in this line:

```
var connection  = mysql.createConnection(globals.database());
```

Save the change, and then we will have to change the declaration at the top of all three model files: model-users, model-photos, and model-albums. In all three files, change line 3 to this:

```
var connection = mysql.createConnection(globals.database());
```

To emphasize the point, all we're doing is adding a "()" after database.

Now we'll put one last finishing touch on our credentials management. We will make our code repository ignore our local credentials, so they don't get pushed to the repo, shared with other developers, or deployed to the App Server. If you're using Git, open the file .gitignore and add the following line:

```
/config/local.js
```

Save this change. If you're using SVN, you want to ignore the file just the same. Commit all these changes to your repository and return to OpsWorks. After you saved your last changes there, you should have been returned to the detail view for the app. You should see at the top right a blue button that reads **Deploy App**. Click the button, to proceed to the Deploy App view. The only thing you need to change here is to add a comment that's of some use to you (see Figure 3-18).

Deploy App

Settings

App	Photoalbums
Command	Deploy ⬍
	Deploy an app. Rails apps have an optional setting named Migrate database. Set Migrate to Yes to migrate the database.
Comment	added dynamic credentials

Advanced »

Instances ⓘ

OpsWorks will run this command on **1 of 1** instances. The assigned recipes are run on all selected instances.

Advanced »

Cancel   **Deploy**

Figure 3-18. *The Deploy App view*

Click **Deploy** at the bottom right and wait for the deployment to complete. If after a few minutes it fails, click **Show** in the Log column and see if you can spot the error. If you get a green check mark next to your hostname, then you should have an app that's now connected to your database. Click on **nodejs-app1** and scroll down to Network Security, locating the Public IP for your instance. Click it, and you should be back at your Hello World screen. Now add **/users/** to the URL.

If you see a pair of empty brackets, congratulations! You requested all users and received all zero of them. This means that your App Server was able to connect to the RDS instance, query the database, and return the results. If you saw an error message instead, then, sadly, something has gone wrong. Check for typos, and if you find none, try retracing your steps.

Stack Commands: Backup Scenario

I briefly discussed the concept of stack commands, which are an OpsWorks tool for running commands on all the instances in your stack. These commands essentially abstract the underlying technology of Chef and give us control over all of our instances in a way that would be more difficult if we had to manage instances individually. We'll use a scenario with our database to explore this in more depth.

RDS Snapshot

Suppose that your database is in an error state and you can't get it back online. Time is passing, and your users cannot access your application. Your Multi-AZ backup isn't working as expected, and every query from the App Server to the RDS layer returns an error. You and your team agree that the best course of action is to deploy a backup database to get your application back online. In a traditional stack, the administrative tasks involved in getting this done could be a nightmare, resulting in significant downtime for your application. Fortunately, we can save a lot of time and energy by using OpsWorks.

The first thing we have to do is grab a snapshot of your database, which we will use to spawn the new instance. If there's nothing wrong with the actual data in your instance, we can take a snapshot right now; otherwise, you would be better off using an automatic snapshot generated by RDS. Navigate to the RDS dashboard and select the **DB Instances** tab. Select your instance from the table and click the **Instance Actions** button to reveal the Actions menu, then select **Take DB Snapshot**.

You will be prompted to name your snapshot. Automated snapshots have the *rds:* prefix in front of them. Name your snapshot something such as **photoalbums-snapshot-[YYYYMMDD]** and click **Yes, Take Snapshot** (see Figure 3-19).

Take DB Snapshot

To take a snapshot of this DB instance you must provide a name for the snapshot. This feature is currently supported for InnoDB storage engine only. If you are using MyISAM, refer to details here.

DB Instance   photoalbums ⓘ

Snapshot Name | photoalbums-snapshot | ⓘ

Cancel   Yes, Take Snapshot

Figure 3-19. *Taking an RDS DB snapshot*

You will be taken to the Snapshots view, where your snapshot will have a status of *creating*. You may also see some of the automated backups in this view. You'll have to wait a few moments for the snapshot to complete before we continue on with the lesson.

When the snapshot has completed, we will create a new instance. Select the snapshot from the list and click **Restore Snapshot** at the top. You will be taken to a view titled Restore DB Instance, though you will recognize the interface from when you created your RDS instance initially. Because we're just running a drill, you can use another **db.t1.micro** instance and disable *Multi-AZ Deployment*. You can name the instance **photoalbums-failover** and click **Launch DB Instance** (see Figure 3-20).

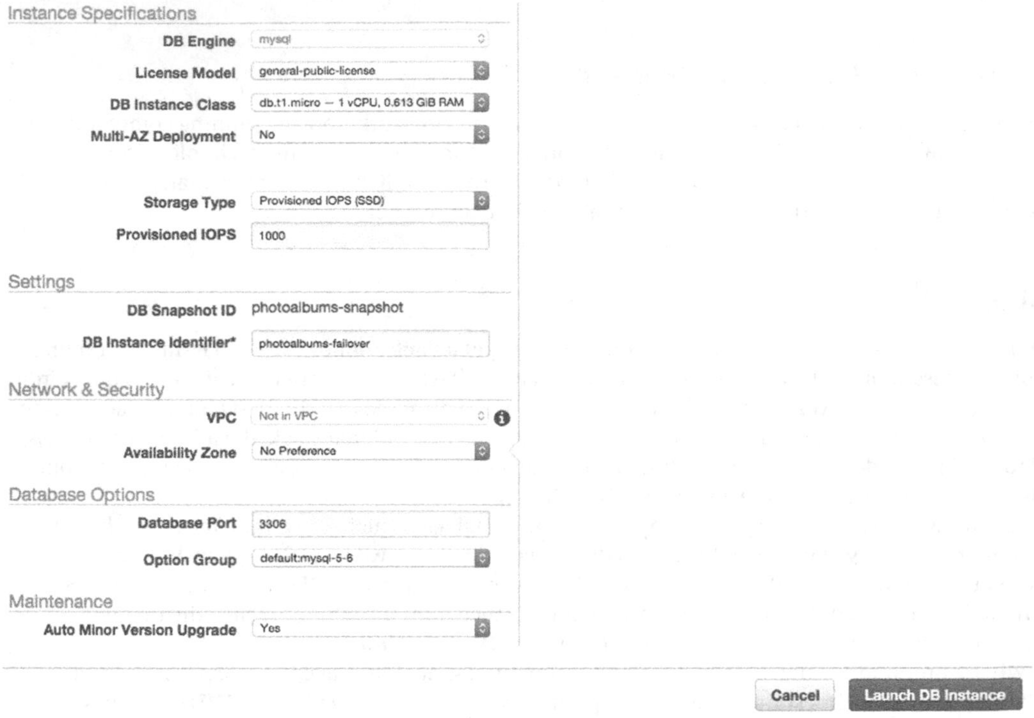

Figure 3-20. *Restoring a DB instance from a snapshot*

Once again, we'll have to wait a few moments for the instance to be created. When the status changes to *available*, we can begin the process of deploying it to our stack.

Creating a New RDS Layer

Return to OpsWorks, and access the Photoalbums stack. Open the Navigation menu and select **Layers**. Click the **RDS photoalbums** layer to view the details for the layer. Before we add our backup database to the stack, we will de-register this layer. At the top right, click the **Deregister** button. You will be prompted to confirm that you want to de-register the layer. After you click the red **Deregister** button, you will be taken to the Resources view, which is empty at this point.

Under the Resources header, there is a submenu that filters your resources by type: Volumes, Elastic IPs, and RDS. Click **RDS**, and you'll see an empty table of RDS instances in your Resources. At the top right, click **Register RDS DB Instances**. This may seem contrary to the way we created our layer before, but we're just being guided by OpsWorks through the same process via a different workflow. Previously, we created an RDS layer and then added an RDS resource. This time, we're adding an RDS resource and then generating a layer automatically.

You will see both of your RDS instances in a table. Select **photoalbums-failover** and input your database credentials in the Connection Details panel below the table, as in Figure 3-21. These should be the same as the credentials of the original database, because this instance is created from a snapshot of that instance. Then, click **Register with Stack**.

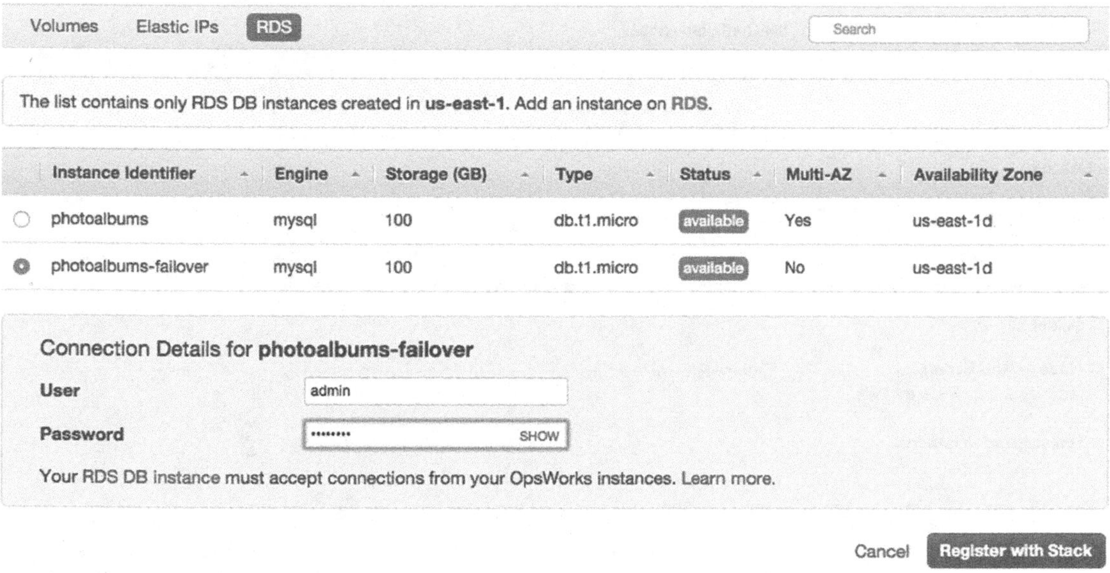

Volumes	Elastic IPs	RDS					Search

The list contains only RDS DB instances created in **us-east-1**. Add an instance on RDS.

Instance Identifier	Engine	Storage (GB)	Type	Status	Multi-AZ	Availability Zone
○ photoalbums	mysql	100	db.t1.micro	available	Yes	us-east-1d
◉ photoalbums-failover	mysql	100	db.t1.micro	available	No	us-east-1d

Connection Details for photoalbums-failover

User	admin
Password	•••••••• SHOW

Your RDS DB instance must accept connections from your OpsWorks instances. Learn more.

Cancel   **Register with Stack**

Figure 3-21. *Adding an RDS resource to the stack*

Connect New Database Layer to App

Open the Navigation menu again, and select **Layers**. You should see that a new RDS layer has been added to your stack, this time entitled RDS: photoalbums-failover. You'll notice that, once again, you have an RDS layer that is not connected to any apps. Click **Connect to App**, which will again take you to the Apps table. In the row next to Photoalbums, click **edit**.

Once again, you must set the Data Source for your app. Change the Data Source type from None to **RDS**. When you do that, you should see photoalbums-failover(mysql) appear in a drop-down, and an empty field for the database name. Type **photoalbums** into the *Database name* field and click **Save** at the bottom-right corner.

Run Stack Command

We've created a new RDS instance from a snapshot of our database, a new OpsWorks layer with it, and connected it to our app. You will recall that the credentials for the RDS layer were copied to our EC2 instances during the Configure phase of deployment. In order to update our credentials, we will have to run the Configure command again on our instances and then deploy to push the new credentials to the instances.

Open the Navigation menu, and select **Stack**. You will be returned to the detail view for the stack. At the top right, you will see a button titled **Run Command**, which you will click. In the Run Command view, you can select from a list of commands, add a comment to your command, and choose on which instances to run the command. Select **Configure** from the Command drop-down, as shown in Figure 3-22. In the *Comment* field, type a message to yourself, such as "configured RDS failover instance credentials." At the bottom-right corner of the view, click **Configure**, to run the command.

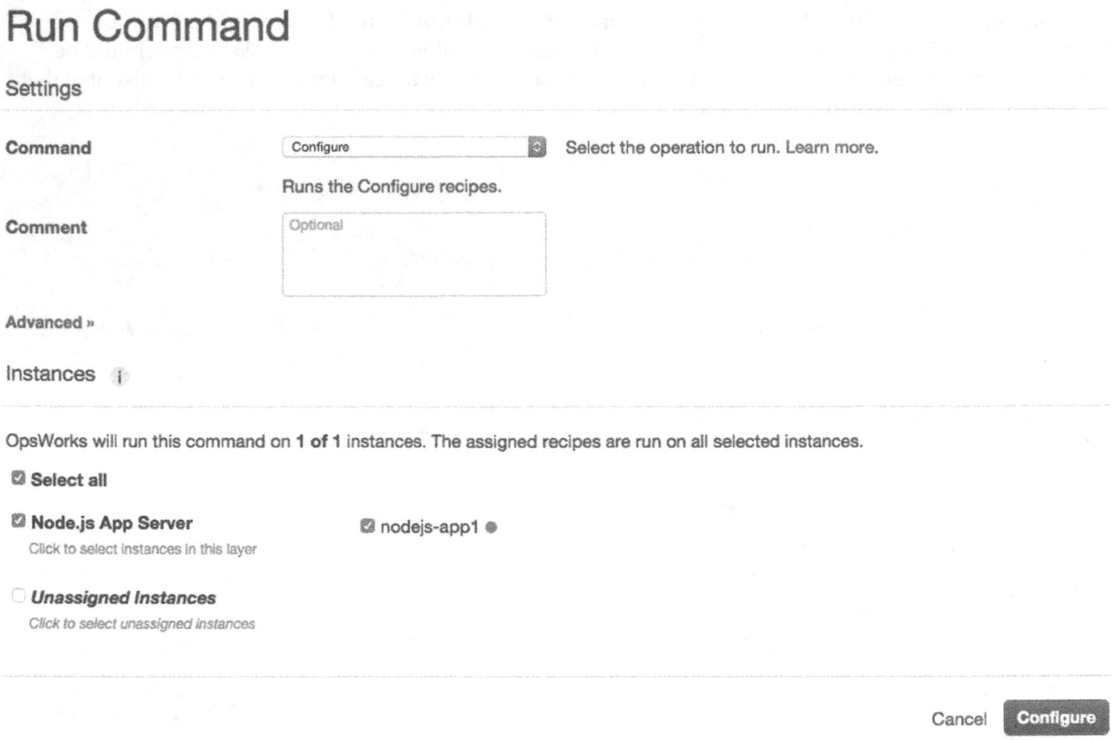

Run Command

Settings

Command	Configure	Select the operation to run. Learn more.
	Runs the Configure recipes.	
Comment	Optional	

Advanced »

Instances ⓘ

OpsWorks will run this command on **1 of 1** instances. The assigned recipes are run on all selected instances.

☑ **Select all**

☑ **Node.js App Server**   ☑ nodejs-app1 ●
  Click to select instances in this layer

☐ *Unassigned Instances*
  Click to select unassigned instances

Cancel   **Configure**

Figure 3-22. *Running the Configure command*

You will be brought to a view with the header Running command configure, where you can see an activity indicator next to your EC2 instance while the command is being executed. Once the command is complete, the opsworks.js file in the root of your app source code will have been updated with the new credentials. Next, run the **deploy** command to deploy this code change to your instances and restart your application.

You can imagine just how useful this workflow can be. We were able to move the app to a backup database in a few minutes, without having to alter any code. Of course, doing this also means that your app is running for several minutes with a database that you're about to swap out, so it's ideally not a procedure you'll ever need to use if your database contains time-sensitive information.

Another way to look at this feature is that it offers you two ways to perform database maintenance. If you have to increase your database storage, convert the storage type, or make some other major configuration change, you can expect some interruption to your application. On the one hand, you could make your changes to the existing database (always taking a snapshot first), and let AWS use the Multi-AZ feature to automatically use the failover database while the maintenance is under way.

Alternatively, you could take a snapshot and create a new database from the snapshot with the configuration changes you want. Then, you would have to add the database instance to your OpsWorks stack and then run the Configure and deploy commands.

Now that this tutorial is complete, let's revert to the original database. In OpsWorks, navigate to Layers and click the title of your RDS layer. At the top right, click **Deregister** and confirm that to detach your database from the stack. Again from the Layers screen, click **+Layer**. Select the **RDS** tab and choose **photoalbums** from the list of RDS instances below. Re-enter the database credentials and click **Register with Stack**. When you return to the Layers screen, click **Connect app** again, then click **edit** next to the App Server. Scroll down to Data Sources and change the Data Source type to **RDS**. Select your original database instance and database name. Click **Save**.

From the Navigation menu, choose **Stack**, and at the top right, click **Run Command**. Change the command to **Configure** and click the button at the bottom right. Finally, navigate to Apps and click **deploy**, next to Photoalbums. Then click **Deploy** at the bottom right and let the deployment run. Now we're connected back to the original database, and you can delete the failover, if you want.

Elastic Load Balancing (ELB)

At this point, we have our app running on a single EC2 instance. We know that while our instance can be scaled to a larger size, this alone may not be enough to handle the incoming traffic to our application. Further, changing the size of an EC2 instance can cause a service disruption, which we'd prefer to avoid.

If you've worked with Node.js extensively, you know that many server-side errors can crash your application, which requires it to be restarted. While OpsWorks will automatically restart your app, it would be a shame for a single error to bring your entire app offline, even for a few seconds.

The solution to both of these problems is to run our app on more than one instance. This can be accomplished with a load balancer, or Elastic Load Balancing (ELB), in AWS terms. With ELB, traffic can be automatically redirected amongst multiple EC2 instances and across multiple availability zones. If an instance crashes, or is in what is referred to as an *unhealthy* state, ELB will stop routing traffic to that instance until it is *healthy* again. The convenience of this being automatic cannot be overstated. If an instance becomes unhealthy, you don't have to worry about manually removing it from your stack, for fear of traffic being routed to a server in an error state.

In Figure 3-23, you can see how a load balancer will work in our application stack. Traffic will be routed to the ELB, which then directs it to the individual instances and forwards the response back to the requester.

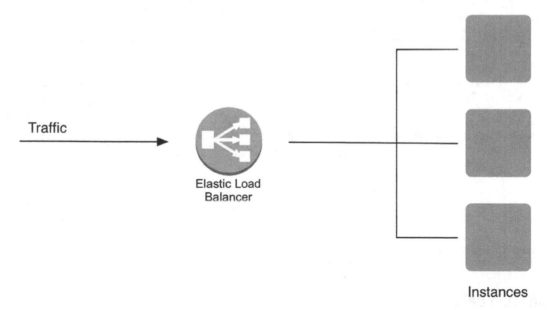

Figure 3-23. An ELB routing traffic to three EC2 instances

■ **Note** ELB can also be used to regulate internal traffic between two layers of an application, not just between the Web and an App Server.

Additionally, using an ELB gives us another useful means of assessing the health of our application. I will be discussing monitoring at a later point, but for the moment, we can do a conceptual analysis of the problem of server health in the cloud. If you have ten servers in your application stack, it would be a quite a task to monitor the health of all instances at all times. If one instance went offline, would it be cause for major concern, immediately? What if you were running the app on a hundred servers? As you can see, with more moving parts, there is also a lot more information to analyze. Instead of monitoring each instance individually, we can monitor various metrics of the ELB instead.

Creating a Load Balancer

ELB does not have its own control panel in AWS. Instead, they are managed in a subsection of EC2. Return to the AWS Console and navigate to EC2. In the left navigation, under the Network & Security header, click **Load Balancers**. Then, at the top of the screen, click **Create Load Balancer**. The Create Load Balancer wizard will open in a modal window, as shown in Figure 3-24.

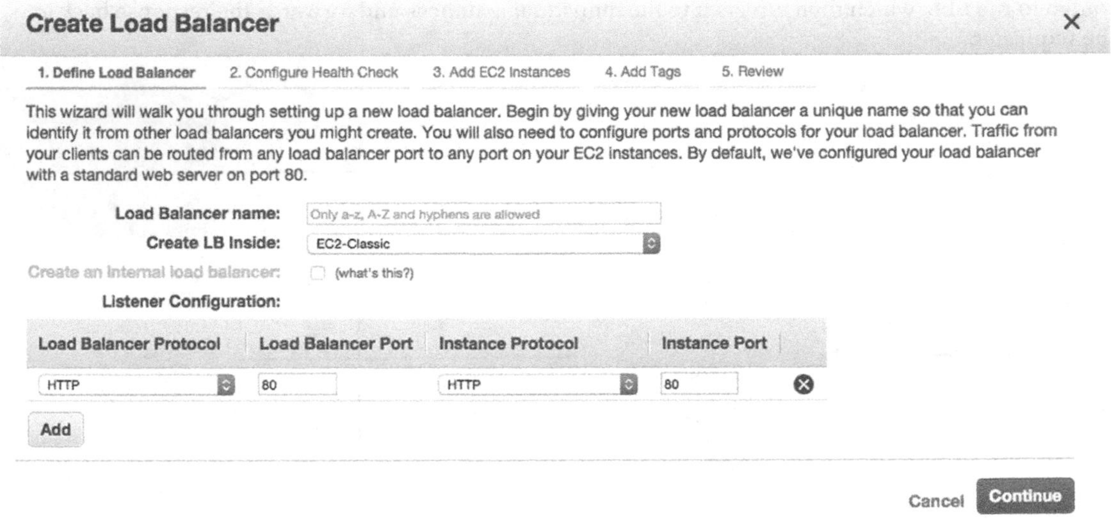

Create Load Balancer   ✕

| 1. Define Load Balancer | 2. Configure Health Check | 3. Add EC2 Instances | 4. Add Tags | 5. Review |

This wizard will walk you through setting up a new load balancer. Begin by giving your new load balancer a unique name so that you can identify it from other load balancers you might create. You will also need to configure ports and protocols for your load balancer. Traffic from your clients can be routed from any load balancer port to any port on your EC2 instances. By default, we've configured your load balancer with a standard web server on port 80.

Load Balancer name: Only a-z, A-Z and hyphens are allowed

Create LB Inside: EC2-Classic

Create an internal load balancer: ☐ (what's this?)

Listener Configuration:

Load Balancer Protocol	Load Balancer Port	Instance Protocol	Instance Port	
HTTP	80	HTTP	80	✕

[Add]

Cancel   **Continue**

Figure 3-24. *Create Load Balancer wizard*

Define Load Balancer

On the first screen of the wizard, you can name your load balancer **photoalbums-elb**. The *Create LB Inside* drop-down can be left as **EC2-Classic**. You would only change this field if you were creating your ELB in a Virtual Private Cloud. Next, you have to open ports via which traffic can be handled by your load balancer. By default, port 80 is opened with the HTTP protocol selected. If you recall, this is also the port on which your application is listening. You can leave and go ahead and click **Continue** to proceed.

Configure Health Check

Earlier, you first heard the terms *healthy* and *unhealthy* to describe instances. These are not empirical terms, and in fact, it is up to us to define them. In the next step, we determine the conditions in which an EC2 instance can be considered healthy and when it can be considered unhealthy. The ELB will perform routine health checks against each instance to which it is assigned.

We will define the parameters for these health checks, which will include a relative path that the ELB will request from each instance. You can see the health check parameters in Figure 3-25.

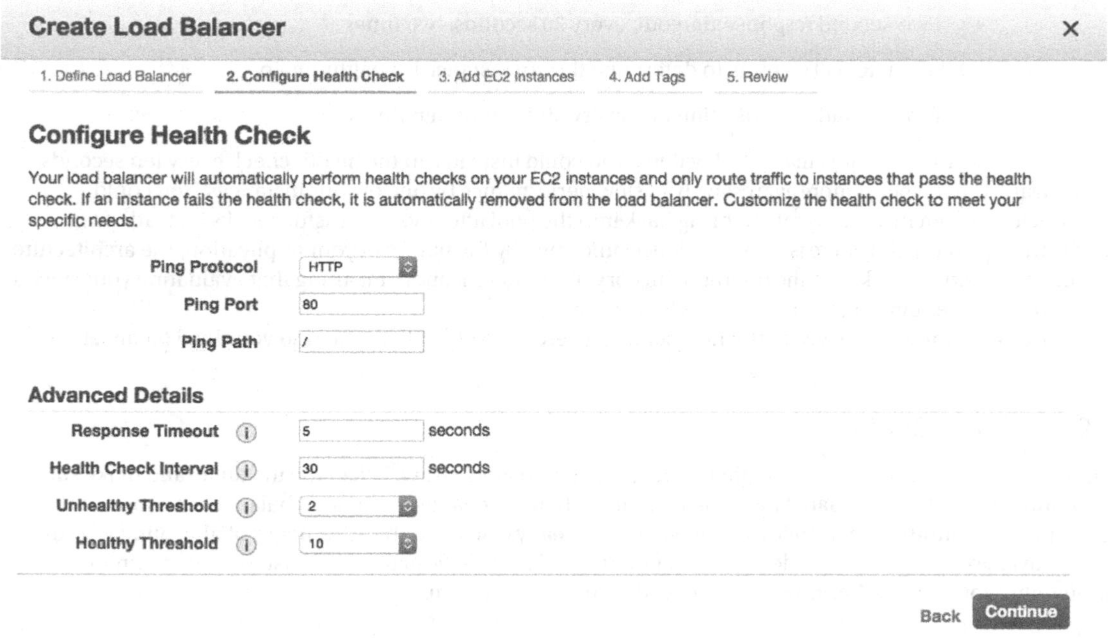

Create Load Balancer   ✕

1. Define Load Balancer   **2. Configure Health Check**   3. Add EC2 Instances   4. Add Tags   5. Review

Configure Health Check

Your load balancer will automatically perform health checks on your EC2 instances and only route traffic to instances that pass the health check. If an instance fails the health check, it is automatically removed from the load balancer. Customize the health check to meet your specific needs.

Ping Protocol	HTTP
Ping Port	80
Ping Path	/

Advanced Details

Response Timeout ⓘ	5 seconds
Health Check Interval ⓘ	30 seconds
Unhealthy Threshold ⓘ	2
Healthy Threshold ⓘ	10

Back   **Continue**

Figure 3-25. *Configuring an ELB health check*

First, we configure the URL request, or *ping*. The *Ping Protocol* should be **HTTP**, and the *Ping Port* should be **80**, the same as our app listens to. Finally, the *Ping Path* is the path along which the request is sent on each instance. Change this to /, which will request the Hello World page of our app. The default value of /index.html would return a 404 error from our app.

The Advanced Details are the more subjective parameters of the health check. First, we have the *Response Timeout*. Each time the EC2 instances are pinged, the load balancer will measure the time it takes to receive a response from the instance. If the instance is slow to respond or completely unresponsive, it will have failed a single health check. The default response timeout is five seconds. For our Hello World page, it seems reasonable to expect it to take fewer than five seconds to generate. In truth, we could probably reduce it further, but five is safe.

Next, we have to determine the frequency with which the health checks are performed, or the *Health Check Interval*. The default is 30 seconds, which means that while the instance is online, the health check will execute every 30 seconds.

A healthy instance may occasionally fail a single health check. It may respond slowly, due to any number of factors. We don't necessarily want to remove an instance from the pool because of a single slow response. Instead, we want to set an *Unhealthy Threshold*, at which point the instance is actually considered to be in the unhealthy state. By default, this threshold is **2**, and the *Healthy Threshold* is **10**. The reason these thresholds are so disparate is to err on the side of caution. Once an instance has become unhealthy, we don't want to prematurely consider it healthy. If the load balancer thought the instance was healthy too early, there would be a risk of more users receiving erroneous responses, or no responses at all.

In the end, the rules for our health checks are such:

- It takes up to 70 seconds to determine that an instance is unhealthy.

  - Five-second response timeout, every 30 seconds, two times

- It takes up to 350 seconds to determine that an instance is healthy again.

  - Five-second response timeout, every 30 seconds, ten times

Of course, these are just the default values. You could instead run the health check every ten seconds, if you wanted to respond more aggressively to slow performance by one of your instances. You could also decide that an instance is safe to bring back into the pool after five successful checks instead of ten. Determining your policy here is its own science, informed by the nature of your application, the architecture of your application stack, and the operating history of your application, meaning that evaluating your stack's performance over time can help you make better decisions.

Click **Continue** to proceed to the next screen, where you will add instances to your load balancer.

Add EC2 Instances

For now, we are only adding the single EC2 instance we created earlier. Select the instance, and make sure that **Enable Cross-Zone Load Balancing** is enabled. If this is enabled, your load balancer can route traffic to instances in multiple availability zones. We have already discussed the advantages of allocating resources across availability zones, so we definitely will want to balance traffic across EC2 instances in different availability zones. Click **Continue** and proceed to the Add Tags step.

Add Tags

By now, you've probably realized that you can very quickly accrue a large number of resources in AWS, some of which are named automatically by AWS and others following your own naming conventions. It can be difficult to track all the moving parts. One way that AWS helps alleviate this problem is through the use of tags. Tags are simply key-value pairs that you can create for many resources in AWS.

■ **Note**   The complete list of taggable resources is available at `http://docs.aws.amazon.com/AWSEC2/latest/UserGuide/Using_Tags.html#tag-restrictions`.

Each resource, be it an EC2 or RDS instance, etc., can have up to ten tags. This can help you organize your resources and can make it easier to keep your billing organized. For instance, if you host the infrastructure for multiple clients on your AWS account, you could tag your assets by client name or client project, to generate billing summaries for each.

Perhaps you were running a production and development stack, and you wanted to determine the cost of spawning additional development environments for longer-term development cycles. You could tag your production resources with "Environment" = "Production" and your dev resources with "Environment" = "Development," to project the cost of additional development environments.

These are just a couple examples. While AWS billing management is outside the scope of this book, it's better to explain what Tags are than to ignore them entirely. Let's add two tags to our ELB, for the sake of getting familiar with them. In the first tag field, type in **Environment** as the key and **Production** as the value, as in Figure 3-26. Then click **Create Tag** and add the key **Stack** with the value **Photoalbums**. Click **Continue** to proceed to the Review step.

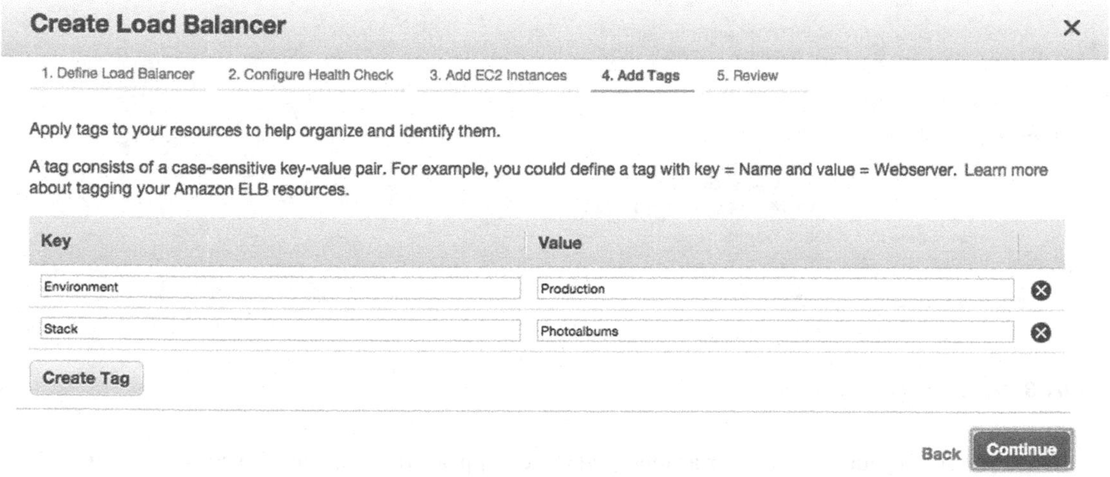

Figure 3-26. *Add ELB tags*

Review

Amazon conveniently allows us to review all our choices before creating the load balancer (see Figure 3-27). Take a moment to review everything, and make sure it looks correct. If you made a mistake, there's an Edit button, which can take you back to each individual step to fix the problem. When you've finished reviewing, click **Create**. In a few seconds, you will see a confirmation that your load balancer was created, and when you dismiss it, you will see your load balancer alone in a table.

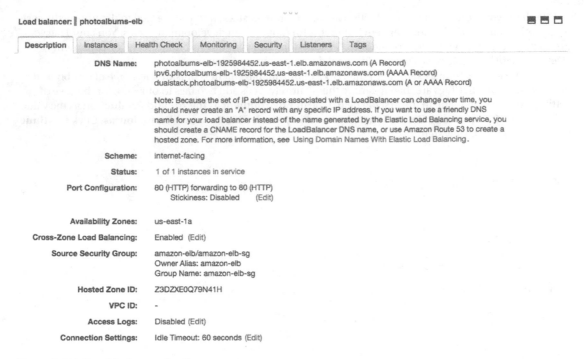

Figure 3-27. *Load balancer details*

When you select your load balancer, a tabbed detail view appears below the list, as shown in Figure 3-27. The Description tab gives you an overview of your load balancer. Front and center, you'll see a *Status* field, which quickly tells you how many of your instances are in service. It should read "1 of 1 instances in service." If your instance becomes unhealthy, this will change from 1 to 0, the point being that *in service* is a euphemism for *healthy*. You can also revisit any of the customizations you made to your load balancer. You can add/edit the tags, open/close ports, and change the configuration of the health check.

You can also manage the instances attached to your load balancer in the Instances tab. However, we will not be doing this here. If we are going to use a load balancer in our OpsWorks stack, we don't want to manually add/remove instances to the load balancer in the EC2 dashboard. Instead, we want to handle load balancing the same way we did the database: by adding an ELB layer in OpsWorks.

OpsWorks ELB Layer

Return to OpsWorks and open the Photoalbums stack. Using the Navigation menu, head to the Layers view and select the **Node.js App Server** layer. In the layer subnavigation, select **Network**. Right at the top, you should see an Elastic Load Balancing header, under which you will see that no ELB has been added. Click **Add an ELB** to attach your ELB to the App Server layer.

The page will refresh, and the *Elastic Load Balancer* field will now show a drop-down from which you can select **photoalbums-elb**. When you do this, a warning will appear, informing you that OpsWorks configuration will now supersede changes made in the EC2 dashboard. This means that if you went back to EC2 and added more instances, the changes would be ignored, because OpsWorks commands will take precedence. Click **Save** to commit your changes, which will again reload the page.

Open the Navigation menu and return to the Layers view. You will see that an ELB layer has been auto-generated and now appears as shown in Figure 3-28.

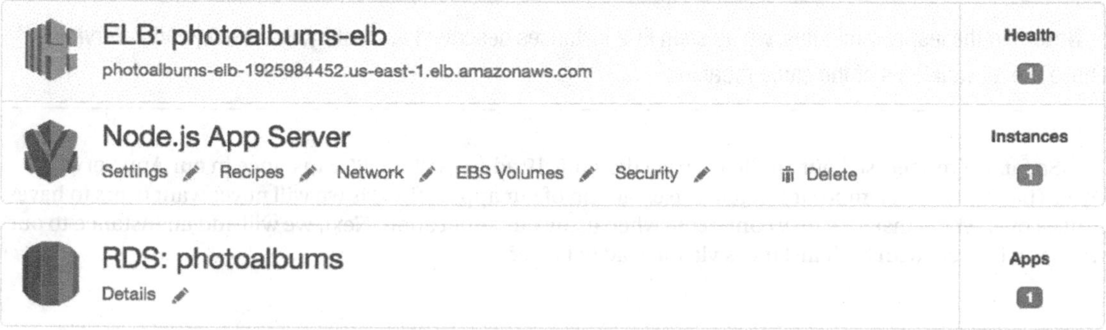

	Health
ELB: photoalbums-elb photoalbums-elb-1925984452.us-east-1.elb.amazonaws.com	[1]
Node.js App Server Settings ✎ Recipes ✎ Network ✎ EBS Volumes ✎ Security ✎ 🗑 Delete	Instances [1]
RDS: photoalbums Details ✎	Apps [1]

Figure 3-28. ELB, App Server, and RDS layers

Click the ELB layer (**ELB: photoalbums-elb**) and you will see the detail view for the layer (see Figure 3-29). First, you will see a public URL next to the *DNS Name*. If you click this, you'll be brought to the Hello World page of our application! You will also see a warning regarding all of your instances being in one availability zone. As discussed previously, it is best practice to duplicate resources in other availability zones. In this case, it's a moot point, because we only have one instance in the App Server layer right now.

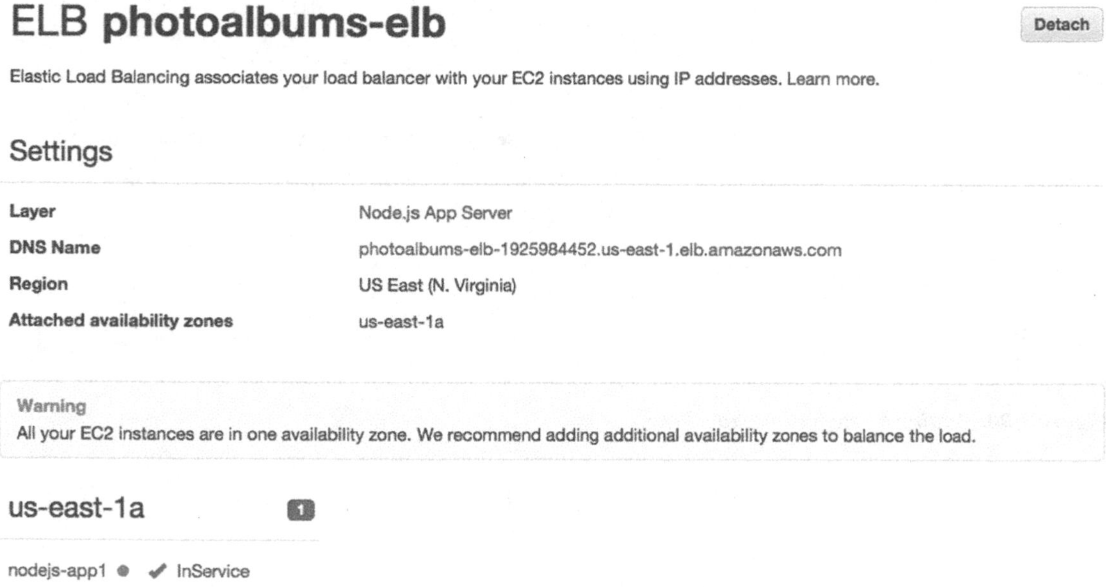

ELB **photoalbums-elb**   `Detach`

Elastic Load Balancing associates your load balancer with your EC2 instances using IP addresses. Learn more.

Settings

Layer	Node.js App Server
DNS Name	photoalbums-elb-1925984452.us-east-1.elb.amazonaws.com
Region	US East (N. Virginia)
Attached availability zones	us-east-1a

> **Warning**
> All your EC2 instances are in one availability zone. We recommend adding additional availability zones to balance the load.

us-east-1a   [1]

nodejs-app1 ● ✔ InService

Figure 3-29. ELB layer view in OpsWorks

At the bottom of the page, you will see a table of all the instances registered with your load balancer, organized by availability zone, and with status indicators to the right of each instance. Because we only have one instance in one availability zone (in this case, us-east-1a), there isn't much information here. But once we've added more instances and availability zones, this section will give you a bird's-eye view of the status of your App Server and a starting point to assess performance problems.

■ **Note** In the last few minutes, we've seen EC2 instances described as healthy, in service, and InService. These are all variations of the same meaning.

So far, we've accessed our application via the static IP address of the EC2 instance in our App Server layer. That was only a temporary step in the evolution of our application, as we will never want users to have control over which instance they connect to when using our application. Next, we will add an instance to our stack and interact with both instances via the load balancer.

Adding a New Instance

Open the Navigation menu, and click **Instances** to return to the Instances view. Click the **+Instance** button at the bottom left to open the instance creation dialog. You can either create a new instance or add an existing one to this layer. The latter case does not allow you to add any instance in your AWS account. Rather, you can only add existing instances that already belong to an OpsWorks layer. If you wanted, you could share computing resources between multiple layers and host two or more layers on a shared instance. Because our stack will only have one App Server layer, we won't be exploring this option, but it's good to know it's there.

Change the new instance size to **t1.micro** (or any small size) and choose a different availability zone than that you chose for the first instance (see Figure 3-30). Then click **Add Instance**.

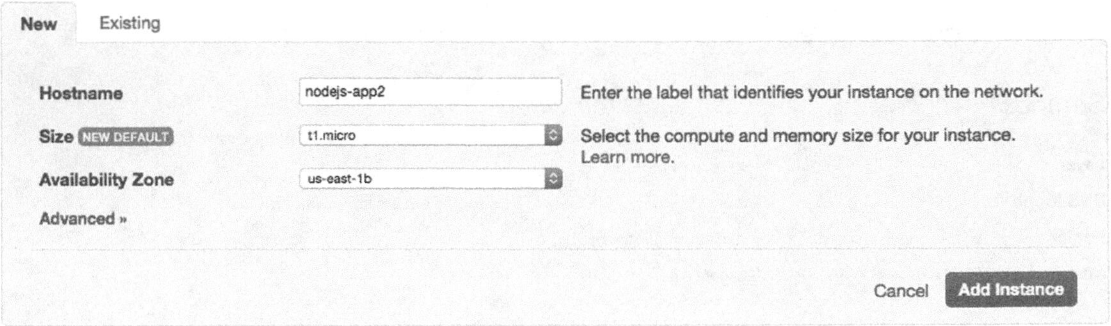

Figure 3-30. *Adding a new instance to a layer*

You will now see your new instance in the table of instances, as in Figure 3-31. It will not start automatically, nor will it have an IP address assigned, as Public IPs are only reserved when an instance is online.

Node.js App Server   **Using ELB:** photoalbums-elb

Hostname	Status	Size	Type	AZ	Public IP	Actions
nodejs-app1	online	t1.micro	24/7	us-east-1a	54.80.114.196	■ stop ssh
nodejs-app2	stopped	t1.micro	24/7	us-east-1b	-	▶ start delete

✚ Instance

Figure 3-31. `App Server Instances overview`

Now that there's more than one instance in the app, this view is starting to become more useful. You can see that the circle at the top left is actually a circle graph depicting the percentage of your instances in one of five possible states. You also have a quick link to the public IP of your active instances, as well as to your ELB. You can start or delete stopped instances and stop or connect via SSH to online instances.

If you recall the lessons about RDS, you may think that you have to run the Configure command before you deploy source code to your new instance. This is not the case. Because you have run the Configure command on your stack after you connected your RDS instance, the credentials that will be deployed to your new instance are up to date. All you have to do is click **start**.

■ **Note**   Occasionally, AWS will not allow new instances to be allocated in a particular availability zone. If us-east-1b is at capacity, and you encounter this error, simply choose us-east-1c or us-east-1d instead.

Your instance will automatically run through a number of statuses in this view, starting with *requested* and finishing with *online*. Click **photoalbums-elb** to navigate back to your load balancer layer. The warning about your instances being in a single availability zone should have disappeared, and you should now see a second column at the bottom listing your instances in us-east-1b. Click the URL next to **DNS Name**, and you will see the Hello World page open in a new window. You're now connecting directly to your load balancer, which is routing requests to your two instances in separate availability zones!

Now that we've gotten this far, let's go ahead and kick the tires a little bit. You should be able to register a new user by submitting a POST request to the register path at your load balancer URL. Open your REST client, and paste in the ELB DNS Name, adding **/users/register**. Add username, password, and e-mail POST parameters and send the request. You should receive the following response:

```
{"message":"Registration successful!"}
```

It seems that your user was successfully registered, and the record was created on the RDS instance. If you recall some details about the sample app in Chapter 1, you will remember there is an API for listing registered users in the application. In your REST client, change to a GET request and remove "register" from the URL, or just open that URL in your browser. You should receive a JSON list of your registered users, like so:

```
[{"username":"admin","userID":1}]
```

Summary

I've covered a lot of ground in this chapter. You learned about some important features of Amazon RDS, created an instance, and created an OpsWorks layer from that instance. We then configured OpsWorks to package the RDS credentials on our App Server instances and reworked the source code to access these credentials, instead of using hard-coded credentials stored in our repository. We also ran through a few scenarios in which we could use the features of RDS and OpsWorks to gracefully handle database failures or to rapidly deploy a backup database.

You also learned about Elastic Load Balancing, Amazon's load-balancing service. We created our first load balancer and configured health checks to identify unhealthy EC2 instances and regulate traffic to healthy instances. We used this load balancer to generate an ELB layer in OpsWorks and added instances in multiple availability zones to the ELB. Last, we tested our progress by registering a user at the ELB's public URL.

In some ways, this is the most difficult chapter, as we have finally created a truly cloud-based application, without dependencies on one single resource. Of course, although we are running our app on two instances, this does not mean it has substantial fault tolerance, nor is it ready for public use. In the next few chapters, you will learn how to give this infrastructure elasticity, responding to heavy traffic by scaling our resources to meet demand. You will also learn more about the various metrics and points of failure in our application stack, and you will learn to use other AWS services to provide caching and accelerated content distribution, to reduce the workload for our App Server and RDS layers.

CHAPTER 4

■ ■ ■

CloudFront and DNS Management

We've already used a lot of AWS services to get this far: EC2, RDS, ELB, IAM, and OpsWorks. In this chapter, we're going to add two more services to our repertoire: CloudFront and Route 53. In these lessons, we will implement Amazon's global content caching tools and get our app published at a top-level web domain. By the end of the chapter, the app will almost be ready for prime time.

In the previous chapters, I've discussed the difference that geographic proximity can make in an app's performance if we're measuring in milliseconds. To optimize our app for a global audience, we could theoretically run a copy of our entire application stack in every AWS region. However, this would be quite expensive and would fragment our resources. If we don't have an unlimited budget, the more we divide our resources by region, the fewer resources we have in each. Our app would lose both some of its elasticity and scalability in this scenario.

Fortunately, we can use CloudFront to accelerate our content distribution around the world. The CloudFront service stores copies of our web content at data centers around the globe, referred to as *edge locations*. When a URL is requested from CloudFront, the user's request is directed to the edge location nearest to the request's geographic origin. This does not mean that CloudFront can serve only static content. Requests to CloudFront can pass through to our app and receive uncached content as well, in cases where that's necessary, such as when a user logs in and receives an authentication token.

As you may have noticed with the public IPs assigned to EC2 instances, IPs and URLs in AWS are dynamic, which could pose a challenge if we want our application stack to be live at a domain of our choosing. You don't want to point your domain to the IP address of one of your instances, nor do you want to route requests directly to the ELB instance. Instead, we'll use the service called Route 53, the DNS manager for AWS.

With Route 53, you can create a hosted zone corresponding to your domain and map various subdomains to different AWS services. You will receive AWS nameservers at which you can point your domain and then configure your DNS records in Route 53.

We will be using these services in conjunction to make our app available worldwide at our chosen domain. Route 53 will direct requests for our domain to CloudFront, which will be serving our app content at the closest possible edge location to our user. In Figure 4-1, you can see how these services work together with our application stack.

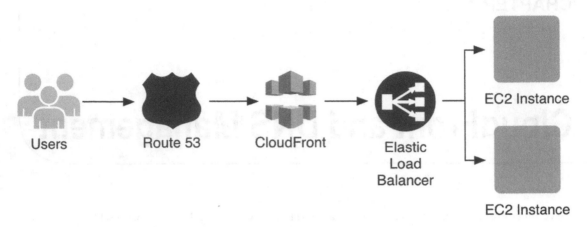

Figure 4-1. *The request route, from Route 53 to EC2 instances in the application stack*

To complete this chapter, you must have registered a domain or be prepared to do so during the lessons. For the purpose of completing the lesson, we will be referring to cloudyeyes.net as the domain—an arbitrary domain that I've registered.

CloudFront

There are many different ways to implement caching into a web application, and CloudFront is merely one of them. Using CloudFront will allow us to cache and serve static assets separately from the application's EC2 instances, in addition to cached response data from the application. The result is a caching mechanism that can drastically reduce the impact of traffic to your application.

In this chapter, we will be setting up CloudFront as a pass-through for requests to our App Server layer. To do so, we have to define the rules by which URL requests to CloudFront are processed and routed to our application stack. In Chapter 5, we will set up an S3 bucket to store all of our images and other static assets. We will then use CloudFront to serve these assets, effectively creating an enterprise-level content delivery network (CDN) in just a few steps.

CloudFront allows you to utilize the functionality of a CDN[1] in your application, completely independent of your application layer. While a CDN is often used just for images and other assets, we will use CloudFront to deliver the entirety of our application to users, with caching rules we define.

■ **Note** In CloudFront terminology, the end user making HTTP requests is known as the *viewer*.

Creating the Distribution

CloudFront rules are organized into what's called a *distribution*. First, we will create a distribution for our application, then we will define rules based on various URL patterns. Log back in to the AWS Console and select **CloudFront** under the Storage and Content Delivery header on the main dashboard. As usual, the create button is at the top-left corner of the main content area (see Figure 4-2). Click **Create Distribution** to begin creating your distribution.

---

[1]For a useful discussion of CDN and performance, see www.webperformancetoday.com/2013/06/12/11-faqs-content-delivery-networks-cdn-web-performance/.

Figure 4-2. The top of the CloudFront dashboard, with the Create Distribution button

AWS presents distribution creation as a two-step process. In actuality, these steps are completely unbalanced. You first choose a delivery method, then go through a lengthy configuration process in the second step.

When you choose a delivery method for your distribution, you select either web or RTMP. RTMP is an Adobe streaming media protocol, which you would use for audio or video streaming. Everything else falls under web distribution, so you can click **Get Started** under the Web Distribution header to proceed.

Configuring the Distribution

Next, you will configure the distribution, as well as define the default origin and cache behavior. The only way to get through this process is to just go through the settings one by one. If you get lost or make a mistake, you can always edit the configuration later.

Origin Settings

You will begin the configuration by defining the Origin Settings, wherein we configure the origin for our distribution (see Figure 4-3). In CloudFront terms, an origin is simply a source (origin) of the content being served by CloudFront. A CloudFront distribution can serve content from more than one origin, a feature we will use to our advantage.

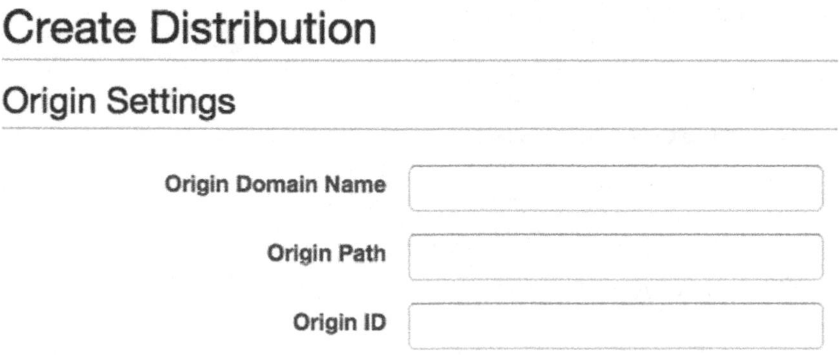

Create Distribution

Origin Settings

Origin Domain Name	
Origin Path	
Origin ID	

Figure 4-3. Origin Settings in a CloudFront web distribution

When you click into the *Origin Domain Name* field, a drop-down will appear, listing all of the S3 buckets and HTTP servers on your AWS account. In our case, the only valid HTTP server is our Elastic Load Balancer, but it is possible for advanced users to employ CloudFront with a web site hosted on a single EC2 instance, for example. Select our load balancer, **photoalbums-elb-[id]. us-east-1.elb.amazonaws.com**, from the drop-down. The *Origin ID*, which is simply a string identifier displayed in CloudFront, will auto-generate something like ELB-photoalbums-elb-[id]. Leave this as is, unless you want to name it something clever.

Set the *Origin Protocol Policy* to **Match Viewer**, which means CloudFront will accept HTTPS connections if the viewer attempts them. We're not using HTTPS currently, but we will later, and we don't want CloudFront to interfere with the setup. Alternatively, if you only wanted to allow HTTP connections, you could control this at the CloudFront level here. Last, you can change the ports from the default of HTTP:80 and HTTPS:443. You'll recall that our application is listening on port 80, so we definitely don't want to change this value.

Default Cache Behavior Settings

When you create a distribution, you define caching rules based on URL path patterns, which I will discuss in greater detail. These rules are referred to as *behaviors*. When we define behaviors, we also establish an order in which requests are compared against our behavior rules. As such, a request is compared against each behavior in order, until it has been matched with a behavior. If a request does not match any behaviors we have declared, then CloudFront requires a default behavior to apply to the request. As such, we will define the default behavior (see Figure 4-4) when we create our CloudFront distribution, and any additional behaviors can be defined after the fact.

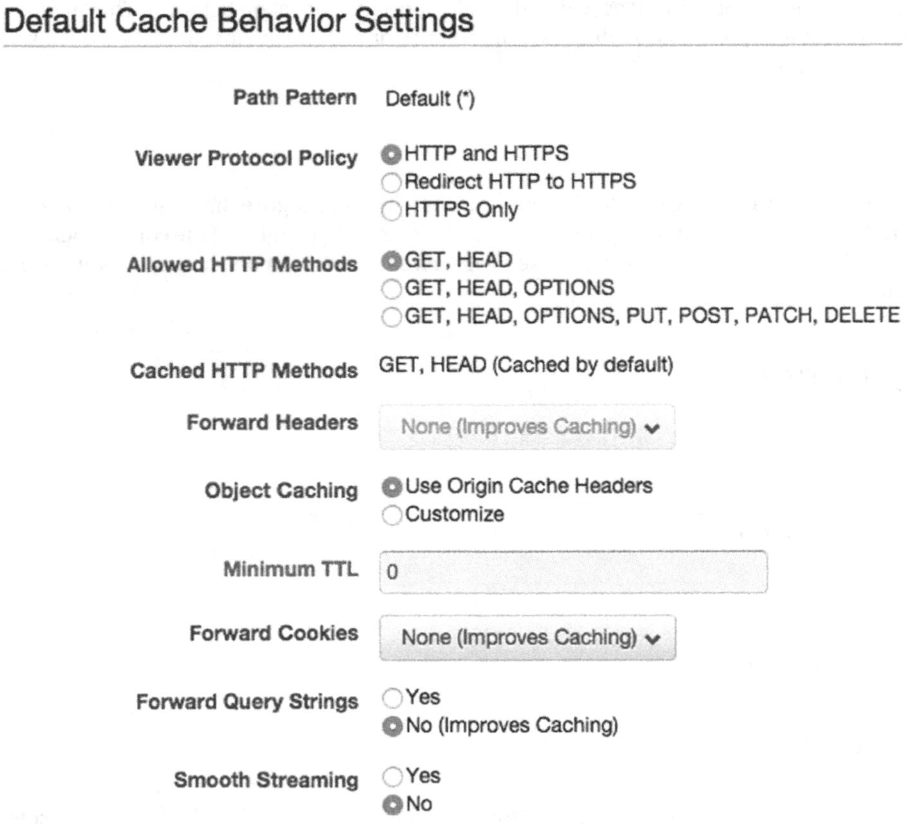

Default Cache Behavior Settings

Path Pattern	Default (*)
Viewer Protocol Policy	◉ HTTP and HTTPS ◯ Redirect HTTP to HTTPS ◯ HTTPS Only
Allowed HTTP Methods	◉ GET, HEAD ◯ GET, HEAD, OPTIONS ◯ GET, HEAD, OPTIONS, PUT, POST, PATCH, DELETE
Cached HTTP Methods	GET, HEAD (Cached by default)
Forward Headers	None (Improves Caching) ⌄
Object Caching	◉ Use Origin Cache Headers ◯ Customize
Minimum TTL	0
Forward Cookies	None (Improves Caching) ⌄
Forward Query Strings	◯ Yes ◉ No (Improves Caching)
Smooth Streaming	◯ Yes ◉ No

Figure 4-4. Distribution Default Cache Behavior Settings

The primary differentiator between behaviors is the path pattern, the URL path syntax that matches the request made by the viewer. For each path pattern you identify, you can configure a unique set of caching rules. You can find a listing of some path pattern examples in Table 4-1.

Table 4-1. *A Few Examples of Valid Path Patterns*

Path Pattern	Explanation
/users/login	Rules for /users/login only
/users/*	Rules for all other requests inside the /users/ directory
*.jpg	Rules for all .jpg files
Default(*)	Default rules

You will notice that the first path pattern in Table 4-1 is the most specific, and the last pattern is the most general. This is intentional, as we will be implementing cache behaviors in this same way. Patterns are checked in descending order, starting at the top of the list. As such, the default of * must be the last rule.

This also means that the default path pattern is not negotiable. If, for example, your default were some value such as /users/*, it would be possible for a request to not match any path patterns you've defined. CloudFront would then not know how to fulfill the request and thus would be unable to generate a response for the user. Therefore, you will see that you can't change the *Path Pattern*, so we'll proceed to the *Viewer Protocol Policy*. At the behavior level, you can determine whether the viewer can access content via HTTP and HTTPS or HTTPS only, or by redirecting HTTP requests to HTTPS. For now, we can leave the default setting, **HTTP and HTTPS**.

Next, we choose the HTTP methods we want to allow, with the *Allowed HTTP Methods* setting. There may be behaviors, or entire applications, which you want to be read-only. In these cases, you would only allow GET, HEAD or GET, HEAD, OPTIONS. In our case, we have to decide whether we would prefer to allow all methods and then restrict them in read-only routes or default to read-only and enable POST in specific routes. Let's go with the latter approach, as there are very few end points that are not read-only. We will therefore select **GET, HEAD**.

The next field is *Cached HTTP Methods*. You may notice that no matter what HTTP methods you allowed in the previous field, you cannot choose to cache PUT, POST, PATCH, or DELETE. This should make some sense to you. If, for example, an HTTP POST request with a user's login information generated an authentication token for that specific user, we would not want the response to be cached by CloudFront. If it were, there would be a risk of returning cached, and wrong, information to the next user. In any case, this field updates based on your previous choice, so we can't change the value there now.

Next, you must decide whether to enable *Forward Headers* as the request is received by CloudFront. If you choose None, your caching will improve significantly—CloudFront will ignore the headers when determining whether to serve a cached copy of the response or request a new copy from the app server.

If for some reason you needed to parse the HTTP request headers in your application, you could either choose All or Whitelist. When you choose Whitelist, you can manually select the individual request headers that are relevant to your application, which I will detail in the next section, but you can skip it if you aren't interested.

SCENARIO: WHITE-LISTING HEADERS

For the sake of argument, let's pretend that we wanted to capture the web page that linked visitors to our application. We can usually find this information in the `Referrer` HTTP header. If we were not forwarding headers from CloudFront, we couldn't access this information, so we will want to white-list just that one specific header.

Choose **Whitelist** from the *Forward Headers* drop-down, and an interface similar to the figure below will appear inline, with a scrolling list of request headers. You'll notice that above the list of headers is a text box in which you can enter a custom header in addition to selecting from the presets, in case you wanted to make up your own request headers for use in an application (see the following illustration).

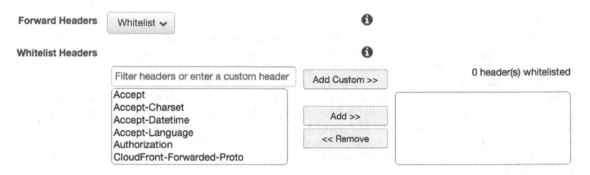

Scroll down the list of headers to find Referrer, and click **Add >>**. When you finish creating this CloudFront distribution, the `Referrer` header will be dynamic in all requests that are run through CloudFront, whereas the other headers will be static.

While scrolling through this list, you may notice a few headers that are unfamiliar:

- `CloudFront-Forwarded-Proto`
- `CloudFront-Is-Mobile-Viewer`
- `CloudFront-Is-Desktop-Viewer`
- `CloudFront-Is-Tablet-Viewer`
- `CloudFront-Viewer-Country`

These are headers that CloudFront adds to your request, based on its own internal logic. For instance, three of the preceding headers help you determine whether the viewer is on a mobile, tablet, or desktop device. AWS maintains its own internal list of devices and checks the `User-Agent` HTTP header, comparing it against their list of devices and generating these headers accordingly. If you were considering using your own device list to identify mobile users, CloudFront does this work for you! You can find more documentation on these headers in the AWS blog here: `http://aws.amazon.com/blogs/aws/enhanced-cloudfront-customization/`.

Now back to the main lesson...

We will choose **None** to forward no HTTP headers to our application. The next two fields, *Object Caching* and *Minimum TTL*, are also coupled. We have to decide here whether we're going to manage the expiration of our cached response programmatically or whether we want to do so in CloudFront. In the former case, we would choose **Use Origin Cache Headers**, and we would have to manually only set our headers with ExpressJS. If you wanted a response to be cached for 60 seconds, you would add the following line before sending a response back to the user:

```
res.set('Cache-Control', 'public, max-age=60'); // cache for up to 60 seconds
```

However, you can also use CloudFront to set this header, by choosing **Customize** for your *Object Caching* and then setting your *Minimum TTL* to **60**. The default max-age in CloudFront is 24 hours, for reference. We will choose the latter route and set our custom TTL to 60 seconds.

Next, we have some additional properties that we can forward from CloudFront to our app server. First is *Forward Cookies*. Once again, our options are None (for better caching), Whitelist, and All. We will choose **None** for now, as we aren't currently using cookies in our application.

Forward Query Strings is a simple Yes/No choice. We can choose **No**, because this is our default behavior; however, we are guaranteed to require query strings in other behaviors we define. It is important that any request that parses query strings have a corresponding CloudFront behavior that forwards them.

SCENARIO: FORWARDING QUERY STRINGS

Imagine that we are not forwarding query strings, and the /user route accepts a GET parameter named id and returns information about the user based on this parameter. The first user logs into our application and sends a request for /user?id=1. She receives the information she asked for, and CloudFront creates a cached object for /user. Then a second user logs in and sends a request for /user?id=2. CloudFront ignores the query string and looks for a cached object for /user. It finds the response that was cached for /user?id=1 and sends it in response to the second user's request.

See what happened? If the query string affects the output, and we aren't forwarding them, then /user?id=1 and /user?id=2 are cached as the same object, and the wrong responses get sent to our users. The second user got the wrong data, because we didn't forward query strings when we should have!

Because we haven't set up user authentication yet, we do not have to preserve cookies. Set *Forward Cookies* to **None** for the time being. In the future, we will have to allow cookies for some behaviors. *Smooth Streaming* can likewise be set to **No**. This is an HTTP protocol created by Microsoft that optimizes streaming media for the client's bandwidth in real time. Not much use for this in our application, is there?

Last in this section is the option to *Restrict Viewer Access* using signed URLs. You can also set this to **No**. You can enable this feature in order to serve private content via CloudFront. If you were to do this, you would have to manage the signed URLs on your own, which is a significant undertaking in its own right.

Distribution Settings

Now that you've configured the default behavior for your distribution, it's time to configure the distribution itself (see Figure 4-5). First, we must select a Price Class, which, as usual, affects both the price and performance of the service.

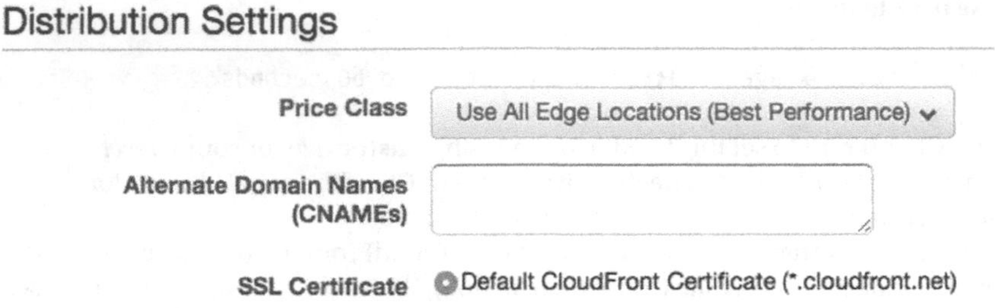

Distribution Settings

Price Class	Use All Edge Locations (Best Performance) ⌄
Alternate Domain Names (CNAMEs)	
SSL Certificate	⦿ Default CloudFront Certificate (*.cloudfront.net)

Figure 4-5. *CloudFront Distribution Settings*

Price Class

Unlike EC2 or RDS, we do not select an instance with built-in computing power. Instead, the pricing is based on both volume of data transferred and regions activated. For each region in which we've enabled CloudFront, we pay for the rate of data transfer in (from CloudFront to the distribution origin) and out of the distribution (to the Internet), as well as number of HTTP and HTTPS requests per region.

Confusing the matter further, the price for data transfer out (to the Internet) per region decreases as the data volume increases. The price tiers are enterprise-scale, so the first price tier includes up to 10TB per month. For the pricing per number of requests, the rate is per 10,000. You can find a complete breakdown of the current rates at: http://aws.amazon.com/cloudfront/pricing/.

To summarize the pricing with a brief example, if you only enabled CloudFront for the United States and Europe, your pricing formula would be as follows:

> US Data In + Europe Data In + US Data Out + Europe Data Out
> + (US HTTP Requests/10,000) + (US HTTPS Requests/10,000)
> + (Europe HTTP Requests/10,000) + (Europe HTTPS Requests/10,000)

Despite the complexity of the pricing, your CloudFront bill is likely to be an order of magnitude less than your EC2 or RDS bill. If you only expect users in the United States and Europe, you could limit your CloudFront distribution to those regions. You can also limit distribution to the United States, Europe, and Asia. But we will go ahead and select **Use All Edge Locations**.

Alternate Domain Names

In this field, you can enter up to 100 CNAMEs from which your CloudFront distribution can be accessed. This is the first place you will use the domain you're using for your application. You will enter it here, including the www but not http://.

SSL Certificate

If we had an SSL certificate, we would configure it here. We will skip this part for now, leaving **Default CloudFront Certificate** selected.

Default Root Object

You can use this field to specify the path to an index file when a viewer enters only the domain into the browser. In our case, you will recall that we have set up this same function in ExpressJS. Our Hello World page is served when users request the "/" path. If, for example, we were using CloudFront to serve a plain HTML file, we would set index.html as the default root object. As such, we don't have to use this feature.

The next several fields pertain to generating logs for CloudFront. We will be exploring logs further in a later lesson. We will leave *Logging* set to **Off** for now. There's also a *Comment* field, which is purely for internal use. You can leave a note for yourself/your team here if need be. Last, *Distribution State* is the on/off switch for the entire distribution. Leave the value set to **Enabled** and review your choices, to make sure everything is configured correctly.

Distribution Settings—Summary

Origin Settings
Origin Domain Name photoalbums-elb-[id].us-east-1.elb.amazonaws.com
Origin ID ELB-photoalbums-elb-[id]
Origin Protocol Policy Match Viewer
HTTP Port 80
HTTPS Port 443

Default Cache Behavior Settings
Viewer Protocol Policy HTTP & HTTPS
Allowed HTTP Methods GET, HEAD
Forward Headers None
Object Caching Use Origin Cache Headers
Forward Cookies None
Forward Query String No
Smooth Streaming No
Restrict Viewer Access No

Distribution Settings
Price Class Use All Edge Locations
Alternate Domain Names www.[yourdomain].com
SSL Certificate Default CloudFront Certificate
Default Root Object (blank)
Logging Off
Comment (blank)
Distribution State Enabled

Finally, click **Create Distribution**. You will be returned to the CloudFront Distributions view, and your distribution will appear in the table with a status of *In Progress*. It will take several minutes for your distribution to be created. However, you can still access the distribution while it's being created.

Distribution Detail View

Click the distribution's ID to proceed to the Distribution detail view. It should look like Figure 4-6.

Figure 4-6. *Distribution detail view*

You'll notice that the organization of CloudFront is a little different from the other services we've used. In the left-hand column, you will see that the secondary navigation is primarily for accessing metrics and reports. This conflicts a bit with the paradigm established in the OpsWorks, IAM, and EC2 dashboards, where the left-hand navigation allowed you to drill down to subsections of the service.

In CloudFront, the distribution subsections are accessed in a tabbed view in the main content area. You begin in the General tab (Figure 4-7), where you see the distribution settings you just created. Note the *Distribution Status*, which can tell you whether your most recent changes to the distribution have propagated (*deployed*), or are still taking effect (*in progress*). The Origins tab lists all the origins for this distribution. The Behaviors tab allows you to define behaviors for viewer requests, based on the URL path of the request. Error Pages allow you to present viewers with custom error pages and HTTP status codes. The Restrictions tab allows you to create geographic restrictions on accessing your content, and you can use the Invalidations tab to clear the CloudFront cache manually.

	Domain Name	Origin ID	Origin Type	Origin Access Identity	Origin Protocol Policy	HTTPS Port	HTTP Port
☐	photoalbums-elb-1925984452.us-east-1.elb.amazonaws.com	ELB-photoalbums-elb-1925984452	Custom Origin	-	HTTP Only	443	80

Figure 4-7. *Distribution origins*

Origins

Click the **Origins** tab, shown in Figure 4-7. In the Origins table, you'll recognize that you created a single origin when you created this distribution. Your only origin right now is the Photoalbums load balancer. This means that requests to the CloudFront instance can only be forwarded to the load balancer, and no other source. In the future, we will be adding a second origin here. While an origin can be included in multiple distributions, you will have to create a record for the origin in each distribution.

■ **Note**   You may be realizing now that there is a lot of potential here. You could create multiple OpsWorks stacks, each with its own load balancer, and serve content from multiple application stacks under a single domain!

Behaviors

The next tab, shown in Figure 4-8, shows the Behaviors for this distribution. When you created your distribution, you also created the default behavior. Each distribution must always have at least one behavior. You'll notice that if you select the default behavior, you can edit it, but you cannot delete it.

General	Origins	Behaviors	Error Pages	Restrictions	Invalidations

CloudFront compares a request for an object with the path patterns in your cache behaviors based on the order of the cache behaviors in your distribution. Arrange cache behaviors in the order in which you want CloudFront to evaluate them.

Create Behavior	Edit	Delete	Change Precedence:	Move Up	Move Down	Save

	Precedence	Path Pattern	Origin	Viewer Protocol Policy	Forwarded Query Strings	Trusted Signers
☐	1	Default (*)	ELB-photoalbums-elb-1925984452	HTTP and HTTPS	No	-

Figure 4-8. Behaviors

If you recall the settings we chose for the default behavior, you will remember that the POST HTTP method is not allowed. However, we do need POST for user registration, login/logout, and for photo and album creation. As such, we will identify and create additional behaviors on a case-by-case basis. We're immediately confronted with a choice: should we create a behavior for every individual route that allows POST? Or should we make group behaviors that are more permissive and less specific? Let's start with /users/. Let's revisit the routes we've defined in the /users/* path.

```
GET  /users/
POST /users/login
POST /users/logout
POST /users/register
GET  /users/user/:user
```

We know that we must allow POST for /users/login, /users/register, and /users/logout. It seems, then, that we could consider logically grouping these together in a single behavior with the path pattern of /users/*. But there are other rules to consider when we design our behaviors. Do we have to accept query strings with any of these paths? There are only two GET routes in /users/, and neither of them accepts GET parameters. And what about cookies? We haven't built our authentication yet, but it seems safe to say that we could need them.

103

It looks like the routes here have enough in common to justify creating a behavior. Click the **Create Behavior** button at the top left. You will see a Create Behavior view that should look familiar. We saw this view nested in the larger Create Distribution view.

In the *Path Pattern* field, input **/users/***, to catch all requests inside the /users/ path. Just so we're clear, this does not just include URLs such as /users/login; it will intercept requests of *any* file type. If your viewer requests /users/profile.jpg or /users/profile.txt, it will be processed by this behavior all the same, unless an earlier behavior in the list catches it first.

Change the *Allowed HTTP Methods* to **GET, HEAD, OPTIONS, PUT, POST, PATCH, DELETE**. Then, change *Forward Cookies* to **All**. You can leave the rest of the settings at their default values. Make sure everything looks like the selections in Figure 4-9, then click **Create**.

Cache Behavior Settings

Path Pattern	/users/login
Origin	ELB-photoalbums-elb-1925984452 ⌄
Viewer Protocol Policy	○ HTTP and HTTPS ○ Redirect HTTP to HTTPS ● HTTPS Only
Allowed HTTP Methods	○ GET, HEAD ○ GET, HEAD, OPTIONS ● GET, HEAD, OPTIONS, PUT, POST, PATCH, DELETE
Cached HTTP Methods	GET, HEAD (Cached by default) ☐ OPTIONS
Forward Headers	All ⌄
Object Caching	● Use Origin Cache Headers ○ Customize
Minimum TTL	0
Forward Cookies	All ⌄
Forward Query Strings	○ Yes ● No (Improves Caching)
Smooth Streaming	○ Yes ● No
Restrict Viewer Access (Use Signed URLs)	○ Yes ● No

Figure 4-9. *Create behavior for* /users/*

Next, we will go through the same process with the /albums/ routes. Albums functionality is pretty limited and includes the following:

```
GET /albums/id/:albumID
POST /albums/upload
POST /albums/delete
```

Seems pretty similar to /users/. Once again, there is no need to forward query strings, but we will want to forward cookies for later. Click **Create Behavior** again, and in the *Path Pattern* field, enter /**albums/***. Change the *Allowed HTTP Methods* to **GET, HEAD, OPTIONS, PUT, POST, PATCH, DELETE**. Then, change *Forward Cookies* to **All**. You can leave the rest of the settings at their default values. Make sure everything looks correct and click **Create**.

The /photos/ route is likewise pretty similar to /users/. The routes defined in /photos/ are as follows:

```
GET /photos/id/:photoID
POST / photos /upload
POST / photos /delete
```

Let's create this behavior with the same rules as well. Once again, click **Create Behavior** and, in the *Path Pattern* field, enter /**photos/***. Change the *Allowed HTTP Methods* to **GET, HEAD, OPTIONS, PUT, POST, PATCH, DELETE**. Then, change *Forward Cookies* to **All**. You can leave the rest of the settings at their default values. Make sure everything looks correct and click **Create**.

If you look at the Behaviors table now, you'll notice that you can conveniently see the Origin, Viewer Protocol Policy, and Forwarded Query Strings values in the table, simply to make it easier to manage your behaviors.

Take another look at the Behaviors table, shown in Figure 4-10. You will see that even though the default behavior was created first, the rest of the behaviors appear above it in the table, in the order that they were created. This is because when CloudFront receives an HTTP request, the request will be checked against each behavior in descending order from the top of the list. The *Precedence* field, numbered upward from 1, indicates the order in which the behaviors are compared. The Default behavior, being the most general, should be the last behavior against which a request is compared. Currently, there is no overlap between our other behaviors, so their ordering doesn't matter too much. If there were, you would want the more specific paths at the top, with a higher precedence, and the more general ones at the bottom. The behavior precedence can be altered by selecting behaviors, clicking **Move Up** or **Move Down**, and **Save**.

| General | Origins | **Behaviors** | Error Pages | Restrictions | Invalidations |

CloudFront compares a request for an object with the path patterns in your cache behaviors based on the order of the cache behaviors in your distribution. Arrange cache behaviors in the order in which you want CloudFront to evaluate them.

Create Behavior | Edit | Delete | Change Precedence: | Move Up | Move Down | Save

	Precedence	Path Pattern	Origin	Viewer Protocol Policy	Forwarded Query Strings	Trusted Signers
☐	1	/users/*	ELB-photoalbums-elb-1925984452	HTTP and HTTPS	No	-
☐	2	/albums/*	ELB-photoalbums-elb-1925984452	HTTP and HTTPS	No	-
☐	3	/photos/*	ELB-photoalbums-elb-1925984452	HTTP and HTTPS	No	-
☐	4	Default (*)	ELB-photoalbums-elb-1925984452	HTTP and HTTPS	No	-

Figure 4-10. *Updated Behaviors table*

Behavior with Query Strings

Let's go ahead and add a behavior that allows query strings. But first, we have to actually create the route in our application. Before we add the behavior, we will finally return to the code editor and add some new functionality to the Photoalbums app. We haven't spent much time talking about larger goals for the sample application, as it is admittedly a bare-bones app. But we can try to add minor features that would be useful for this app and for web app development in general.

One common use of query strings (or GET parameters) is for searching or filtering content by one or more parameters. It would be useful to add a basic search function to photos, so users can search photos globally for matching text in the caption field. Open /routes/photos.js and find the space between the /id/:id route and /upload route. Paste the code from Listing 4-1 here.

Listing 4-1. The /photos/search Route

```
/* GET photo search */
router.get('/search', function(req, res) {
    if(req.param('query')){
        var params = {
        query : req.param('query')
        }
        model.getPhotosSearch(params, function(err, obj){
        if(err){
          res.status(400).send({error: 'Invalid photo search'});
        } else {
          res.send(obj);
        }
        });
    } else {
        res.status(400).send({error: 'No search term found'});
    }
});
```

As you can see, this route simply accepts a string in the query parameter and passes it to model.getPhotosSearch. If the query is missing, an error is returned instead. The structure of the controller logic is similar to that of the other routes we've created. We don't directly pass the GET parameters into the model. Instead, we construct a params object on which we could perform any additional operations we needed. For example, if we wanted to filter profanity from the search queries, we could easily plug in that functionality with this pattern.

Next, we have to add the getPhotosSearch function to the model. Navigate to /lib/models/model-photos.js. Beneath the getPhotosByAlbumID function, paste the code from Listing 4-2.

Listing 4-2. getPhotosSearch Function in model-photos.js

```
function getPhotosSearch(params, callback){
  var query = 'SELECT photoID, caption, albumID, userID FROM photos WHERE caption LIKE "%' +
  params.query + '%"';
  connection.query(query, function(err, rows, fields){
    if(err){
      callback(err);
    } else {
```

```
    if(rows.length > 0){
      callback(null, rows);
    } else {
      callback(null, []);
    }
  }
});
}
```

This function also follows the same pattern as the other model functions we've created. We select several photo fields and use the SQL operator LIKE to filter the photos by the value of caption. We run the query and return the results to the controller. We have to be sure to make this function public, by adding the following line to the bottom of the file:

```
exports.getPhotosSearch = getPhotosSearch;
```

Deploy Code Changes

We're ready to push our code changes to our application stack. You could also test locally first, if you still have the local database running. Commit your changes to your code repository. In the AWS Console, navigate back to OpsWorks. Click the **Photoalbums** stack. Open the **Navigation** menu and click **Apps**. Click the **deploy** button to return to the Deploy App view. In the *Comment* field, add a note to the effect of "added photo search method," then click **Deploy**.

Add New Behavior

Navigate back to CloudFront and click your distribution. Open the **Behaviors** tab and click **Create Distribution** again. This time, we're creating a behavior for a specific path, so we'll enter it directly into the *Path Pattern*: **/photos/search**. This time, we'll leave *Allowed HTTP Methods* set to the default of **GET, HEAD**. Likewise, *Forward Cookies* can be set to **None**, as this is a public method that requires no authentication. Set *Forward Query Strings* to **Yes** and click **Create**.

When you're returned to the Behaviors table, you'll see that the new behavior is the fourth in the list, with a precedence of 4. This won't work, as requests will get caught by the /photos/* behavior before they will reach this one. Select the new behavior and click **Move Up**, then click **Save**. Your behaviors table should now look like Figure 4-11.

	Precedence	Path Pattern	Origin	Viewer Protocol Policy	Forwarded Query Strings	Trusted Signers
☐	1	/users/*	ELB-photoalbums-elb-1925984452	HTTP and HTTPS	No	-
☐	2	/albums/*	ELB-photoalbums-elb-1925984452	HTTP and HTTPS	No	-
☐	3	/photos/search	ELB-photoalbums-elb-1925984452	HTTP and HTTPS	Yes	-
☐	4	/photos/*	ELB-photoalbums-elb-1925984452	HTTP and HTTPS	No	-
☐	5	Default (*)	ELB-photoalbums-elb-1925984452	HTTP and HTTPS	No	-

Figure 4-11. *Behaviors table with new behavior*

With our code deployed and our behavior in place, we should be ready to test. The first time we tested our code hosted on AWS, we accessed the EC2 instance directly. The next test, we ran our requests at the load balancer's URL. This time, we've added another intermediary layer between our instances and the user, and we're going to use the CloudFront URL instead.

Return to the **General** tab and locate the *Domain Name*. It should be formatted like [unique-identifier].cloudfront.net. Open this URL in your browser, and you should see the Hello World page. Now, let's create a few photos to make sure our behaviors are working correctly. Before we can upload a photo, we need both a userID and an albumID. If you created a user before, you can get his/her ID at /user/:username (but most likely the userID will be 1). If you haven't, then open your REST client and make a POST request to /users/register with the following parameters: username, email, and password.

When you have your userID, create an album by making a POST to /albums/upload with parameters for userID and title. You should receive the albumID in the response to your request. Next, we can create the photo objects (yes, there are still no file uploads attached to them). Make a POST request to /photos/upload with your userID, albumID, and the caption "Hello World." If you get an ID in response, your photo was created successfully (of course, you could also tell that from the status code 200). In order to test search, we will want to have a few photos. Make another request with the caption "Hello Chicago," and then a third with the caption "Goodbye New York."

By now we have three photos, which is enough to test a few searches. In your REST client or browser, make a request to the path /photos/search?query=Hello. You should see two photo entries: "Hello World" and "Hello Chicago." Change your request to /photos/search?query=Hello%20World, and you should only see one entry.

Caching

Now it's time to see CloudFront's caching in action. Make another POST request to /photos/upload, this time with the caption "Hello London." Then, make another GET request to /photos/search?query=Hello. The response should be lightning fast, but if you look closely at the JSON, you will not see your most recent photo, "Hello London." This is because after the first request, CloudFront is now storing a cached object for the address /photos/search?query=Hello. It will continue to send the same response to all requests for this URL, until the object expires. But when does it expire?

Each object stored in the cache is linked to a behavior, and its expiration is determined by the value of several fields in the corresponding behavior, shown in Figure 4-12.

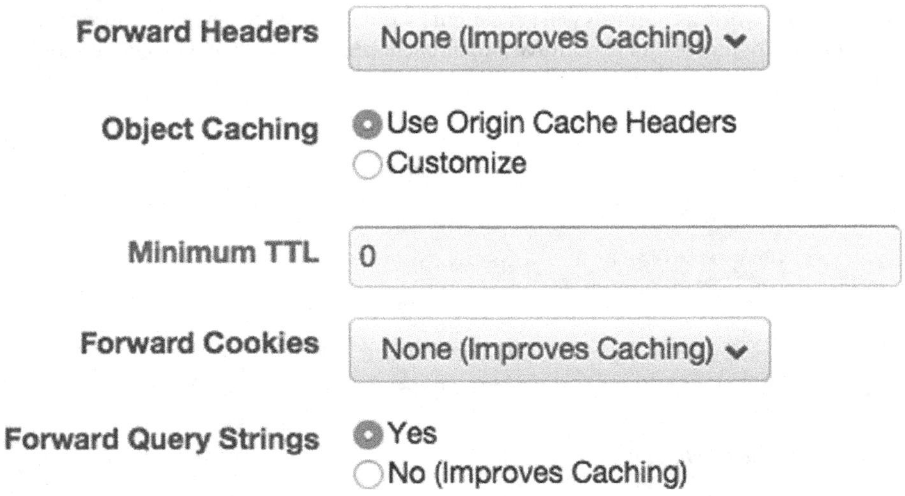

Figure 4-12. Important CloudFront behavior fields when determining object caching

There are two basic factors to determining how long an object stays in the cache: Minimum TTL and the HTTP request headers. As you can see in Figure 4-12, the behavior for /photos/search employs Use Origin Cache Headers to determine the caching of the object. With this setting, we must control the caching of our responses programmatically. If we change the setting to Customize, we can specify the number of seconds that an object will stay in the cache, in which case CloudFront will override any Cache-Control:max-age headers sent by our application. However, CloudFront has a default expiration of 24 hours and will not cache an object for a shorter amount of time without some effort on our part.

FORWARDED QUERY STRINGS

It's important to note how the other settings can impact the caching as well. Because we are forwarding query strings, this means that they are factored into the way objects are stored in CloudFront. This means that /photos/search?query=hello and /photos/search?query=goodbye are stored as distinct objects in the cache. If they weren't, both searches could yield the same result.

One easy way to test this is to force your results to refresh by adding a unique query string to the request. For instance, /photos/search?query=hello&time=4815162332 is different from /photos/search?query=hello&time=4211138 and will force CloudFront to retrieve a new response for the origin.

You should see in your search request the header shown in the following code:

Request Header
Accept: text/html,application/xhtml+xml,application/xml;q=0.9,image/webp,*/*;q=0.8
Accept-Encoding: gzip,deflate,sdch
Accept-Language: en-US,en;q=0.8
Cache-Control: max-age=0
Connection: keep-alive
Host: d23xpp2aiwzqtf.cloudfront.net
If-None-Match: W/"fe-4203691681"

Response Header
Connection: keep-alive
Date: Mon, 24 Nov 2014 23:51:35 GMT
ETag: W/"180-2935506378"
X-Powered-By: Express
Age: 1196 X-Cache: Hit from cloudfront
Via: 1.1 f519cbbbbf1657343dde8ed4d32a9966.cloudfront.net (CloudFront)
X-Amz-Cf-Id: l1UWAownAiSOIHoVoXGuw5dHo3Rt_9POCx5eqCL-Dqus4BijxF-oWg==

As you can see, the Cache-Control header in the *request* is set to max-age=0, but this header is conspicuously absent from the *response*. While you might think this means that CloudFront has to refresh the object, in practice, this is not the case. As stated previously, the default Minimum TTL of 0 actually means 24 hours, and without the origin overriding this directive, the Minimum TTL takes precedence. In our current scenario, the *browser* will only cache the response for 0 seconds, but CloudFront will retain the object in its cache for 24 hours.

With our /photos/search behavior, we face the age-old question of how long to cache our response. On the one hand, caching our results will reduce the workload for our application stack, as the requests can be processed completely by CloudFront without ever burdening the application layer or database. On the other hand, user or client expectations for an enterprise app often mean we must provide near-instantaneous results. Our code change is only going to take a few minutes to make and deploy; however, first, we have to remove our cached objects from CloudFront.

Invalidations

Unfortunately, we can't simply deploy our code and test it again. There are already objects in CloudFront's cache for the URLs in question, so CloudFront will continue to serve a response with the old response headers. This brings us to another feature of CloudFront distributions: invalidations.

An *invalidation* is essentially a command to remove an object from CloudFront edge caches. You can't simply clear your cache in-browser, as the invalidation has to be sent to CloudFront caches globally. Because CloudFront caches your content in data centers around the globe, it will take a few moments to undo that.

At first glance, you might think, "Why can't I just programmatically invalidate my caches on the fly when content is updated but otherwise use maximum caching on my responses?" In theory, the concept makes sense: store cached copies of all your responses in CloudFront and generate new ones only when the content of the responses has changed. While it sounds nice, unfortunately, CloudFront invalidations are far from instantaneous. Although you could invalidate your caches programmatically using the AWS SDK (indeed, everything we do in the console can be done programmatically), you'll see in a moment that there is a significant delay between when you create an invalidation and when the operation is completed.

In CloudFront, open your distribution again and click the **Invalidations** tab. You will see an empty table of your invalidations. Click the **Create Invalidation** button at the top, which will open a modal text area, shown in Figure 4-13. Add the two paths you wish to invalidate, separated by a line break, as follows:

```
/albums/id/1
/photos/search?query=Hello
```

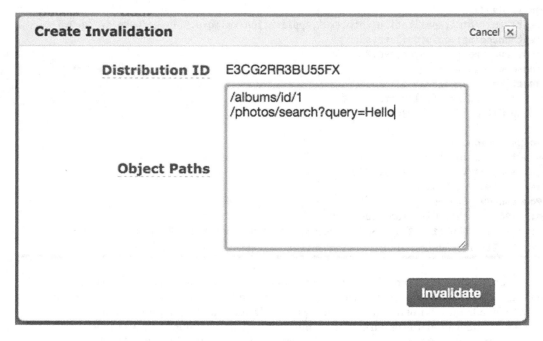

Figure 4-13. Creating a CloudFront invalidation

Go ahead and click the **Invalidate** button. You will see your invalidation appear in the table, with a status of InProgress. It will take a few minutes for the change to take effect, at which point the status will change to Completed. You'll also notice that each invalidation has a unique ID and a timestamp. Now we can make our code changes, and we'll be ready to test as soon as the code is deployed. Note that we only invalidated the cache before pushing our fix to save some time, because no one else is using the app. In a production setting, you should deploy your changes before invalidating the cache.

Controlling Caching

Let's make two changes, reflecting two different scenarios. First, we want photo search results to be instant. Let's instruct CloudFront to *never* cache the results. Of course, this is going to be a problem down the road with a large user base, but at least we will know how to do it. Second, we will use the Expires request header to make a request route expire at a specific interval.

In our first scenario, we are going to configure our request headers such that neither the browser nor CloudFront will ever attempt to cache the response. In your code editor, navigate to /routes/photos.js. Locate the handler for the **/search** rout, and paste the following line at the beginning of the function:

```
res.header('Cache-Control', 'no-cache, no-store');
```

This should be straightforward, as we're simply passing a key-value pair to the response header using ExpressJS syntax. It belongs at the beginning of the function, so as to avoid copy-pasting. To recap, the function should look like Listing 4-3.

Listing 4-3. /photos/search with Cache-Control Header

```
router.get('/search', function(req, res) {
  res.header('Cache-Control', 'no-cache, no-store');
  if(req.param('query')){
    var params = {
      query : req.param('query')
    }
    model.getPhotosSearch(params, function(err, obj){
      if(err){
        res.status(400).send({error: 'Invalid photo search'});
      } else {
        res.send(obj);
      }
    });
  } else {
    res.status(400).send({error: 'No search term found'});
  }
});
```

Next, we'll add our second use case. Let's say that the response when requesting an album by ID can be cached by CloudFront for ten seconds. This will keep the response up to date without taxing the servers as much as disabling the cache entirely. Open /routes/albums.js and find the handler for the **/id/:id** route. At the top of the function, add the following two rows:.

```
res.header("Cache-Control", "public, max-age=10");
res.header("Expires", new Date(Date.now() + 10).toUTCString());
```

Your handler should look like Listing 4-4.

Listing 4-4. /albums/id/:albumID with Cache-Control Header

```
router.get('/id/:albumID', function(req, res) {
  res.header("Cache-Control", "public, max-age=10");
  res.header("Expires", new Date(Date.now() + 10000).toUTCString());
  if(req.param('albumID')){
    var params = {
      albumID : req.param('albumID')
    }
    model.getAlbumByID(params, function(err, obj){
      if(err){
        res.status(400).send({error: 'Invalid album ID'});
      } else {
        res.send(obj);
      }
    });
  } else {
    res.status(400).send({error: 'Invalid album ID'});
  }
});
```

The response takes the current date and adds ten seconds (in milliseconds) to it, then sets the header. One thing to note is that this ten seconds will not be exact, as it will still take time to retrieve the data from the model before sending the response. If you want it to be as close to perfect as possible, set the header in the callback for model.getAlbumByID instead.

You might be wondering why the header is set at the top instead, then. There are other possible responses, such as the 400 error sent when the album ID is missing from the URL, or when no album is found for the provided ID, the latter of which could be caused by some sort of database error. It is possible for CloudFront to cache the error response the user would see, resulting in this error being shown to other users, perhaps incorrectly. In this scenario, CloudFront could backfire by prolonging errors on the client side unnecessarily. As such, it's best to make all responses include the Expires header. You could set the header each time a response is sent from this route, but it would just make the listing look messier. After all, what good is a code sample if it's too cluttered?

Anyway, go ahead and commit your changes to your code repository. In the AWS Console, navigate back to OpsWorks. Click the Photoalbums stack. Open the **Navigation** menu, and click **Apps**. Click the **deploy** button to return to the Deploy App view. In the *Comment* field, add a note to the effect of "added Cache-Control headers," then click **Deploy**. Give OpsWorks a few minutes to push your code.

Testing CloudFront Caching

Once deployment is complete, let's test the albums route first. Make a GET request to /albums/id/1 in your browser (making sure to clear your local cache) or REST client. Take a look at the response headers. They should look similar to Listing 4-5.

Listing 4-5. New and Improved, Ten-Second Cache Response Headers

```
Response Header
Cache-Control:public, max-age=10
Connection:keep-alive
Content-Length:631
Content-Type:application/json; charset=utf-8
Date:Wed, 26 Nov 2014 01:29:02 GMT
ETag:W/"277-3646801943"
Expires:Wed, 26 Nov 2014 01:29:02 GMT
Via:1.1 a2c541774483a4b9c153c3cb7c7a7753.cloudfront.net (CloudFront)
X-Amz-Cf-Id:pcxqjO3svkFItzzQ3KWi4OK5jJf4eGXs91PCQLjv2liWf9f7iP-KaQ==
X-Cache:Miss from cloudfront
X-Powered-By:Express
```

The important parts of the response header are bolded. First, you can see that the Cache-Control header we added appears verbatim. The Expires header should appear roughly ten seconds after the current time, accommodating for differences in time zones. You'll also see a header we didn't add, X-Cache. The first time, this might read "Miss from cloudfront." Make a couple more requests in rapid succession, and you'll see "Hit from cloudfront." This header informs you whether CloudFront provided a cached response (a hit) or had to retrieve a new response from the origin (a miss).

However, your browser or REST client may also be conforming to the caching headers, caching the X-Cache header, thus you might not see the expected result. If this is the case, you'll have to test using cURL. Open your command-line interface (Terminal), and type the following command:

```
curl -I http://[cloudfront-id].cloudfront.net/albums/id/1
```

If you get a response header with a miss from CloudFront, run the command a few more times. You should receive a hit on the second or third request.

You will also notice the X-Amz-Cf-Id header. You may have deduced that this is a CloudFront ID for the request. If you enable logging in CloudFront, this is the unique ID for each request received by CloudFront. If you ever have to seek support from AWS in debugging CloudFront issues, it may ask you for the X-Amz-Cf-Id requests with which you are experiencing issues.

Next, let's test our no-caching solution for photo searching. To demonstrate this, we will do a search, upload another photo, and then run the search again. First, search for photos with the words "New York," by making a request to /photos/search?query=New%20York. You should see something similar to Listing 4-6.

Listing 4-6. No-Cache Response Headers and Body

```
Response Header
Cache-Control:no-cache, no-store
Connection:keep-alive
Content-Length:67
Content-Type:application/json; charset=utf-8
Date:Wed, 26 Nov 2014 04:23:44 GMT
ETag:W/"43-3955827999"
Via:1.1 b05dafe95c8baade280459c121e622be.cloudfront.net (CloudFront)
X-Amz-Cf-Id:zhNlH4MXzU9G7Mrb5tVgBq8qtMLlW3XONjZsmEZOmQ5MhXmCqdJxAg==
X-Cache:Miss from cloudfront
X-Powered-By:Express
```

```
Response Body
[{"photoID":3,"caption":"Goodbye New York","albumID":1,"userID":1}]
```

Once again, the important headers are bolded. You can see our Cache-Control header at the top. Our first search got a **Miss from cloudfront** in the X-Cache header. This makes sense, as this should be the first search we've run since we invalidated the object in our cache. Now let's create another photo and search again to make sure we get the results we expect.

Make a new POST to /photos/upload with the same album and user IDs as before and the caption "Hello New York." When you get a 200 response back, run the search query again. Your response should look like Listing 4-7, with the new photo showing up almost instantly in the next search.

Listing 4-7. Search Results Showing Up Instantly in the Next Request

```
Response Header
Cache-Control:no-cache, no-store
Connection:keep-alive
Content-Length:132
Content-Type:application/json; charset=utf-8
Date:Wed, 26 Nov 2014 04:35:58 GMT
ETag:W/"84-3303063004"
Via:1.1 2b0986af7f8d32d3d4b4cf9330702abf.cloudfront.net (CloudFront)
X-Amz-Cf-Id:KTpgTxO9XBebAzuSOMSP1f2EkrcRGfqijMFz3Fc6xGqI93TPXsnldw==
X-Cache:RefreshHit from cloudfront
X-Powered-By:Express

Response Body
[
  {
    "photoID":3,
    "caption":"Goodbye New York",
    "albumID":1,
    "userID":1
  },
  {
    "photoID":10,
    "caption":"Hello New York",
    "albumID":1,"userID":1
  }
]
```

This time, the value of the X-Cache header is **RefreshHit from cloudfront**. This means that CloudFront recognized that it needed to refresh the request, and it did so. This is exactly what we wanted to happen!

The difference between these two scenarios may be confusing, owing to the browser's behavior, as *both CloudFront and the browser respond to the same HTTP response headers*. With the /albums/id/1 request, both CloudFront and the browser were responding to the header instructions to cache the response, so more often than not, the browser would cache the entire response, including the response headers. You can validate this by keeping an eye on the X-Amz-Cf-Id header and watching for it to change.

In the case of the /photos/search response, the browser obeys the Cache-Control: no-cache, no-store header, so a new request is always made to CloudFront, which in turn response to the header by always forwarding the request to the origin.

While there are a number of other possible scenarios, we have covered the two primary caching policies you will generate programmatically from your origin. In case you find yourself having to accommodate some unusual scenario beyond what was demonstrated here, AWS provides a table of all possible use cases for origin response headers at http://docs.aws.amazon.com/AmazonCloudFront/latest/DeveloperGuide/Expiration.html.

Cache Statistics

We've run some tests to see when CloudFront is serving our content and when the origin is. Fortunately, it's easy to get a statistical breakdown of how our objects are behaving. In the left-hand navigation, under the Reports & Analysis header, you will see a number of reports that paint a picture of CloudFront's performance. First, click **Cache Statistics**, which will present you with a series of graphs. At the top, you'll see a series of fields that you can use to filter all of the graphs on the page. Choose a **Start Date** and **End Date** that includes the range of dates you've been working on in this chapter. Change the **Web Distribution** to your distribution, and click **Update**.

The first graph, *Total Requests*, is self-explanatory. The second graph, *Percentage of Viewer Requests by Result Type*, is shown in Figure 4-14. Here you can see your requests broken down by Hits, Misses, and Errors. Interestingly, RefreshHits are not shown in the chart. Still, the percentage of requests that are Hits is a good metric to watch. This tells you essentially when CloudFront is saving your application from doing work, because every hit is a request that was handled by CloudFront. As you can see in Figure 4-14, the number of hits drastically decreased when the new caching rules were applied.

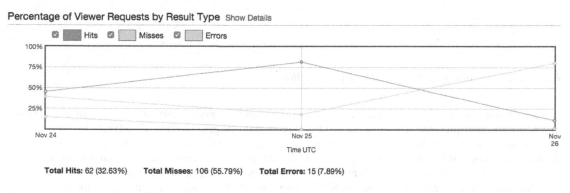

Figure 4-14. Percentage of Viewer Requests by Result Type

Feel free to review the other graphs at your own pace. We will return to the CloudFront reports later, when discussing ways to monitor the health of our application stack. Next, click **Popular Objects** in the CloudFront navigation. Once again, you will see a view with filtering tools at the top. Choose a date range that corresponds with the days you've worked on this chapter and click **Update**. You should see a table similar to that in Figure 4-15.

	Object	Requests ▲	Hit	Miss	Hits %	Bytes From Misses	Total Bytes	Incomplete	2xx	3xx	4xx	5x
								Viewing 1 to 13 of 13 Items				
1	/albums/id/1	82	18	64	21.95%	64.40 KB	74.44 KB	0	76	6	0	0
2	/photos/search	76	44	13	57.89%	6.46 KB	44.47 KB	0	19	44	13	0
3	/stylesheets/style.css	14	0	13	0.00%	7.10 KB	7.52 KB	0	11	3	0	0
4	/photos/upload	7	0	7	0.00%	2.39 KB	2.39 KB	0	7	0	0	0
5	//photos/upload	3	0	3	0.00%	1.03 KB	1.03 KB	0	3	0	0	0
6	/albums/upload	1	0	1	0.00%	367 B	367 B	0	1	0	0	0
7	/users/register	1	0	1	0.00%	381 B	381 B	0	1	0	0	0
8	/photos/id/1	1	0	1	0.00%	429 B	429 B	0	1	0	0	0
9	/photos/id/2	1	0	1	0.00%	432 B	432 B	0	1	0	0	0
10	/photos/id/3	1	0	1	0.00%	435 B	435 B	0	1	0	0	0
11	/	1	0	1	0.00%	541 B	541 B	0	1	0	0	0
12	/favicon.ico	1	0	0	0.00%	0 B	1.64 KB	0	0	0	1	0
13	/phots/search	1	0	0	0.00%	0 B	1.64 KB	0	0	0	1	0

Figure 4-15. *Popular objects in CloudFront distribution*

This is a handy breakdown, as you can identify where exactly users are getting hits and misses and how much output the application is generating that could potentially be generated by CloudFront instead.

You can also see which requests are received the most, if you're looking for a starting point to either optimize your code or improve the effectiveness of CloudFront. Equally important, you can see which objects are responding with 4XX or 5XX errors, which is invaluable diagnostic information.

The next section, *Usage Reports*, is also full of useful metrics for measuring your application's traffic. Feel free to explore it as well, but there's nothing critical to this lesson. I will be discussing *Monitoring and Alarming* in Chapter 7, so you don't need to review it now.

GEO-RESTRICTIONS

Another feature that may be helpful at the enterprise level is geo-restriction, or blocking traffic to/from specific parts of the world. While you may have had to perform this blocking at the software level previously, or relied on network administrators to do so, with CloudFront, you can use this feature quite easily.

Let's pretend that we only want our application to be available in the United States. Return to the CloudFront dashboard and select your distribution again. Click the **Restrictions** tab, which will take you to a table of restrictions. The user interface here is a little funny. The only actual restriction in the table *is* Geo-Restriction. Click the **Edit** button above the table. You will be confronted with a single setting: Enable Geo-Restriction. Hmmm….Let's choose **Yes**.

There are two means of enabling geo-restriction: White listing and blacklisting. In short, you can either choose which countries to allow (white list), or choose which countries to disallow (blacklist). Because we only want to allow one country, it would be more logical to **Whitelist** the United States than to blacklist every other country. Select **US -- United States** and click **Add >>** (see following illustration), then click **Yes, Edit**.

Enable Geo-Restriction	⊙ Yes	❶
	○ No	
Restriction Type	⊙ Whitelist	❶
	○ Blacklist	
Countries		❶

```
GB -- UNITED KINGDOM
US -- UNITED STATES              Add >>          US -- UNITED STATES
UM -- UNITED STATES MINOR OUTLY
UY -- URUGUAY                   << Remove
UZ -- UZBEKISTAN
VU -- VANUATU
```

Cancel   **Yes, Edit**

You will be returned to the Restrictions tab in the distribution view, where you will see that Geo-Restriction has a status of Enabled and Type set to Whitelist. Once again, your distribution will have a status of InProgress while the changes take effect.

■ **Note**   If you want to test geo-restrictions, you could instead blacklist your current country and attempt to access your app via the CloudFront URL.

Now that I've covered the basic features and use case of CloudFront, it's time to move on to the final service we have to configure before your application is hosted at a domain name. Return to the AWS Console and select **Route 53**.

Route 53

How do we point our domain to the application? If you've worked with DNS before, you may have noticed several locations at which we could point our domain: the public IP for one of our instances, the URL of our load balancer, or the URL of our CloudFront instance. There would be a few limitations with any of these approaches.

First and foremost, we want to adhere to the principles set out in Chapter 1: scalability and elasticity. Obviously, the IP addresses of our EC2 instances are unreliable, and if we add new instances but our domain is pointing to only a single instance, we cannot scale properly. A DNS change can take up to 72 hours to propagate. Right now, we can make any number of changes to our configuration and see the results in seconds or minutes. We want to preserve this ability regardless of what goes wrong. If we have to launch a clone of our application stack for any reason, the load balancer address will change. We can't say with certainty that our CloudFront URL is never going to change either. It just might, and we want to be prepared!

For best results, we will use Route 53 to configure our DNS. We will configure our domain to point to AWS nameservers, and then we can add our CNAMES, A records, MX records, etc., in Route 53. We can use the www and app subdomains for different purposes, or we could make www and dev subdomains point to the respective production and development application stacks. In this lesson, we're simply going to learn about the service and set up our application stack at www.[your-domain].com. Let's begin!

We're going to assume that you already have reserved a domain that you want to use, and you know how to use the web portal for your domain registrar. If you don't have a domain yet, you can actually register one in Route 53 by clicking **Registered Domains** in the left-hand navigation and following the steps from there. Our focus, however, will be working with existing domains.

From the Route 53 dashboard, you will see your Resources right at the top: 0 hosted zones, 0 health checks, and 0 domains. The set of records for a domain is collected under the entity known as a *hosted zone*. This is distinct from domains, which are simply the domains that you have registered from Route 53.

Click **Hosted Zones** at the top left and click **Create Hosted Zone** at the top. Instead of taking you to a new view or presenting a modal pop-up, this time, the creation tool will appear in a container on the right-hand side of the screen (see, each AWS service has a subtly unique interface). In the *Domain Name* field, enter your domain name without the http:// or www. Enter a *Comment* labeling the hosted zone and leave the *Type* field set to **Public Hosted Zone** (see Figure 4-16). Click **Create** at the bottom of the view.

Your hosted zone will appear in the table shortly (you may have to click the refresh button at the top right). Select it and click **Go To Record Sets**.

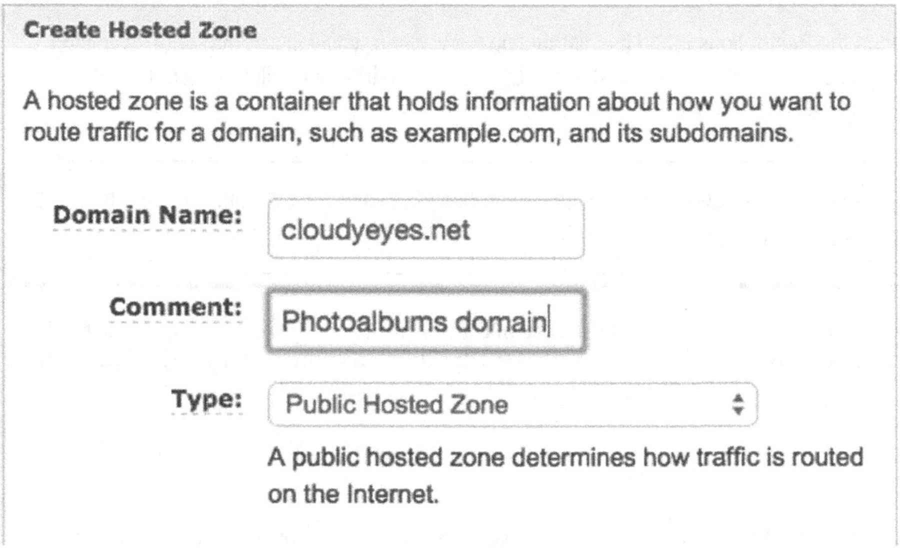

Figure 4-16. *Create Hosted Zone in Route 53*

The Record Sets view, shown in Figure 4-17, is a two-panel layout with your hosted zone records on the left and the detail/editing view on the right. Once you've created a hosted zone, AWS will automatically generate four AWS nameserver addresses as the value of a record with the type **NS** (nameserver). Go back to your domain registrar and change the nameservers for your domain to these addresses, in order. As you may know, it can take up to 72 hours for DNS changes to propagate. You'll also see an SOA, start of authority, record. You most likely won't have to touch it, but it's a necessary part of domain registration.

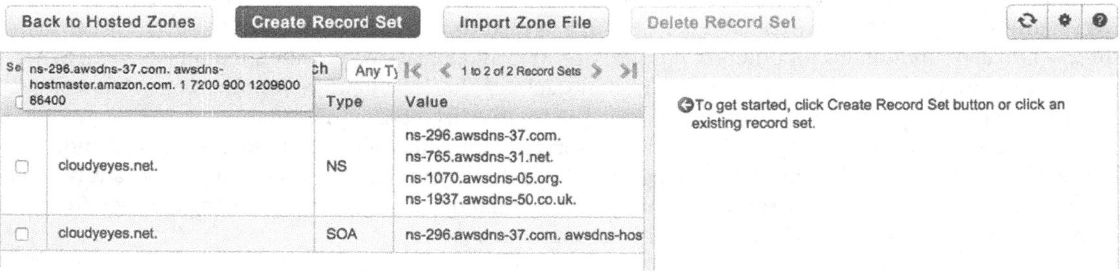

Figure 4-17. *Record sets*

We'll assume that you're ready to press onward while your domain change is propagating. The next task is to route requests from your domain to CloudFront. To do this, we'll create an A record and point it to our www subdomain.

At the top of the screen, click **Create Record Set**. You'll see that the panel on the right side of the screen will update with the interface elements you need in order to create a record set. In the *Name* field, you enter the subdomain for which you want to create a record. Enter **www** into the field. The *Type* field should be set to **A – IPv4 address**, so only change the value of the field if that's not the case.

The next field, entitled *Alias*, has a number of secondary options attached to it. The term "alias" is shorthand for "alias for an AWS resource." You're really selecting whether you want to link directly to an AWS resource you've created or if you want to manually configure it. If you select **No**, then you can set the TTL and enter an IP address directly into the *Value* field. Select **Yes**, and you will see the interface changes. Now you're prompted to enter the target name for an *Alias Target*. If you click into the field, a drop-down will appear listing all of your eligible AWS resources, as in Figure 4-18. You should see both your load balancer and your CloudFront distribution.

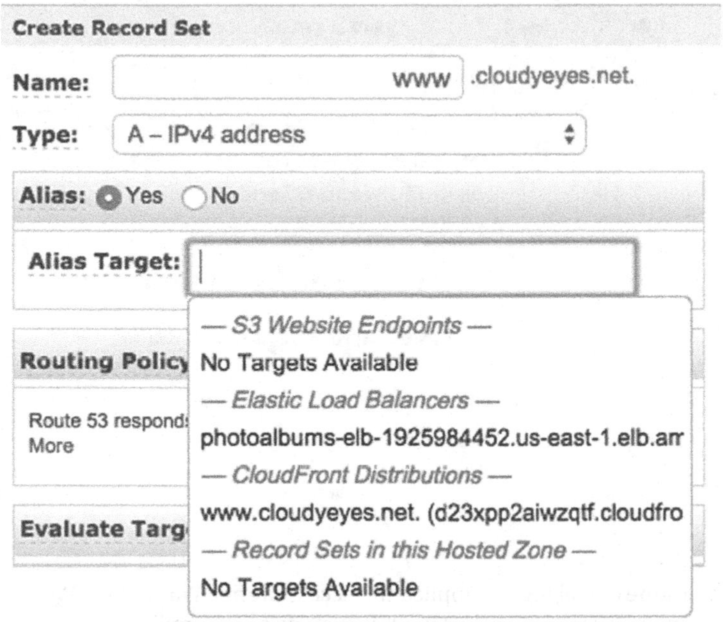

Figure 4-18. Selecting your record set alias target

Select your CloudFront distribution from the drop-down and you'll see a little yellow warning icon appear next to the field. This icon is to remind you to set your alternate domain in the CloudFront distribution. Fortunately, we did this earlier, so we don't need to worry about it.

Next, is the *Routing Policy* for our subdomain. We're going to leave it set to **Simple**, but it's good to know what you can do with this policy. By taking advantage of the routing policy, you can create multiple records for the same subdomain that work in unison to route users to the best possible AWS resource. While tutorials on these are outside the scope of the lesson, I will discuss a couple of situations in which routing policies could be useful.

Imagine a scenario in which, instead of using CloudFront, you wanted to set up an entire application stack in each AWS region. First, you would clone your application stack and configure the different stacks for different regions. Then, you would head over to Route 53 and create a www record set with **Routing Policy: Geolocation**. You would select **Default**, and create your record set. You could then create a www record for each continent, giving you eight www records in total. You would then point each respective stack to the nearest load balancer to that continent (there would be some duplicates, as Antarctica, for one, does not have any AWS data centers).

Under another scenario, imagine you simply wanted to have a backup application stack ready to handle requests when the main stack is not performing well. First, you would clone your application stack in OpsWorks. Then, you would create two record sets with **Routing Policy: Failover**. One record set would be **Failover Record Type: Primary**, and the other would be **Failover Record Type: Secondary**. Of course, you would need some metrics to determine the point at which requests are routed to the backup stack. You would create a health check on your subdomain and determine the parameters by which healthiness is determined. Then, when your application stack is performing slowly or suffers an outage, Route 53 would automatically route traffic to the backup stack.

These are just a couple examples, but you can see the utility of using Route 53 for your DNS records. Go ahead and click **Create** to finish constructing your record set with a **Simple** routing policy. Your record set should appear immediately, with the type listed as **A** (ALIAS), as shown in Figure 4-19. Once you've given your DNS change time to propagate, you should finally be able to access your Hello World page at your domain!

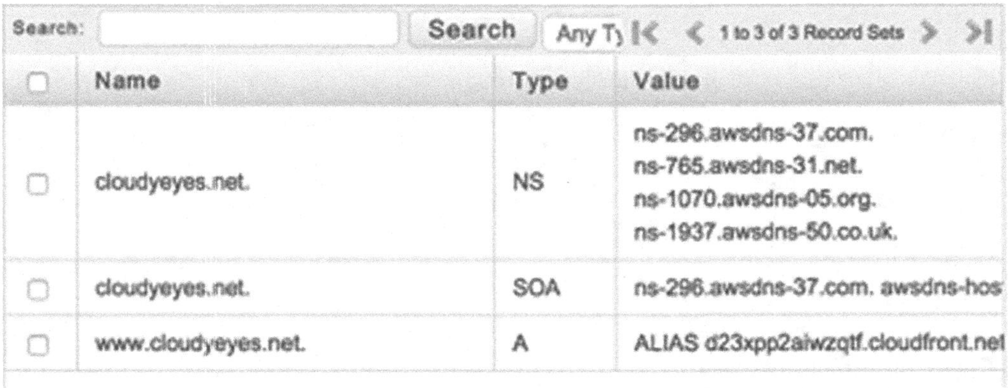

	Name	Type	Value
☐	cloudyeyes.net.	NS	ns-296.awsdns-37.com. ns-765.awsdns-31.net. ns-1070.awsdns-05.org. ns-1937.awsdns-50.co.uk.
☐	cloudyeyes.net.	SOA	ns-296.awsdns-37.com. awsdns-hos
☐	www.cloudyeyes.net.	A	ALIAS d23xpp2aiwzqtf.cloudfront.net

Figure 4-19. *ALIAS record created*

Summary

In this chapter, we reached the major milestone of making our application accessible at a World Wide Web domain. It wasn't easy, but we've made tremendous progress thus far in launching a web application. By using CloudFront, we've optimized our application performance with caching and accelerated content delivery. However, there are a couple of major pieces missing.

For starters, we have a photo-sharing app that doesn't accept any photo uploads! We will be adding this functionality in the next chapter, but it was important that we set up CloudFront first, as we will be writing our code with CloudFront in mind.

It's also important to remember the basic principles we're trying to adhere to: scalability and elasticity. While we have some incredible resources at our disposal, we haven't truly achieved either of these yet. You'll be tackling issues of application health and monitoring in a later lesson, but it's important to remember that the end of the road is not a matter of getting our application online. *Keeping* our application online no matter what is the real objective.

CHAPTER 5

■ ■ ■

Simple Storage Service and Content Delivery

Now that our application is live on the Web, it's time to build out some core functionality: image uploads. One would think that we could have done this from the beginning, but that is not the case. While we have used many AWS services with little coding, this functionality is one exception. We are building our photo upload and viewing functionality based on our AWS architecture. To do this, we will make our first attempt to directly interact with AWS services programmatically, using the AWS SDK.

We will be doing some work in the console, then quickly add the SDK to our application package and start coding. We will have to create an S3 (Simple Storage Service)[1] bucket, the AWS service designed to provide file storage for static assets. We'll also have to configure the S3 bucket and corresponding IAM policy.

If our application were to take off, we would expect thousands or millions of file uploads and downloads. If we were to store these files on our EC2 instances, it would create a large number of problems. First, the sheer volume of disk space consumed by our media would require us to scale up our instance storage capacity. In fact, each instance would need a copy of every image, so there would be a massive waste of resources from this redundancy. Second, it could cause a significant bottleneck if our instances were responsible for sending users the images, purely in the memory used by retrieving and sending all of the content.

Third, this would create a major synchronization problem. All of the data stored on EC2 instances is ephemeral, with persistent data stored in our RDS database. If a user uploaded a photo to one instance, it would create a situation in which the image would have to be copied to all other running instances. In short, it's a bad idea to use instances for file uploads.

In this chapter, we will brush aside these problems by using S3 to store our static content. Because S3 provides high availability and redundancy with unlimited file storage, we can keep all our static content in one place. We will revise our application so that it uploads images to an S3 bucket. With the AWS SDK, we will be able to programmatically upload files, set their permissions, and access them from a public URL. Then, we will use CloudFront to distribute the images to our users.

---

[1]Also see the S3 documentation at http://aws.amazon.com/documentation/s3/.

Using S3 in the Application

Using S3 for static content storage will save us a lot of the headaches described previously, as well as significantly reduce the overall weight of our application. Further, if we ever have to replace our instances, stack, or database, we can rely on S3 staying in service independent of our application stack. While S3 buckets are created in specific regions, they are redundant within the region, minimizing the risk of problems from an availability zone outage.

Of course, with the S3 bucket being created in a particular region, there is the potential for images to be stored geographically far from our users. This is where CloudFront can help us, by storing copies of our files in edge locations. In order to maximize the effectiveness of CloudFront, we will use versioning in our file naming and give our images long life spans in CloudFront. These two services will work in unison to serve as what's commonly known as a content delivery network, or CDN.

Take note of Figure 5-1. This is an update to a diagram of our system that we saw earlier. This time, it's been updated to reflect the new role the S3 bucket will play. While many of the requests received by CloudFront will be routed to the load balancer, requests for media will bypass the application stack entirely and go to the S3 bucket instead. Likewise, the EC2 instances in our application stack will be able to connect directly to the S3 bucket to transfer files to it.

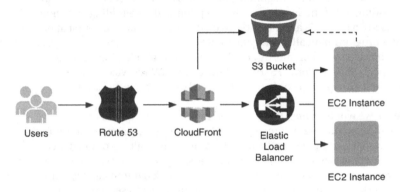

Figure 5-1. *Our system, updated for this lesson*

Creating an S3 Bucket

To begin, we will create an S3 bucket in the AWS Console. Log in and navigate to S3. If you haven't been here before, it's somewhat similar to the Route 53 interface: list of buckets on the left, detail view on the right. Click the **Create Bucket** button at the top-left corner. A modal view will appear, prompting you to name your bucket and choose a region. Name your bucket something such as **photoalbums-cdn**.

■ **Note**   S3 identifiers are unique, so you won't be able to name your bucket exactly the same as in the preceding text. Try something similar that also reflects your preferences.

From the *Region* drop-down, choose **US Standard** (the region names do not conform to the us-east, us-west convention we're used to), as in Figure 5-2.

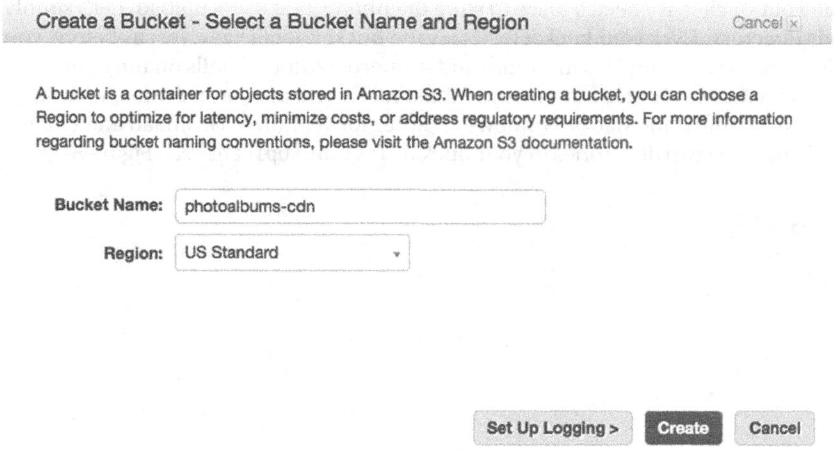

Create a Bucket - Select a Bucket Name and Region   Cancel x

A bucket is a container for objects stored in Amazon S3. When creating a bucket, you can choose a
Region to optimize for latency, minimize costs, or address regulatory requirements. For more information
regarding bucket naming conventions, please visit the Amazon S3 documentation.

Bucket Name: photoalbums-cdn

Region: US Standard ▾

Set Up Logging >   Create   Cancel

Figure 5-2. *Selecting a bucket name and region*

You now have the option of either creating the bucket now or setting up logging for the bucket. For a
production app, you may find that the logging is useful, so let's enable it now. Click **Set Up Logging ➤**. In
the next view, choose your bucket as the target bucket for storing your logs (see Figure 5-3). Leave the other
fields as they are and click **Create**.

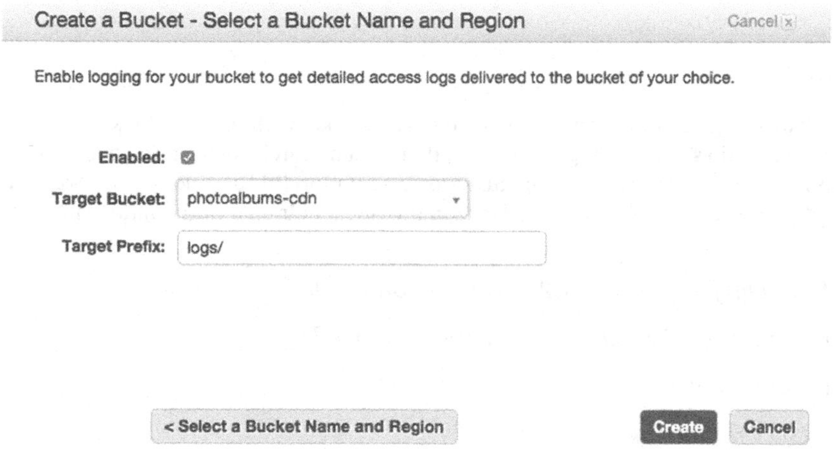

Create a Bucket - Select a Bucket Name and Region   Cancel x

Enable logging for your bucket to get detailed access logs delivered to the bucket of your choice.

Enabled: ☑

Target Bucket: photoalbums-cdn ▾

Target Prefix: logs/

< Select a Bucket Name and Region   Create   Cancel

Figure 5-3. *Setting up logging for your bucket*

The S3 bucket itself is simple to interact with. Each bucket contains its own directory structure. You can
create as many directories as you want and nest them as deeply as you want. In terms of file management,
there are some limitations to interacting with an S3 bucket in the console. You cannot move a file from one
directory to another; you have to download it and re-upload it in the new directory. You cannot delete a
directory or bucket without first deleting its contents. Instead, AWS recommends that you determine the life
cycle of your files when you are designing the system to begin with. For instance, if you want to delete log
files after 30 days, it's best to determine that now and configure the bucket's behavior accordingly. But this is
a whole topic unto itself.

Now that we have created our bucket, we need a place to store the photos that users upload. Let's simply store these files in a **/uploads** directory. Click your bucket to access the bucket detail view. Just as before, you will see a list on the left (a list of directories and files this time) and properties/other details on the right.

In the top-left corner, click the **Create Folder** button. An untitled folder will appear in the list, with its name ready to be edited, just like in Finder for Mac or Windows Explorer for Windows. Go ahead and enter the name **uploads**. You should now see two directories in your bucket: logs and uploads (see Figure 5-4).

| Upload | Create Folder | Actions ⌄ |

All Buckets / photoalbums-cdn

	Name
☐ 📁	logs
☐ 📁	uploads

Figure 5-4. *Bucket contents list*

Enabling S3 Access in IAM

By now, it should not be surprising that we need to head over to Identity and Access Management to configure our application to upload assets to our S3 bucket. In the first chapter, there was an optional lesson wherein you may have created an IAM user with permission to read/write from an S3 bucket. We need similar functionality again, although there is more than one possible approach here.

Storing Credentials

The main issue is not whether we *can* give our instances access to the S3 bucket with the AWS SDK, but how we manage the credentials when we do so. According to Amazon, there is a hierarchy of best practices when it comes to using credentials in your code. In the JavaScript SDK documentation (http://docs.aws.amazon.com/AWSJavaScriptSDK/guide/node-configuring.html), Amazon provides their recommendations in order as follows:

1. *Loaded from IAM roles for Amazon EC2 (if running on EC2),*

2. *Loaded from the shared credentials file (~/.aws/credentials),*

3. *Loaded from environment variables,*

4. *Loaded from a JSON file on disk,*

5. *Hardcoded in your application*

The first three recommendations are specific to the AWS environment, whereas the latter two are more common, platform-agnostic techniques. While we want to follow Amazon's recommendation, there is a catch that it will impair our ability to develop in the local environment. This is a pitfall that's not unique to Amazon but occurs with a number of platforms as a service (PaaS) providers.

The first recommendation, "Loaded from IAM roles for Amazon EC2," is not going to be difficult to implement. Being both the top recommendation and the easiest, we will be pursuing this strategy shortly. However, we want to preserve as much functionality in our local development environment as possible. There is no way to simulate an IAM EC2 role in your local environment, so we will have to take a different approach to enable local development. We can, however, create an IAM user and employ its credentials with the AWS SDK in the local environment. To do so, we will also be supporting the fourth recommendation.

Implementing IAM Roles

Let's implement the IAM role approach first. To begin, let's return to OpsWorks to jog your memory. Navigate to your application stack and click **Stack Settings** (see Figure 5-5).

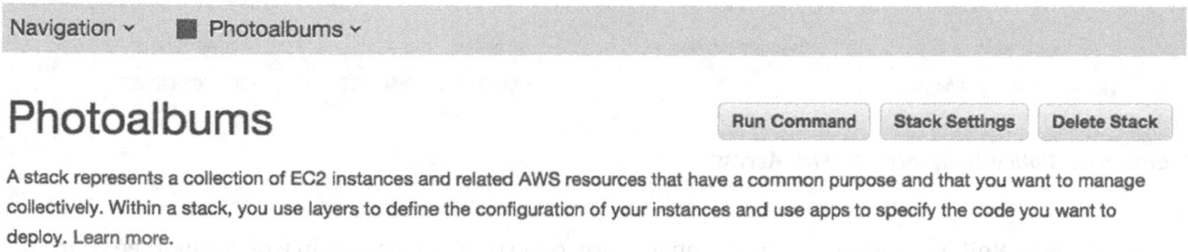

Navigation ⌄   ■ Photoalbums ⌄

Photoalbums

| Run Command | Stack Settings | Delete Stack |

A stack represents a collection of EC2 instances and related AWS resources that have a common purpose and that you want to manage collectively. Within a stack, you use layers to define the configuration of your instances and use apps to specify the code you want to deploy. Learn more.

Figure 5-5. *Access application stack settings via the Stack Settings button at the top right*

In the Stack Settings view, you will see many of the configuration decisions we made at the beginning (see Figure 5-6). You will find a setting called *Default IAM instance profile*, which should be set to a long identifier ending with **aws-opsworks-photoalbums-ec2-role**. When we set this value earlier, we created the IAM role that is deployed to every EC2 instance in our application stack. So much of the work is already done!

IAM role	arn:aws:iam::061246224738:role/aws-opsworks-photoalbums-service-role
Default SSH key	aws-opsworks-photoalbums-key
Default IAM instance profile	arn:aws:iam::061246224738:instance-profile/aws-opsworks-photoalbums-ec2-role
Hostname theme	Layer Dependent

Figure 5-6. *Stack Settings*

Navigate to IAM and select **Roles** from the left-hand navigation. In the list of roles, select **aws-opsworks-photoalbums-ec2-role**. Under the Permissions header, you will see that we have not created any policies for this role yet. We simply have not needed any. We now have to give this role read/write permissions for S3 buckets. For the sake of lesson clarity, we'll be enabling global access to S3, but in the future, we may want to restrict access to specific S3 buckets. As you can see, we are again faced with highly subjective decisions to make about our practices and organization methods. It's more of an art than a science.

Click **Attach Policy** to head to the policy selection view. Scroll down in the policy table until you find **AmazonS3FullAccess** and select it, as in Figure 5-7.

Attach Policy

You can have up to two managed policies attached.

Filter: Policy Type ▾	Search			Showing 104 results
	Policy Name ⬍	Attached Entities ⬍	Creation Time ⬍	Edited Time ⬍
☑ 📖	AmazonS3FullAccess	0	2015-02-06 13:40 EST	2015-02-06 13:40 EST

Figure 5-7. *Policy Template—S3 Full Access*

Click **Apply Policy** at the bottom right. You'll return to the user detail view, in which you'll see your policy listed (see Figure 5-8).

▾ Permissions

Managed Policies ⌃

The following managed policies are attached to this role. You can attach up to 2 managed policies.

Attach Policy

Policy Name	Actions
📖 AmazonS3FullAccess	Show Policy | Detach Policy

Figure 5-8. *EC2 Service Role Permissions*

And that's it! Now when we use the AWS SDK, it will automatically detect the permissions for the EC2 service role and use those credentials. You can see why Amazon recommends this approach: at no point are credentials exposed to anyone, and the risk of human error is negligible.

■ **Note**   At a later point, we may want our application to have more than just S3 permissions. We will simply return to this IAM role and attach additional policies to expand the permissions.

Using IAM User Credentials

For our secondary approach, we will create credentials that we can use for local development but that we will not check in to our repository or deploy to production.

Looking back to an earlier IAM lesson, I discussed that you always have a choice between creating an IAM user and configuring its permissions or creating group permissions and adding a user to the group. Once again, we can choose either approach. At this point, I've covered how to create IAM users, groups, and roles, so there's little need to rehash each one. If you want to create an IAM group, give it the proper policies and create a user within that group. Feel free to do so and exercise what you've learned already. In the interest of being succinct, we will simply create an IAM user and apply the policy to the user itself.

Select **Users** in the left navigation of IAM and click **Create New Users**. When prompted for a name, enter **photoalbums-stack**. Make sure the box to generate an access key is checked and click **Create**. On the next screen, click **Download Credentials**. When the file downloads, keep it secret; keep it safe. Then, click **Close** to return to the users list.

Click your user to proceed to the user detail view. We have a user and its credentials, now we just have to give it the necessary permissions. We will be following the exact same steps we took when we created a policy for the IAM role. Under the Permissions header, click **Attach Policy**. We're back at the managed policy selection view. Scroll down until you find *AmazonS3FullAccess*. Select the box next to it and click the **Attach Policy** button. You'll return to the user defail view, where you'll see your policy has been added.

We have completed both IAM methods, which we will soon put to use in our code. Before we do so, we have to make a brief stopover in OpsWorks.

Adding OpsWorks Environment Variables

In Chapter 3, we moved our database credentials out of our source code and into a file generated by OpsWorks by connecting our application layer to a database layer. Unfortunately, we can't do the same thing with an S3 bucket. You may recall, however, that we used OpsWorks Environment Variables in our code to determine where we should look for those database credentials. We'll be using a similar approach to connect to our S3 bucket. We don't have to store our IAM credentials in Environment Variables, but we should do so for the S3 bucket name. The reason for this is simple: it will make it easy to change the S3 bucket in our app, and it will make it easier to create a new application stack. If we have to create a dev stack, or a copy for any reason, we can also create a new S3 bucket and swap out the name in OpsWorks easily.

Navigate to OpsWorks in the AWS Console and select your application stack. Using the Navigation menu, select **Apps**. When you see the apps list view, click **edit** next to the Photoalbums app (see Figure 5-9).

Navigation ⌄ ▇ Photoalbums ⌄

Apps

An app represents code stored in a repository that you want to install on application server instances. When you deploy the app, OpsWorks downloads the code from the repository to the specified server instances. Learn more.

Name	Type	Data Source	Last Deployment	Actions
Photoalbums	Node.js	photoalbums	2014-11-26 02:07:44 UTC	⟳ deploy ✎ edit 🗑 delete

➕ App

Figure 5-9. *Return to OpsWorks Apps list view*

In the Apps editing view, scroll down to the Environment Variables header (see Figure 5-10). You should see the variable you've already created, titled "ENVIRONMENT." Add a variable with the key **S3BUCKET** and a value equal to the name of the S3 bucket you created earlier. Then click **Save** at the bottom right.

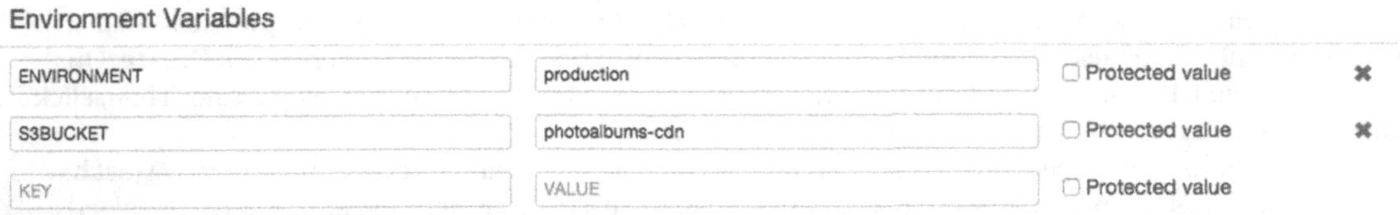

Environment Variables

ENVIRONMENT		production		☐ Protected value	✖
S3BUCKET		photoalbums-cdn		☐ Protected value	✖
KEY		VALUE		☐ Protected value	

Figure 5-10. *New Environment Variables*

When we redeploy our app, the environment variables will be accessible. But we have one more task before we start coding, which is to change the default server configuration of our instances.

Developing with the AWS SDK

Until now, our AWS lessons have relied entirely on the AWS Console. This does not mean you have to use it, but it is simply easier to learn and easier to teach. In fact, most of what we've done so far could also be achieved programmatically using the AWS SDK. In some cases, it's significantly faster to work in the AWS Console. In other cases, and particularly with tasks that you want to be automated, it will make a lot more sense to use the SDK and script the behavior you want.

The AWS SDK is available in a variety of languages and platforms, including JavaScript, which will be our choice. You can find the complete list of AWS SDK tools here: `http://aws.amazon.com/tools/`. Getting set up with the AWS SDK is easy.

Updating Dependencies

We will have to add the AWS SDK to our app, as well as the *multer* middleware package. For those who have used ExpressJS before, ExpressJS version 4 is a little different. Several of the middleware dependencies have been removed, and we'll have to add them to our package individually, based on the functionality we need to support. We will be using multer for accepting file uploads and writing them to a temporary directory.

In your code editor, open `package.json` in the root directory. At the beginning of your list of dependencies, you will add the AWS SDK node module and multer, so your dependencies JSON should look like Listing 5-1.

Listing 5-1. `package.json` Dependencies

```
"dependencies": {
  "aws-sdk": "2.0.*",
  "multer": "^0.1.3",
  "express": "~4.8.6",
  "body-parser": "~1.6.6",
  "cookie-parser": "~1.3.2",
  "mysql": "2.0.*",
  "morgan": "~1.2.3",
  "serve-favicon": "~2.0.1",
  "debug": "~1.0.4",
  "jade": "~1.5.0"
  }
```

Next, we have to reinstall our application locally, to install the new packages. In your command-line interface, navigate to the project directory and type the following:

npm install

The `aws-sdk` and `multer` node modules and their respective dependencies should begin downloading, which will print to the console something such as Listing 5-2.

Listing 5-2. AWS SDK Installing

```
npm http GET https://registry.npmjs.org/aws-sdk
npm http 200 https://registry.npmjs.org/aws-sdk
npm http GET https://registry.npmjs.org/aws-sdk/-/aws-sdk-2.0.29.tgz
npm http 200 https://registry.npmjs.org/aws-sdk/-/aws-sdk-2.0.29.tgz
npm http GET https://registry.npmjs.org/xml2js/0.2.6
npm http GET https://registry.npmjs.org/xmlbuilder/0.4.2
npm http 200 https://registry.npmjs.org/xml2js/0.2.6
npm http GET https://registry.npmjs.org/xml2js/-/xml2js-0.2.6.tgz
npm http 200 https://registry.npmjs.org/xmlbuilder/0.4.2
npm http GET https://registry.npmjs.org/xmlbuilder/-/xmlbuilder-0.4.2.tgz
npm http 200 https://registry.npmjs.org/xml2js/-/xml2js-0.2.6.tgz
npm http 200 https://registry.npmjs.org/xmlbuilder/-/xmlbuilder-0.4.2.tgz
npm http GET https://registry.npmjs.org/sax/0.4.2
npm http 200 https://registry.npmjs.org/sax/0.4.2
npm http GET https://registry.npmjs.org/sax/-/sax-0.4.2.tgz
npm http 200 https://registry.npmjs.org/sax/-/sax-0.4.2.tgz
aws-sdk@2.0.29 node_modules/aws-sdk
├── xmlbuilder@0.4.2
└── xml2js@0.2.6 (sax@0.4.2)
```

Once the installation completes, you can start using the `aws-sdk` module in your code. It will also be installed on your EC2 instances automatically the next time you deploy your code. Let's start writing our upload code!

First, we must configure the express app instance to use multer. Open /`server.js` and add the following line among your variable declarations at the top, as follows:

var multer = require('multer');

The "header" (not really, but in spirit) should now look something like Listing 5-3.

Listing 5-3. The `server.js` "Header"

```
var express = require('express');
var path = require('path');
var favicon = require('serve-favicon');
var logger = require('morgan');
var cookieParser = require('cookie-parser');
var bodyParser = require('body-parser');
var multer = require('multer');
var debug = require('debug')('photoalbums');
var routes = require('./routes/index');
var users = require('./routes/users');
```

```
var photos = require('./routes/photos');
var albums = require('./routes/albums');
var globals = require('./lib/globals');
var mysql = require('mysql');
var app = express();
```

Next, we will tell the express instance to use multer as middleware and pass in the destination for file uploads as a parameter. A little farther down in the code, you will see a series of app.use() statements, configuring express. After app.use(bodyParser{...}), add the following:

app.use(multer({dest: './tmp/'}));

Your app.use() block should now be as in Listing 5-4.

Listing 5-4. server.js Express App Configuration

```
app.use(logger('dev'));
app.use(bodyParser.json());
app.use(bodyParser.urlencoded({ extended: false }));
app.use(multer({dest: './tmp/'}));
app.use(cookieParser());
app.use(express.static(path.join(__dirname, 'public')));
```

Save your changes to the file, as we're done here. Next, we want to set up our app to use the OpsWorks Environment Variables we created. We'll use a similar approach to how we access database credentials. If the code is running in the production environment, we'll use the environment variables. If not, we will default to a local copy of credentials.

Accessing Environment Variables

In the case of the local credentials, this means that the credentials would still be exposed to developers. But because both the IAM credentials and the bucket name are stored in Environment Variables, you could easily create a separate bucket and IAM user for local development, restricting that user's access to a single dev bucket. You could try this as an exercise on your own, if you're interested in practicing this level of security.

Open /lib/globals.js. We will add a function almost identical to database(), called awsVariables(). As you can imagine, we will again check for the ENVIRONMENT variable, and if it's there, use the new variables we created. If it's not defined, we'll load a local configuration instead. You want your globals file to look like Listing 5-5.

Listing 5-5. Complete /lib/globals.js

```
module.exports = {
  applicationPort  : 80,
  database : function(){
    if(process.env.ENVIRONMENT){
      var opsworks = require('./../opsworks');
      var opsWorksDB = opsworks.db;
      var rdsConnection = {
        host : opsWorksDB.host,
        port : opsWorksDB.port,
```

```
          database : opsWorksDB.database,
          user : opsWorksDB.username,
          password : opsWorksDB.password
        };
        return rdsConnection;
      } else {
        var local = require('./../config/local');
        var localConnection = local.db;
        return localConnection;
      }
    },
    awsVariables : function(){
      if(process.env.ENVIRONMENT){
        var variables = {
          bucket : process.env.S3BUCKET
        }
        return variables;
      } else {
        var local = require('./../config/local');
        return local.awsVariables;
      }
    }
  }
}
```

Next, we have to update our local config file. Open /config/local.js, in which you will add an awsVariables object. The properties of this object should be mapped to those in /lib/globals.js, so your code should look like Listing 5-6, using the key/secret we generated for our IAM user. While it's up to you to decide how to manage these credentials, remember that you don't need to commit them to the repository if you don't want to, or you could commit the file with blank strings for the key and secret values.

Listing 5-6. Local Config File

```
module.exports = {
  db : {
    host : 'localhost',
    port : 3306,
    database : 'photoalbums',
    user  : 'root',
    password : 'root'
  },
  awsVariables : {
    bucket : 'photoalbums-cdn',
    key : 'AKIAINJDCDGH3TBMN7AA',
    secret : '8RJHMIGriShsKjgs;8W3B8gIRXC/vOQXDhcVH2RwMAw'
  }
}
```

Handling File Uploads

Now we've done all of the configuration and can start writing our upload code. Fortunately, we don't have to make any changes to the model, though we do have to alter the database schema. We will be making all of our changes in /routes/photos.js.

The major tasks remaining in this file are significant. When the user makes a POST to /photos/upload, we want the following actions to be taken:

1. User input is validated (user ID, album ID, and image are required).

2. Image is written to /tmp folder.

3. Image is uploaded from /tmp folder to S3 bucket.

4. Image is deleted from /tmp folder.

5. Final image URL is generated.

6. Entry is created in database, including URL.

7. User receives success message.

Along the way, there are a number of things that could go wrong, which we want to plan for: the user could include invalid input; there could be a problem reading/writing the image on the EC2 instance; or there could be a failure to upload to S3 or write to the database. The bad news is that proper error handling in complex Node.js apps can look a bit messy to read. The good news is that we can accomplish all of these steps with relatively little code.

First, we will have to enable access to globals to the router, as well as the fs module. Though the file system module is built into Node.js, you must declare it to access it directly. The top of the router will now look like the following:

```
var express = require('express');
var router = express.Router();
var model = require('./../lib/model/model-photos');
var globals = require('./../lib/globals');
var fs = require('fs');
```

Next, the route for /upload requires a complete rewrite. Replace it with Listing 5-7.

Listing 5-7. New POST/upload Route

```
router.post('/upload', function(req, res) {
  if(req.param('albumID') && req.param('userID') && req.files.photo){
    var params = {
      userID : req.param('userID'),
      albumID : req.param('albumID')
    }
    if(req.param('caption')){
      params.caption = req.param('caption');
    }
    fs.exists(req.files.photo.path, function(exists) {
      if(exists) {
        params.filePath = req.files.photo.path;
        var timestamp = Date.now();
```

```
      params.newFilename = params.userID + '/' + params.filePath.replace('tmp/', timestamp);
      uploadPhoto(params, function(err, fileObject){
        if(err){
          res.status(400).send({error: 'Invalid photo data'});
        } else {
          params.url = fileObject.url;
          delete params.filePath;
          delete params.newFilename;
          model.createPhoto(params, function(err, obj){
            if(err){
              res.status(400).send({error: 'Invalid photo data'});
            } else {
              res.send(obj);
            }
          });
        }
      });
    } else {
      res.status(400).send({error: 'Invalid photo data'});
    }
  });
  } else {
    res.status(400).send({error: 'Invalid photo data'});
  }
});
```

There's a lot happening here, so let's take it down step-by-step. First, the form data is validated. In addition to albumID and userID being required, we are now requiring a file with the imaginative name photo to be submitted. Most of the code is wrapped in this condition, and if it fails, an HTTP 400 error is sent in response to the request.

As we often do, we next construct a params object based on the request parameters. The required albumID and userID are included, and if a caption is found, it is also included. Captions are optional, and we never access them directly in this route. Because we're using multer, when a file is included in the POST, it is automatically written to the /tmp folder (which we specified in server.js). The copy stored in the /tmp folder does not retain its original name but is instead assigned a random identifier, to alleviate concerns of duplicate file names. It's not inconceivable that two users uploading photos from the same smartphone could have identical image names. Any files included in requests are automatically assigned a path property, pointing to their location on the server. This saves us quite a bit of trouble!

Next, we begin using the fs module. First, we use fs.exists() to check that the file is indeed located at the path we expect, accessible via req.files.photo.path. If it cannot be found here, an error is sent to the user and our route is stopped. If the file is found, then we add the file's path to our params objects. We also create a params property called newFilename, which will be the final file name when the file is uploaded to S3. Because our app is running on several instances simultaneously, even with the random file name, there is still a chance of file names conflicting. To alleviate this, we prepend a timestamp to the file name, making the names even more unique. Additionally, we are also including a directory with the user's ID in the path. The chances of a file name collision with these techniques are astronomically small.

Now that our params object is ready, we send it to the uploadPhoto() method, which we've yet to review. If that is successful, our image will be written to S3, and our params object will be assigned a url property. Finally, we delete the params properties we no longer need and send the finished object to the model.createPhoto() function. If that operation is successful, we return an HTTP 200 status to the user with a photo ID.

In /routes/photos.js, scroll down to the end of the routes, but before the module.exports declaration at the bottom. We will add private functions here, for use only in this file. First, we will add the uploadPhoto() function, shown in Listing 5-8.

Listing 5-8. uploadPhoto() Function

```
function uploadPhoto(params, callback){
  fs.readFile(params.filePath, function (err, imgData) {
    if(err){
      callback(err);
    } else {
      var contentType = 'image/jpeg';
      var uploadPath = 'uploads/' + params.newFilename;
      var uploadData = {
        Bucket: globals.awsVariables().bucket,
        Key: uploadPath,
        Body: imgData,
        ACL:'public-read',
        ContentType: contentType
      }
      putS3Object(uploadData, function(err, data){
        if(err){
          callback(err);
        } else {
          fs.unlink(params.filePath, function (err) {
            if (err){
              callback(err);
            } else {
              callback(null, {url: uploadPath});
            }
          });
        }
      });
    }
  });
}
```

First and foremost, this function reads the file from the /tmp directory. Then an upload path is set, using the file name from the params object. An object named uploadData is constructed, using the key-values required by the AWS SDK. We construct this object in preparation for uploading the image to S3, at which point it will be referred to as an object.

The Bucket key uses the bucket declared in our globals, which were ultimately set in an OpsWorks Environment Variable. The Key is simply the path in the S3 bucket. The Body contains the image data we retrieved with fs.readFile(). ACL stands for *Access Control List* and represents the permissions for the object when it's created on S3. Last is the ContentType, which is hard-coded to 'image/jpeg'.

As an additional exercise, you could set the ContentType dynamically, by reading it with fs and passing it to this function in the params object.

Next, we pass the uploadData object to putS3Object(). When the upload is complete, the image is removed from the /tmp directory using fs.unlink(). Last, the S3 object path is returned in the callback. You'll recall that this relative path is what is passed to model.createPhoto(), from where it is being written to the database.

We'll add the last function, putS3Object(), below uploadPhoto(). This function (see Listing 5-9) simply handles the upload to S3, using the AWS SDK. Add the following function to /routes/photos.js:

Listing 5-9. putS3Object() Function

```
function putS3Object(uploadData, callback){
  var aws = require('aws-sdk');
  if(globals.awsVariables().key){
    aws.config.update({ accessKeyId: globals.awsVariables().key, secretAccessKey: globals.
awsVariables().secret });
  }
  var s3 = new aws.S3();
  s3.putObject(uploadData, function(err, data) {
    if(err){
      callback(err);
    } else {
      callback(null, data);
    }
  });
}
```

Let's break it down line by line. First, the aws-sdk is loaded. Then, we check whether globals. awsVariables().key is defined. You'll recall that it's only defined locally, for the use case wherein we use IAM user credentials. If you never want to use this approach, you could eliminate this if statement entirely. But if you're using an IAM user for S3 permissions, then the key and secret must be passed to aws.config. update(). If we're instead relying on the IAM role of the instance, then the AWS SDK obtains the credentials automatically, and we never have to call aws.config.update().

Then, we simply call s3.putObject(). As mentioned previously, an S3 bucket's contents are referred to ambiguously as *objects*, regardless of type. We already constructed the necessary parameters prior to this function, so it's short and simple.

Just to be clear on how this all works, let's take a quick look at model.createPhoto(). Open /lib/ model/model-photos.js. Near the top of the file, you should see the code in Listing 5-10.

Listing 5-10. Model createPhoto() Function

```
function createPhoto(params, callback){
  var query = 'INSERT INTO photos SET ? ';
  connection.query(query, params, function(err, rows, fields){
    if(err){
      callback(err);
    } else {
      var response = {
        id : rows.insertId
      };
      callback(null, response);
    }
  });
}
```

We have not made any changes to this function. Because it sets values based on the contents of the params object parameter, any changes to the controller and database will automatically be reflected here. You can see that the value returned is simply the ID of the photo.

However, if you look at the other methods in the model, you'll see that we are selecting specific fields for output to the user. We will have to make a few changes to our other SQL statements. After all, it would be ridiculous to have a photo album web app that didn't actually show any photos. It could probably raise $50 million in VC funding anyway.

First, find function getPhotoByID(). Add url to the query variable, so the function now appears as in Listing 5-11.

Listing 5-11. Model getPhotoByID() Function

```
function getPhotoByID(params, callback){
  var query = 'SELECT photoID, caption, url, albumID, userID FROM photos WHERE published=1
AND photoID=' + connection.escape(params.photoID);
  connection.query(query, function(err, rows, fields){
    if(err){
      callback(err);
    } else {
      if(rows.length > 0){
        callback(null, rows);
      } else {
        callback(null, []);
      }
    }
  });
}
```

Likewise, we want to include the URL when photos are selected by album ID. Once again, update the SQL query only (see Listing 5-12).

Listing 5-12. Model getPhotosByAlbumID() Function

```
function getPhotosByAlbumID(params, callback){
  var query = 'SELECT photoID, caption, url, albumID, userID FROM photos WHERE published=1
AND albumID=' + connection.escape(params.albumID);
  connection.query(query, function(err, rows, fields){
    if(err){
      callback(err);
    } else {
      if(rows.length > 0){
        callback(null, rows);
      } else {
        callback(null, []);
      }
    }
  });
}
```

Last, we want to include the URL for photos retrieved via search (see Listing 5-13).

Listing 5-13. Model getPhotosSearch() Function

```
function getPhotosSearch(params, callback){
  var query = 'SELECT photoID, caption, url, albumID, userID FROM photos WHERE caption LIKE
"%' + params.query + '%"';
  connection.query(query, function(err, rows, fields){
    if(err){
      callback(err);
    } else {
      if(rows.length > 0){
        callback(null, rows);
      } else {
        callback(null, []);
      }
    }
  });
}
```

And we're now done coding! Commit your changes to your repository. Return to OpsWorks and deploy your app. You can do that without directions by now. The deployment process has a lot of work to do this time. It's adding your OpsWorks Environment Variables to each instance, updating the IAM role, and running your Chef JSON. When your code is retrieved from your repository, OpsWorks will find the new dependencies listed in your package.json file and automatically install them along with the rest of your app. In the meantime, we have a few more tasks to finish before this lesson is complete.

Updating the Database Schema

You've probably noticed that our database schema no longer reflects the values we need. We'll have to make a quick change to the *photos* table. In your MySQL client (ideally MySQL Workbench), connect to your RDS instance. Expand the **photoalbums** database in the left-hand navigation and expand *Tables* to reveal **photos** (see Figure 5-11).

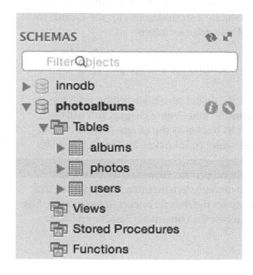

Figure 5-11. *RDS instance tables*

Control-click on the table, and select **Alter Table** from the tool tip menu. You should see the table schema appear in the center column. Add a url column of type Varchar(250), as in Figure 5-12. If you prefer to execute the raw SQL query, here it is:

`` ` ALTER TABLE photoalbums.photos ADD url VARCHAR(250) NOT NULL;` ``

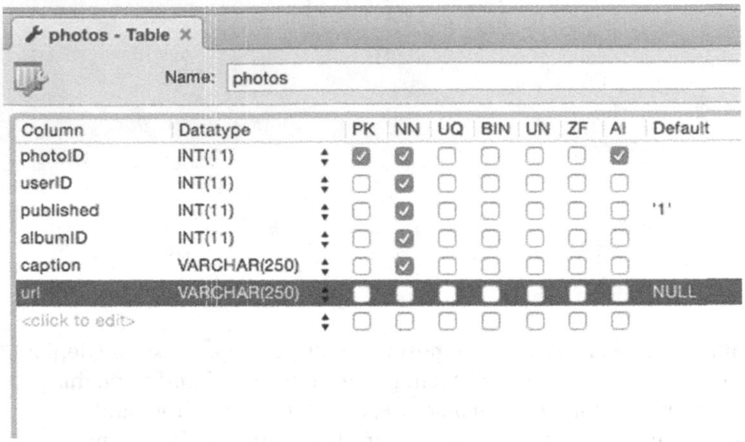

photos - Table ×										
Name:	photos									
Column	**Datatype**		**PK**	**NN**	**UQ**	**BIN**	**UN**	**ZF**	**AI**	**Default**
photoID	INT(11)	↕	☑	☑	☐	☐	☐	☐	☑	
userID	INT(11)	↕	☐	☑	☐	☐	☐	☐	☐	
published	INT(11)	↕	☐	☑	☐	☐	☐	☐	☐	'1'
albumID	INT(11)	↕	☐	☑	☐	☐	☐	☐	☐	
caption	VARCHAR(250)	↕	☐	☑	☐	☐	☐	☐	☐	
url	VARCHAR(250)	↕	■	■	■	■	■	■	■	NULL
<click to edit>		↕	☐	☐	☐	☐	☐	☐	☐	

Figure 5-12. *The photos table schema*

If you are keeping your local environment up to date, be sure to make the same change to your local database.

Integrating with CloudFront

In Chapter 4, we created a CloudFront instance with which to serve our application. In doing so, we registered the load balancer of our application stack as an *origin* for requests to the CloudFront instance. Next, we will do the same thing with the S3 bucket. The S3 bucket will be a second origin for the CloudFront instance and automatically store copies of our assets in the CloudFront edge locations.

Creating CloudFront S3 Origin

Using the Services menu, navigate to CloudFront in the AWS Console. Select your distribution from the Distributions list on the CloudFront landing page. Click the **Origins** tab and **Create Origin**. You will once again be in the Create Origin view, from which you will select your S3 bucket as the *Origin Domain Name*. A drop-down appears when you begin editing the field. When you select your bucket, an Origin ID will be auto-generated. You can leave this as is.

Currently, we're not planning to make the photos in our application private. However, we very well could want to make user content private (or at least restricted) at a later date. As a first step in supporting this functionality, we have to restrict direct access to the bucket. When we set the *Restrict Bucket Access* value to **Yes**, the S3 URLs will no longer be public, and users will only be able to access the content at CloudFront URLs.

Because we're restricting bucket access, we will have to create a CloudFront Access Identity with permissions to access the S3 buckets. While this may sound like something you manage in IAM, these identities are entirely managed within CloudFront. Select **Create a New Identity** to generate a new CloudFront origin access identity. In the *Comment* field, you can enter a string to identify the identity you're creating, something like **access-identity-photoalbums-cloudfront**.

Next, you will be asked if you want to *Grant Read Permissions on Bucket*. This is a convenient method to update the policy on your S3 bucket, so you don't have to do this manually. Select **Yes, Update Bucket Policy**. If everything looks like Figure 5-13, click **Create** to proceed.

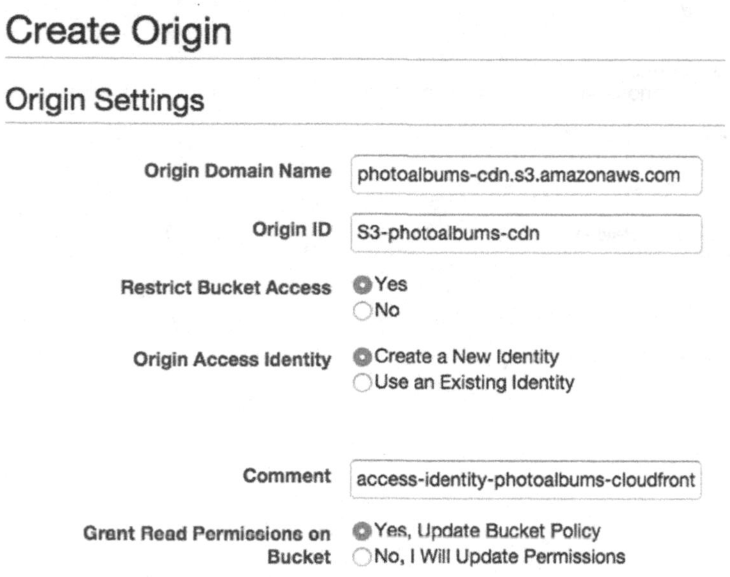

Create Origin

Origin Settings

Origin Domain Name	photoalbums-cdn.s3.amazonaws.com
Origin ID	S3-photoalbums-cdn
Restrict Bucket Access	◉ Yes ◯ No
Origin Access Identity	◉ Create a New Identity ◯ Use an Existing Identity
Comment	access-identity-photoalbums-cloudfront
Grant Read Permissions on Bucket	◉ Yes, Update Bucket Policy ◯ No, I Will Update Permissions

Figure 5-13. *Creating a CloudFront Origin for the S3 bucket*

CloudFront S3 Behavior

Now that we have created a CloudFront origin for our S3 bucket, we have to create the behavior that will route requests to that origin. Select the **Behaviors** tab. You should recognize this view from when we were experimenting with caching behavior in Chapter 4. You'll notice that so far, all of our behaviors have the same origin: the load balancer from our application stack. But as discussed before, it would be a waste of resources to make our application serve the image uploads to users. This time, we will create a behavior that originates in the S3 bucket, completely removing the application stack from the equation.

Click **Create Behavior** at the top-left corner. Once again, you have to input a path pattern for the behavior. In the *Path Pattern* field, enter **/uploads/*** to catch all requests to the uploads folder. In the *Origins* field, expand the drop-down and choose the origin you just created, which corresponds to the S3 bucket.

Leave the other fields alone until we reach *Object Caching*. Because we will not be sending custom origin headers from our application stack, we want CloudFront to control the TTL for these assets. Select **Customize** and in the *Minimum TTL* field, enter **43200** (seconds), for 12 hours. Assets retrieved from our S3 bucket will be refreshed in CloudFront after a minimum of 12 hours, which you can certainly change to any other value if you have a preference.

Going through the rest of the options, we will not forward query strings or cookies or change any other value. Review your choices to be sure they match Figure 5-14 and click **Create**.

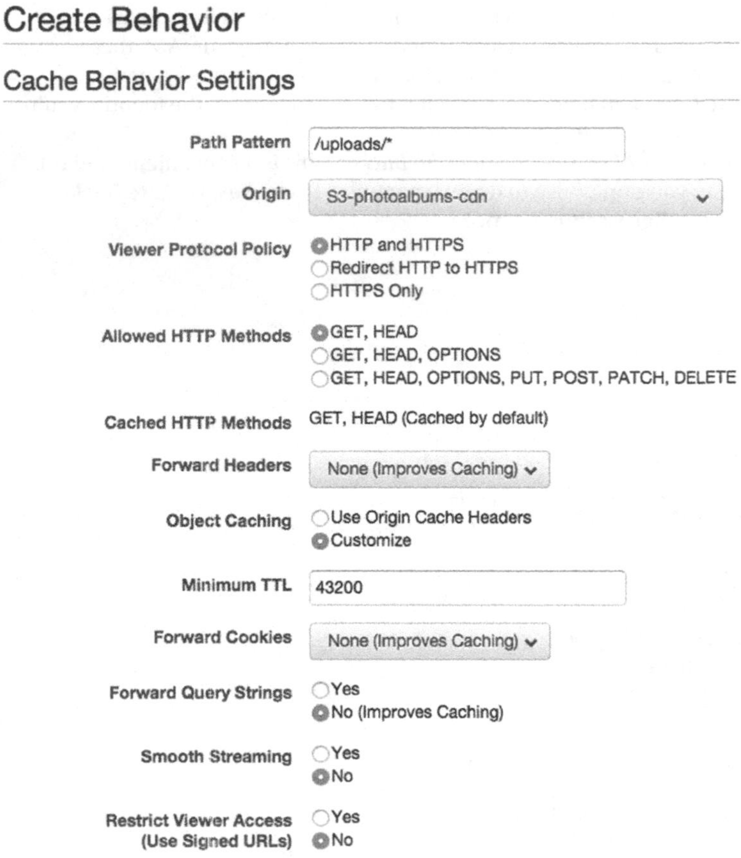

Create Behavior

Cache Behavior Settings

Path Pattern	/uploads/*
Origin	S3-photoalbums-cdn ⌄
Viewer Protocol Policy	● HTTP and HTTPS ○ Redirect HTTP to HTTPS ○ HTTPS Only
Allowed HTTP Methods	● GET, HEAD ○ GET, HEAD, OPTIONS ○ GET, HEAD, OPTIONS, PUT, POST, PATCH, DELETE
Cached HTTP Methods	GET, HEAD (Cached by default)
Forward Headers	None (Improves Caching) ⌄
Object Caching	○ Use Origin Cache Headers ● Customize
Minimum TTL	43200
Forward Cookies	None (Improves Caching) ⌄
Forward Query Strings	○ Yes ● No (Improves Caching)
Smooth Streaming	○ Yes ● No
Restrict Viewer Access (Use Signed URLs)	○ Yes ● No

Figure 5-14. *Create CloudFront behavior for /uploads/**

You'll notice that the new behavior appears at the bottom of the behaviors list, except for Default(*), which is always at the bottom. There's no need to move this behavior to the top of the list, as there is no conflict with our existing behaviors. Once again, it will take a few moments for the changes in CloudFront to propagate. You can keep an eye on the *Status* field in the distributions list, waiting for yours to change from *In Progress* to *Deployed*.

Now it's time for the moment of truth! Find a jpeg image file that you want to use to create a photo. We're assuming you've created a user and album already in production. If you haven't, make those requests now, and you should have a userID of 1 and albumID of 1. Now make a POST request to www.[your domain]. com/photos/upload. Include the following parameters in your form data:

```
albumID: 1
userID: 1
caption: 'my first real photo'
```

The file key should be *photo*, and be sure to set the Content-Type to **application/x-www-form-urlencoded**. If the request is successful, you will still receive the photo ID in response.

```
{"id":21}
```

Your response headers should look like Listing 5-14. You'll notice that the `X-Cache` header shows a miss from CloudFront. The response should *never* be a hit from CloudFront, or you would without a doubt be seeing the wrong data.

Listing 5-14. Photo Upload Response Headers

```
Content-Type: application/json; charset=utf-8
Content-Length: 9
Connection: keep-alive
Date: Mon, 15 Dec 2014 21:02:57 GMT
X-Powered-By: Express
X-Cache: Miss from cloudfront
Via: 1.1 eadedd3fe9e82c51cc035044b3a5f3fa.cloudfront.net (CloudFront)
X-Amz-Cf-Id: yRWUsgyOTSh4xw5NcKfX-ne2-N7EU9yUIQYot9J82xcF1elqiRgBnw==
```

Next, let's validate that the data we uploaded to the application was stored correctly and is now accessible. Open your browser to `www.[your domain].com/photos/id/21` (replacing 21 with the ID you received). You should see JSON similar to the following:

```
[
  {
    "photoID":21,
    "caption":"my first real photo",
    "url":"uploads/1/141867737733318085bdee7f0a1577a57200e59c65306.jpg",
    "albumID":1,
    "userID":1
  }
]
```

There's a URL for the image! Next, as long as the CloudFront behavior changes are complete, you should be able to access the image at your domain. Copy the URL, add it to your domain, and try to view it in your browser. You should see your image!

Finishing Touches

Congratulations! You now have a CDN in your application! This is a major breakthrough moment for the application. This would be a good time to go back and apply a couple of the lessons you've learned to improve functionality. A few small changes could go a long way in improving our application.

The URLs in our web app API are all relative. While this may be fine, many developers would prefer an absolute URL in this scenario. We should be able to support both. The current setup is also a problem for local development, as we are still uploading files to S3, even when we're running the app on the local database. So, while there is a web-accessible version of `uploads/1/141867737733318085bdee7f0a1577a5720` `0e59c65306.jpg`, the image cannot be found at `http://localhost:8081/uploads/1/141867737733318085b` `dee7f0a1577a57200e59c65306.jpg`. So, our first task is to switch our images to absolute URLs and make the URLs correct, even in the local environment.

We can also improve how CloudFront caches our images. By default, the cached URLs in the /uploads/* path will be cached in CloudFront for 24 hours. However, we know for certain that these images are not going to change at all. We aren't supporting any image retouching or cropping, and even if we were, we would use versioned file naming. Right now, 24 hours is no big deal. But if we were serving thousands or millions of users, why not reap the benefits of CloudFront? Thus the other finishing touch will be to simply store the images in CloudFront for significantly longer than 24 hours.

Absolute URLs

The first task, though it's the harder one, is still pretty easy. If you thought we could use Environment Variables to store the domain, you are correct! Not only will this allow us to access our S3 images when developing locally, it will also make it easy to clone our stack for dev, change domains, etc.

First, return to OpsWorks and select your stack. Navigate to the **Apps** view in the stack and click **edit** in the column next to your app. Scroll down to the Environment Variables header and add the value `http://www.[your domain].com` for the key *DOMAIN* (see Figure 5-15). Then, click **Save** at the bottom of the page.

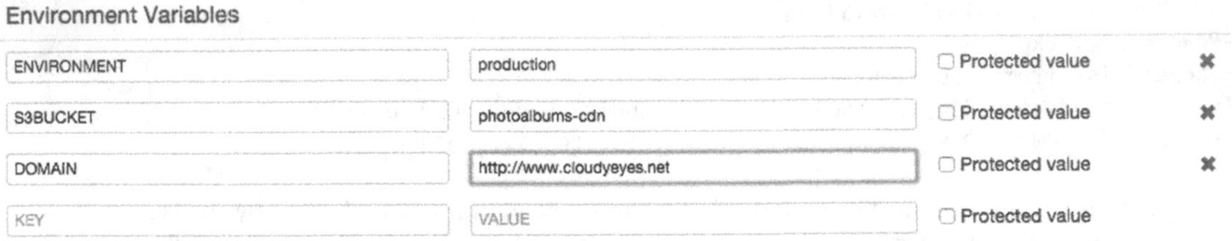

Environment Variables

ENVIRONMENT	production	☐ Protected value	✖
S3BUCKET	photoalbums-cdn	☐ Protected value	✖
DOMAIN	http://www.cloudyeyes.net	☐ Protected value	✖
KEY	VALUE	☐ Protected value	

Figure 5-15. *Adding another Environment Variable to OpsWorks*

Now that that's set, we can make our code changes, then start a new deployment. Return to your code editor, and we'll make the changes one by one. The first thing we have to do is add the new variable to our globals. Open `/libs/globals`, in which we will add the domain variable. The `awsVariables()` function should look like Listing 5-15.

Listing 5-15. Adding Another Environment Variable to the Code Base

```
awsVariables : function(){
  if(process.env.ENVIRONMENT){
    var variables = {
      bucket : process.env.S3BUCKET,
      domain : process.env.DOMAIN
    }
    return variables;
  } else {
    var local = require('./../config/local');
    return local.awsVariables;
  }
}
```

We're also going to go a step further with globals. While we only have to convert relative URLs to absolute URLs for photos right now, it's conceivable that we may need this functionality elsewhere as well. Let's add a function called `absoluteURL()` to the globals, so that we can easily reuse our code. After `awsVariables :function(){}`, add a comma, followed by the code in Listing 5-16.

Listing 5-16. `absoluteURL()` Helper Function

```
absoluteURL : function(path){
  if(this.awsVariables().domain){
    return this.awsVariables().domain + '/' + path;
  }
  return path;
}
```

This function is simple, but it may save us a lot of copy-paste in the future. It accepts a relative path as a parameter and prepends the domain and a forward slash to it, if the domain is defined. If not, it will fail silently without a crash.

We will also need the domain variable in our local file. Head over to /config/local.js and add your domain to the awsVariables object there.

Currently, we are not doing any post-query operation on the data in the database. We simply retrieve the objects and properties we need and send them back to the respective controller. Unfortunately, that party has come to an end. We're not going to write the domain to the database, but, instead, we'll add it to the response before the database data is returned from the model. Further, it's conceivable that this would be the first of many post-query operations we perform on data retrieved from the database. As such, we can add a private function to the model, from which we can organize our modifications to the data.

Open /lib/model/model-photos.js and scroll to the bottom. After the deletePhotoByID() method, add the code from Listing 5-17.

Listing 5-17. formatPhotoData() Helper Function

```
function formatPhotoData(rows){
  for(var i = 0; i < rows.length; i++){
    var photo = rows[i];
    if(photo.url){
      photo.url = globals.absoluteURL(photo.url);
    }
  }
  return rows;
}
```

This function is simple, iterating through photos retrieved from the database and calling our absoluteURL() helper function on those photos that have a url property. If we need to do any other post-query operations on all photos, we can add them to this loop later.

Next, we have to make sure each method that retrieves photos uses this function, which means we have to make a change in three places. Scroll up to function getPhotoByID() and find the line that reads as follows:

```
callback(null, rows);
```

Replace this with the following:

```
callback(null, formatPhotoData(rows));
```

The function should now look as follows:

```
function getPhotoByID(params, callback){
  var query = 'SELECT photoID, caption, url, albumID, userID FROM photos WHERE published=1
AND photoID=' + connection.escape(params.photoID);
  connection.query(query, function(err, rows, fields){
    if(err){
      callback(err);
    } else {
```

```
      if(rows.length > 0){
        callback(null, formatPhotoData(rows));
      } else {
        callback(null, []);
      }
    }
  });
}
```

Last, we must make the same change to getPhotosByAlbumID() and getPhotosSearch(). Make these changes, then commit your code to the repository. Head back to OpsWorks and deploy your application. Wait a few minutes for the deployment to complete, and when it does, refresh the /photos/id/21 path in your browser. You should now see the absolute path to your image, like so:

```
[
  {
    "photoID":27,
    "caption":"test",
    "url":"http://www.cloudyeyes.net/uploads/1/1418498633152f1fe581691cc3aa20577958626077976
.jpg",
    "albumID":1,
    "userID":1
  }
]
```

Enhanced Image Caching

For your final task of this chapter, you'll increase the TTL for the /uploads/* path in CloudFront. Return to CloudFront in the AWS Console and select your distribution from the distributions list. Then, click the **Origins** tab. Select the **/uploads/*** path pattern, as in Figure 5-16, and click **Edit**.

General	Origins	**Behaviors**	Error Pages	Restrictions	Invalidations

CloudFront compares a request for an object with the path patterns in your cache behaviors based on the order of the cache behaviors in your distribution. Arrange cache behaviors in the order in which you want CloudFront to evaluate them.

Create Behavior	Edit	Delete	Change Precedence:	Move Up	Move Down	Save

	Precedence	Path Pattern	Origin	Viewer Protocol Policy	Forwarded Query Strings	Trusted Signers
☐	1	/users/*	ELB-photoalbums-elb-1925984452	HTTP and HTTPS	No	-
☐	2	/albums/*	ELB-photoalbums-elb-1925984452	HTTP and HTTPS	No	-
☐	3	/photos/search	ELB-photoalbums-elb-1925984452	HTTP and HTTPS	Yes	-
☐	4	/photos/*	ELB-photoalbums-elb-1925984452	HTTP and HTTPS	No	-
☑	5	/uploads/*	S3-photoalbums-cdn	HTTP and HTTPS	No	-
☐	6	Default (*)	ELB-photoalbums-elb-1925984452	HTTP and HTTPS	No	-

Figure 5-16. *Edit CloudFront behavior*

Locate the *Object Caching* field and change the value from Use Origin Cache Headers to **Customize**. There's no gain in using the origin cache headers. Because requests to /uploads/* never even make it to our application stack, we cannot programmatically control the caching behavior as we did with some of the other paths. By switching to *Customize*, we can input a minimum TTL, or essentially life span, of the cached objects in CloudFront edge locations. After selecting **Customize**, put the number **604800** in the *Minimum TTL* field. This will store cached objects for one week (in seconds). We could just as easily set it to two weeks, or a year! One week seems ample for now, though. Finally, click **Yes, Edit**, and your changes will begin to take effect. You can check on this by watching the Distribution Status, which will now be set to *InProgress*. Remember: It takes several minutes for changes in CloudFront to propagate.

Summary

Another chapter down, with some big changes to our application. And yet we had to write very little code to add some powerful tools to our software. I hope you're getting used to the idea of using the AWS Console to make sweeping changes to our infrastructure. It can be a little nerve-wracking to wield such power so casually. With that in mind, we've only barely scratched the surface of what you can do with the AWS SDK. In the next few chapters, we will continue to use the SDK to add more features.

■ ■ ■

CHAPTER 6

Simple Email Service

While our application has come a long way, there are still a few more features we have to build before it's ready for prime time. The most obvious, of course, is the lack of security on user accounts. You don't even have to log in to upload to someone else's album. Security truly is an illusion in this case. Not to worry, though, I'll cover this topic in the grand finale in Chapter 8.

In truth, there are quite a few pieces our application is missing before it's truly production-ready. If this were strictly a programming book, we would still have to go through tutorials on building an admin portal, a flagging system for inappropriate content, and social-networking features. Unfortunately, there isn't time to build a complete enterprise application in these lessons. Our focus remains building a scalable and elastic application on AWS, and the cost of that is focusing on features that are integrated into AWS services, as opposed to features that you can learn from older and wiser developers in another Node.js programming book.

That being said, there are still a few features we can build with the synergy between AWS and some good old-fashioned programming. Because our app is interacted with entirely as a web service, it feels a little flat, doesn't it? I've uploaded so many travel photos, and all I get in response is JSON this, JSON that. The way to my heart is my inbox, and it's time to let our app send some mail!

Introducing Simple Email Service

Regardless of content, any web application with user-generated content can benefit from a notification system of some kind, be it e-mail or mobile push notifications. Amazon offers a few different services to support notifications, but we will be focusing on Amazon Simple Email Service (SES). Amazon SES is designed to allow you to programmatically generate e-mail notifications of any type and volume. From mass-marketing campaigns to password reset e-mails, you can use Amazon SES to send both static and dynamic content at any volume.

If you've built a server-side application in any language before, there's a good chance you have had to generate an e-mail before. If you used PHP, you've probably spent some time carefully formatting parameters for the mail() function. Tedious as it is, this sort of approach works just fine on a small scale. But imagine if your application has thousands or millions of users. Suddenly, there is a resource-management concern from simply generating e-mail.

Amazon provides a solution to this problem by allowing you to separate the workload of sending mail from your application stack. Instead, we will use the AWS SDK to send a command to Amazon SES, which will send the mail on our behalf. This will provide significant resource savings, and our application stack will remain unburdened by the task of being a mail server. We're also spared from the hassle of configuring our own mail server. And we won't have to watch the e-mails we worked so hard to generate go straight to the spam folder.

Much to our relief, Amazon SES has a free tier. At the time of this writing, you can send 62,000 e-mails per month for free. After that, you pay $.10 per thousand e-mails. In addition to the fee for sending mail, your mail is included in the data transfer out from the EC2 rate table, and you also pay $.12 per GB of attachments. In all, it's quite reasonable, and it's likely that your SES costs will be an order of magnitude lower than your RDS or EC2 bill.

Exploring the SES Dashboard

We're going to add a few e-mails to our application, which we will be generating programmatically in our code. Before we do this, there are a few tasks we have to carry out in the AWS Console. Let's begin by configuring SES. In the AWS Console, locate **SES** in the *Application Services* column on the right side of the page and click it. We'll begin the process here, in the SES dashboard. As you can see on your screen (and in Figure 6-1), there is a lot happening in this dashboard.

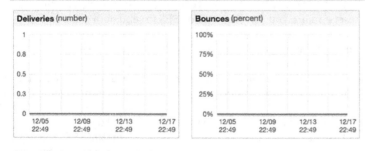

Figure 6-1. *SES dashboard*

As in many other AWS dashboards, the left column of the view is the secondary navigation. In the main content area, you are immediately greeted by a warning that your account has "sandbox" access. By default, all AWS accounts are created in sandbox mode, restricting the ability of AWS customers to send mass e-mails to the public. This is merely an anti-spam precaution, as it's easy to request production access. I'll discuss this in more detail later, but for now, be aware that you cannot send e-mails to anyone and everyone at the moment.

Immediately below the warning, you can see a quick snapshot of Your Amazon SES Sending Limits. You'll notice that the *Sending Quota* is currently 200 e-mails per 24-hour period. This quota is in effect until you request production access to SES. To be clear, this means 200 recipients. If you send 20 e-mails with 10 recipients each, you will meet your quota.

Below Your Amazon SES Sending Limits, you will see a header titled Your Amazon SES Metrics. In this section, you can view the results of messages sent by SES, viewable in actual numbers or rate (percentage). If you've ever worked with e-mail marketing software before, you will recognize the terminology: deliveries, bounces, complaints, rejects. If you are only using SES to send notifications to subscribed and registered users, these metrics may not be valuable to you. But if you ever plan to terrorize your users with e-mail marketing, these can be useful metrics.

SES Verification

While we're in sandbox mode, there are significant restrictions as to whom we can e-mail. Any addresses we use as senders or recipients must be verified. In Figure 6-2, notice Verified Senders in the left navigation.

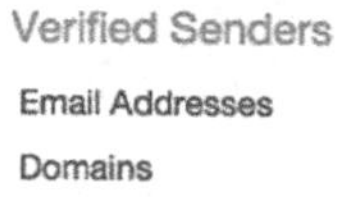

Verified Senders

Email Addresses

Domains

Figure 6-2. SES Verified Senders

There are two levels at which you can verify SES addresses: the individual e-mail address level and the domain level. For verified e-mail addresses, you verify each individual e-mail address manually. You can then send e-mail to and from the verified address. If you verify at the domain level, then you can send e-mail from any address at the domain. For instance, you might want to validate the domain to send e-mails from support@yourdomain.com in one case and donotreploy@yourdomain.com in another case. Verified domains only allow you to send e-mail from the domain in question. You could not, for example, verify gmail.com and be allowed to send e-mail to the millions of Gmail users.

For development purposes, it would be ideal to send e-mails from our application's web domain to the registered user. While we're in development, registered users must also have verified e-mail addresses in SES. Later, we will request production access to SES, enabling us to send e-mails to all users. But we don't have to do that to finish development and testing.

E-mail Address Verification

Let's begin by verifying an e-mail address—your own personal e-mail. Under the Verified Senders header shown in Figure 6-2, click **Email Addresses**. You will see a table of verified addresses, of which there are now zero. Click **Verify a New Email Address** at the top of the page. A modal window, as shown in Figure 6-3, will appear above the page. Enter your e-mail address and click **Verify This Email Address**.

Figure 6-3. *Verifying an e-mail address*

After a few moments, the modal window will inform you that the verification e-mail has been sent. When you close out of the modal and return to the main view, your address will appear in the table with a status of *pending verification* (see Figure 6-4).

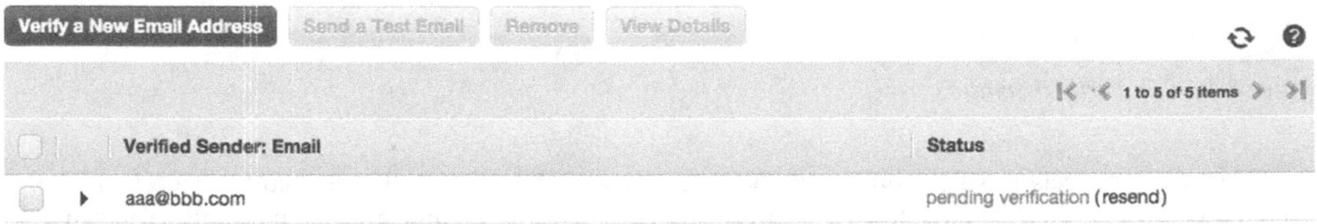

Figure 6-4. *SES verified e-mail addresses*

Check your inbox for an e-mail with the subject *Amazon SES Address Verification Request in region [your current region]*. You'll see a lengthy verification URL, which you should click to confirm the address. If you don't click the link within 24 hours, it will expire, and the verification status of your e-mail address will change to *failure*. The link will take you to an AWS page congratulating you on verifying your e-mail address. A celebration is in order!

When you refresh the e-mail addresses list, the status of your address should now be *verified*. Let's run a quick test. Select your address and click **Send a Test Email**. A modal window will appear, allowing you to populate the *To*, *Subject*, and *Body* fields for an e-mail (see Figure 6-5). You can click **More options** to add additional e-mail headers such as Bcc:. Make yourself the recipient as well: fill out a message and click **Send Test Email**.

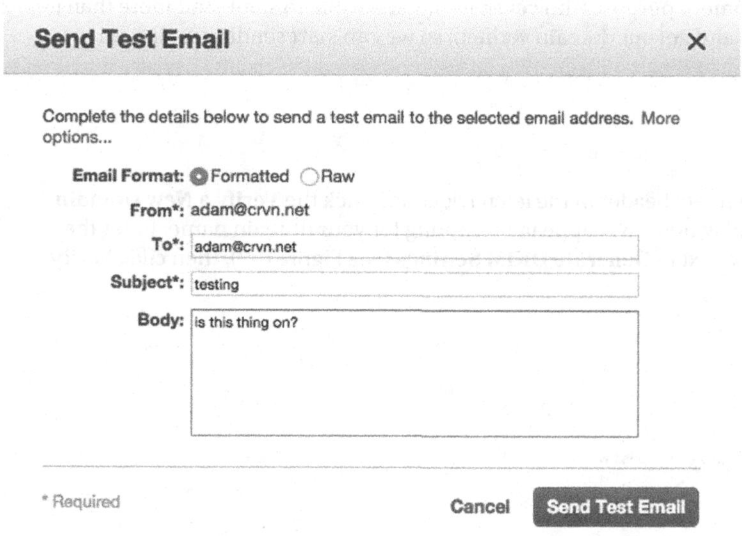

Send Test Email ✕

Complete the details below to send a test email to the selected email address. More options...

Email Format: ◉ Formatted ◯ Raw

From*: adam@crvn.net

To*: adam@crvn.net

Subject*: testing

Body: is this thing on?

* Required   Cancel   **Send Test Email**

Figure 6-5. *SES Send Test Email*

In a few moments, you should receive the e-mail. Now let's try to send an e-mail to someone else. Select your e-mail from the list and click **Send a Test Email** again. This time, in the *To:* field, put a different address belonging to a friend or another of your own addresses, then click **Send Test Email** again. This time, you'll encounter an error, as shown in Figure 6-6, because the recipient must also be a verified e-mail address.

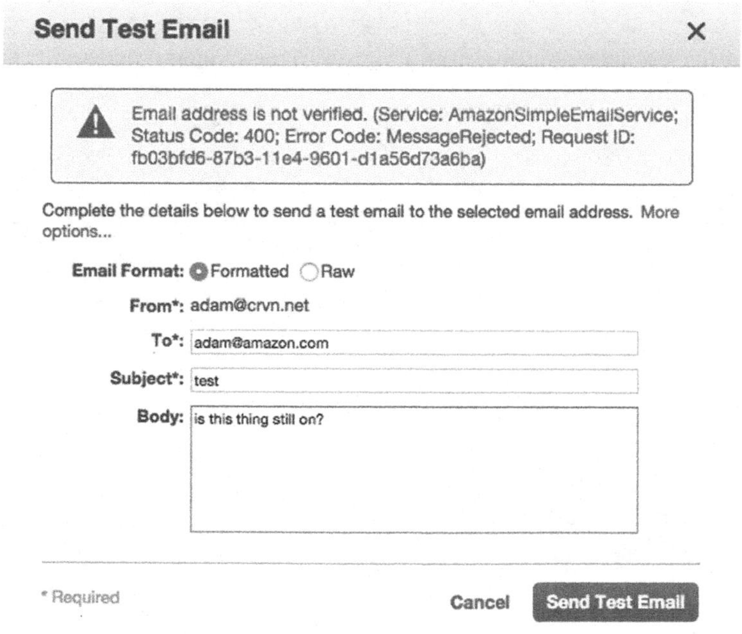

Send Test Email ✕

⚠ Email address is not verified. (Service: AmazonSimpleEmailService; Status Code: 400; Error Code: MessageRejected; Request ID: fb03bfd6-87b3-11e4-9601-d1a56d73a6ba)

Complete the details below to send a test email to the selected email address. More options...

Email Format: ◉ Formatted ◯ Raw

From*: adam@crvn.net

To*: adam@amazon.com

Subject*: test

Body: is this thing still on?

* Required   Cancel   **Send Test Email**

Figure 6-6. *SES Send Test Email again*

151

It's as simple as that. For development purposes, however, we must be able to send mail more than just to and from ourselves. Let's go ahead and get our domain verified, so we can start sending mail from the application.

Domain Verification

Select **Domains** under the Verified Senders header in the left navigation. Click the **Verify a New Domain** button at the top. Once again, a modal window will appear, prompting for your domain name. Enter the domain name and click the check box next to **Generate DKIM Settings** (see Figure 6-7), then click **Verify This Domain**.

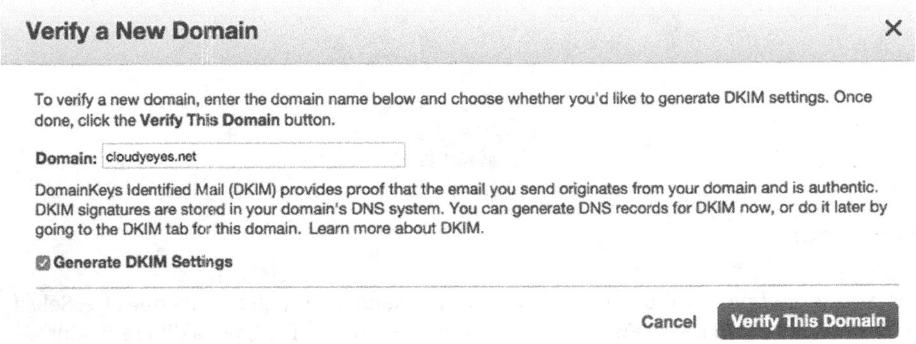

Verify a New Domain   ✕

To verify a new domain, enter the domain name below and choose whether you'd like to generate DKIM settings. Once done, click the **Verify This Domain** button.

Domain: cloudyeyes.net

DomainKeys Identified Mail (DKIM) provides proof that the email you send originates from your domain and is authentic. DKIM signatures are stored in your domain's DNS system. You can generate DNS records for DKIM now, or do it later by going to the DKIM tab for this domain. Learn more about DKIM.

☑ **Generate DKIM Settings**

Cancel   **Verify This Domain**

Figure 6-7. *Verifying a domain*

In a moment, a new modal view will appear, shown in Figure 6-8.

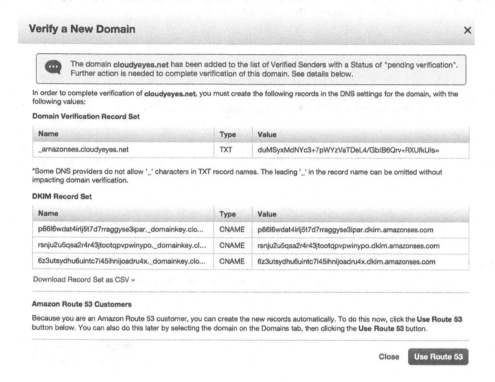

Figure 6-8. *Verify domain DNS records*

These DNS records must be created at your host, in order to complete domain verification. Additionally, the DKIM records should ideally be created. DKIM, or DomainKeys Identified Mail,[1] is essentially a cryptographic method for verifying that mail claiming to be sent from a domain is in fact originating from said domain. By enabling DKIM at the domain level, we reduce the risk of our application messages ending up in the spam folder.

If you were managing your DNS elsewhere, you would have to create TXT and CNAME records, as shown in the modal view. However, you'll notice a **Use Route 53** button at the bottom right. Because we're using Route 53 to manage our DNS, we can have the configuration done for us automatically. Click this button to proceed.

---

[1]For more on the exciting world of DKIM, check out the official site at www.dkim.org.

Instead of being redirected to Route 53, another modal view will appear, ready to carry out some Route 53 tasks. You will see tables for the domain verification and DKIM record sets and have check boxes above each table with which to toggle the creation of those records (see Figure 6-9).

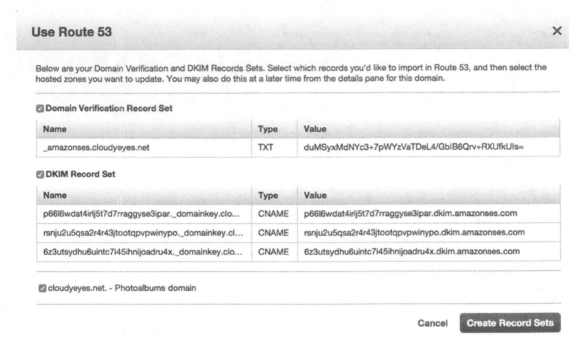

Figure 6-9. *Creating DNS records in Route 53*

Click **Create Record Sets** to create them automatically. In a few moments, you'll be returned to the Verified Sender: Domain table, shown in Figure 6-10, which will list your domain, with a status of *pending verification.*

Figure 6-10. *Verified domains*

As a sanity check, let's validate that the records were created properly. Open the AWS services menu and navigate to Route 53. Select **Hosted Zones** and choose your domain name from the table that appears. At the top, click **Go To Record Sets** to view the DNS records associated with your domain. Sure enough, you should see three CNAME records and one TXT record, with names and values corresponding to what we generated in SES (see Figure 6-11). As this is effectively a DNS change, it may take up to 72 hours for your domain to be verified. Anecdotally, it takes much less time than that using Route 53. In any case, our domain will not be immediately verified.

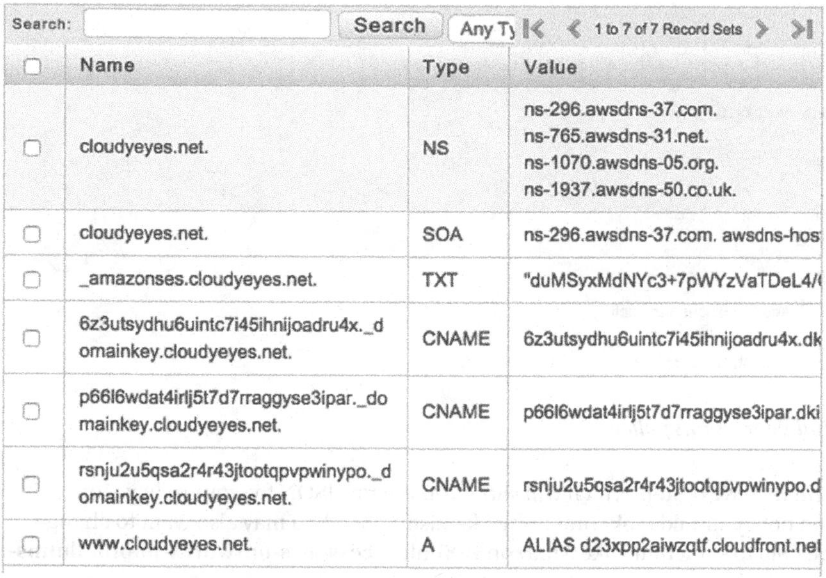

Search:		Search	Any Ty |< < 1 to 7 of 7 Record Sets > >|
☐	Name	Type	Value
☐	cloudyeyes.net.	NS	ns-296.awsdns-37.com. ns-765.awsdns-31.net. ns-1070.awsdns-05.org. ns-1937.awsdns-50.co.uk.
☐	cloudyeyes.net.	SOA	ns-296.awsdns-37.com. awsdns-hos
☐	_amazonses.cloudyeyes.net.	TXT	"duMSyxMdNYc3+7pWYzVaTDeL4/(
☐	6z3utsydhu6uintc7i45ihnijoadru4x._d omainkey.cloudyeyes.net.	CNAME	6z3utsydhu6uintc7i45ihnijoadru4x.dk
☐	p66l6wdat4irlj5t7d7rraggyse3ipar._do mainkey.cloudyeyes.net.	CNAME	p66l6wdat4irlj5t7d7rraggyse3ipar.dki
☐	rsnju2u5qsa2r4r43jtootqpvpwinypo._d omainkey.cloudyeyes.net.	CNAME	rsnju2u5qsa2r4r43jtootqpvpwinypo.d
☐	www.cloudyeyes.net.	A	ALIAS d23xpp2aiwzqtf.cloudfront.net

Figure 6-11. *Route 53 record sets for SES*

Managing SES Permissions with IAM

In the meantime, we can finish getting set up in AWS. By now, you've probably concluded that we will be generating SES mail from the EC2 instances in our application stack, using the AWS SDK. Last time we used the AWS SDK to control another service, we had to manage permissions in IAM in order to allow our instances to run the commands. We'll be going through the same process again here.

Navigate to the IAM dashboard. Select **Roles** from the navigation and you will see the list of IAM roles we've created. Locate **aws-opsworks-photoalbums-ec2-role** in the list and click it. Under the Permissions header, you should see the policy we created in the previous chapter giving this role permission to upload to S3 buckets. The name of the policy describes its utility. Rather than modify the existing policy, we'll add an inline policy for our new permissions. Click **Create Role Policy** to begin the policy generation process again. With the **Policy Generator** header selected, click **Select**. In the Edit Permissions view, select **Amazon SES** from the AWS Service dropdown, and **All Actions(*)** from the Actions dropdown (see Figure 6-12).

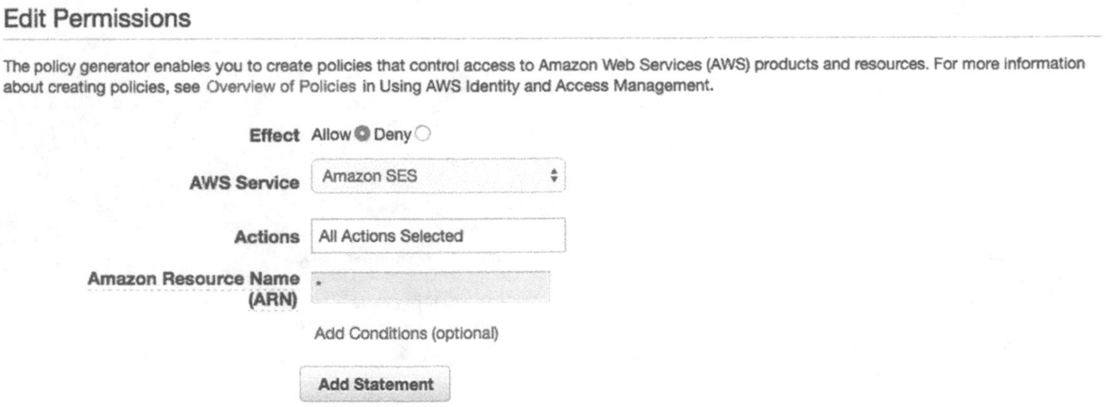

Edit Permissions

The policy generator enables you to create policies that control access to Amazon Web Services (AWS) products and resources. For more information about creating policies, see Overview of Policies in Using AWS Identity and Access Management.

Effect	Allow ⦿ Deny ○
AWS Service	Amazon SES ⬍
Actions	All Actions Selected
Amazon Resource Name (ARN)	.

Add Conditions (optional)

Add Statement

Figure 6-12. *Amazon SES full permissions policy*

Click **Add Statement** and then **Next Step**, which will show you the raw JSON for your policy along with an auto-generated name. The policy should look something like Listing 6-1. You may also want to change the name in the Policy Name field to something like **AmazonSESFullAccess-aws-opsworks-photoalbums-ec2-role**. Click **Apply Policy** at the bottom right.

Listing 6-1. SES Full-Access IAM Policy

```
{
  "Version": "2012-10-17",
  "Statement": [
    {
"Sid": "Stmt1424445811000",
      "Effect": "Allow",
      "Action": [
        "ses:*"
      ],
      "Resource": "*"
    }
  ]
}
```

When you return to the detail view for the role, the permissions/policies should look something like those in Figure 6-13.

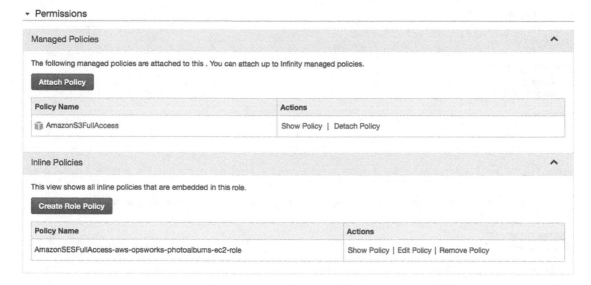

Figure 6-13. *EC2 Instance role policies*

We also want to be able to use the SES functionality in the local development environment. This means that we also have to give the same permissions to the photoalbums-s3 user whose credential we use locally. Select **Users** from the IAM navigation, and select the **photoalbums-stack** user (or whichever user you're using for local development). Scroll down in the user detail view until you see the Permissions header. Click the link to create an inline policy for this user.

Once again, you will scroll down a list of policy templates until you find Amazon SES Full Access. You will allow all permissions for the service, click **Add Statement**, and then click **Next Step**. You can once again review the policy you've selected. The *Policy Document* should appear just like the one we saw previously in Listing 6-1.

Click **Apply Policy** to return to the user detail view. This user should now have two policies: one managed policy for S3 access and one inline policy for SES permissions (see Figure 6-14).

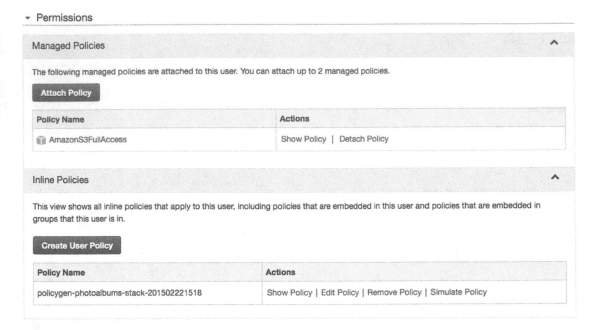

Figure 6-14. *IAM user policies*

Using SES with the AWS SDK

Now we're all set to start integrating SES into our application! For the time being, let's add some pretty standard functionality. When a new user registers, we'll send her a registration confirmation e-mail. We won't force her to activate the account in the e-mail; it will simply be a welcome message.

Before we get into the thick of it, we once again have to determine how to make our addresses dynamic, that is, avoid hard-coding them into the application. After all, we want our code to work as well in a dev environment as it does in the production environment. The e-mail address from which registration e-mails are sent should be something like donotreply@yourdomain.com. It's probably a reasonable decision to always assume that the sender should be "donotreply." We also have the domain stored in an OpsWorks Environment Variable—in the wrong format. There are a few approaches we could take here.

1. Store specific e-mail addresses, such as contact@yourdomain.com in OpsWorks Environment Variables, and access them programmatically.

2. Use the existing DOMAIN environment variable and programmatically trim http://www off the beginning, to make it usable in constructing e-mail addresses dynamically.

3. Make a new environment variable for the mail domain and use that.

All three of these approaches (and probably a few others I didn't think of) are perfectly valid. To keep things simple, we're going to use the second approach, which will save us the trouble of making new environment variables. At this point, however, you should feel confident about your ability to use any of the preceding approaches to construct an e-mail address dynamically in this context.

Globals

Open /lib/globals.js in your code editor and scroll to the end. After the absoluteURL() function, paste the following:

```
rootDomain : function(){
return this.awsVariables().domain.replace('http://www.','');
}
```

This simple function will convert http://www.yourdomain.com to simply yourdomain.com. We call it rootDomain and not just mailDomain, because we could potentially need the root domain at some later point. In the interest of clarity, your globals file should now be as in the following Listing 6-2:

Listing 6-2. Updated Globals

```
module.exports = {
  applicationPort : 80,
  database  : function(){
    if(process.env.ENVIRONMENT){
      var opsworks = require('./../opsworks');
      var opsWorksDB = opsworks.db;
      var rdsConnection = {
        host   : opsWorksDB.host,
        port : opsWorksDB.port,
        database : opsWorksDB.database,
        user : opsWorksDB.username,
        password : opsWorksDB.password
      };
      return rdsConnection;
    } else {
      var local = require('./../config/local');
      var localConnection = local.db;
      return localConnection;
    }
  },
  awsVariables : function(){
    if(process.env.ENVIRONMENT){
      var variables = {
        bucket : process.env.S3BUCKET,
        domain : process.env.DOMAIN
      }
      return variables;
    } else {
      var local = require('./../config/local');
      return local.awsVariables;
    }
  },
```

```
  absoluteURL : function(path){
    if(this.awsVariables().domain){
      return this.awsVariables().domain + '/' + path;
    }
    return path;
  },
  rootDomain : function(){
    return this.awsVariables().domain.replace('http://www.','');
  }
}
```

Mail.js

While we could put most of the rest of our code in the users route, it might make more organizational sense to have a separate class for handling all of our SES transactions. After all, we may want to generate e-mails for other purposes elsewhere in our application. It seems safe to say that e-mail communication deserves its own proxy class.

Create a new file called mail.js in the /lib directory. You could, of course, name it something such as ses.js, if you prefer. First, we must include the dependencies for this file. We'll require access to our globals.js, as well as the AWS SDK. At the top of the file, paste the following lines:

```
var aws = require('aws-sdk');
var globals = require('./globals');
```

For now, we're only adding registration e-mails. However, we should structure this file with the assumption that we will be adding other mail functionality in the future. As such, we will be writing two functions: one to construct the content for the registration e-mail and another to send the SES mail.

First, add the sendEmail() function to mail.js (see Listing 6-3). This function will simply send the SES mail with the parameters passed to it. It will remain a private function.

Listing 6-3. sendEmail Function

```
function sendEmail(params, callback){
  if(globals.awsVariables().key){
    aws.config.update({ accessKeyId: globals.awsVariables().key, secretAccessKey:
    globals.awsVariables().secret });
  }
  var ses = new aws.SES({region:'us-east-1'});
  var recipient = params.username + '<' + unescape(params.email) + '>';
  var sesParams = {
    Source: params.messageSource,
    Destination: {
      ToAddresses: [recipient],
      BccAddresses: params.bccAddress
    },
    Message: {
      Subject: {
        Data: params.subject,
        Charset: 'UTF-8'
      },
```

```
      Body: {
        Text: {
          Data: params.messageText,
          Charset: 'UTF-8'
        },
        Html: {
          Data: params.messageHTML,
          Charset: 'UTF-8'
        }
      }
    },
    ReplyToAddresses: [emailSender()]
  }
  ses.sendEmail(sesParams, function(err, data){
    callback(err, data);
  });
}
```

You'll notice a similar pattern to our S3 upload functionality. If an IAM key is found, meaning we're in the local environment, then call `aws.config.update()` to use our local credentials. Then, we initialize an instance of SES from the SDK. To use SES, you must set the region as well. In our case, it's `'us-east-1'`. The rest of the function is populating SES parameters with the values sent in the `params` object. Last, `ses.sendEmail()` sends the e-mail.

Next, we will create the `sendRegistrationConfirmation()` function. This function will construct the parameters passed to `sendEmail`. To add other e-mails to our application, we will merely replicate the `sendRegistrationConfirmation` functionality. Add the code in Listing 6-4 to `mail.js`.

Listing 6-4. sendRegistrationConfirmation Function

```
function sendRegistrationConfirmation(params, callback){
  var emailParams = {
    username : params.username,
    email : params.email
  };
  emailParams.messageSource = emailSender();
  emailParams.bccAddress = [];
  emailParams.subject = 'Registration Confirmation';
  emailParams.messageText = 'You have successfully registered for Photoalbums.
                             Your username is ' + emailParams.username + '.';
  emailParams.messageHTML = 'You have successfully registered for Photoalbums.
                             Your username is <strong>' + emailParams.username + '</strong>.';
  sendEmail(emailParams, callback);
}
```

As you can see, we generate our e-mail subject and message in both plain text and HTML. You'll notice that the `messageSource` is set to `emailSender()`. Because we will conceivably be sending multiple system e-mails to users, a reusable function is a good way to minimize code duplication. The `emailSender()` function should be added to `mail.js` as well.

```
function emailSender(){
  return 'donotreply@' + globals.rootDomain();
}
```

161

With the preceding code, we use the root domain originating in the OpsWorks environment variable to construct an e-mail address for the sender.

Last, we have to make sendRegistrationConfirmation() a public method. At the end of the file, add the following line:

```
exports.sendRegistrationConfirmation = sendRegistrationConfirmation;
```

User Registration Route

Next, we integrate this new functionality into our application. For now, we're only adding mail functionality to the users route. Open /routes/users.js. At the top of the file, include mail in the file:

```
var mail   = require('./../lib/mail');
```

Locate the /register route, to which you will be adding the mail.sendRegistrationConfirmation() function. We don't want to send the registration e-mail until we have successfully created the user account in the database. The route should appear as follows (Listing 6-5):

Listing 6-5. New User Registration Code

```
router.post('/register', function(req, res) {
  if(req.param('username') && req.param('password') && req.param('email')){
    var email = unescape(req.param('email'));
    var emailMatch = email.match(/\S+@\S+\.\S+/);
    if (emailMatch !== null) {
      var params = {
        username: req.param('username').toLowerCase(),
        password: req.param('password'),
        email: req.param('email').toLowerCase()
      };

      model.createUser(params, function(err, obj){
        if(err){
            res.status(400).send({error: 'Unable to register'});
        } else {
            mail.sendRegistrationConfirmation({username: req.param('username'),
            email: req.param('email')}, function(errMail, objMail){
          if(errMail){
            res.status(400).send(errMail);
          } else {
            res.send(obj);
          }
        });
        }
      });
    } else {
      res.status(400).send({error: 'Invalid email'});
    }
  } else {
    res.status(400).send({error: 'Missing required field'});
  }
});
```

■ **Note** In the production environment, you might want to check for duplicate e-mail addresses during registration.

Deployment and Testing

Those are all the code changes we need! Commit your code to your repository; navigate over to OpsWorks; and select your application stack. Select **Apps** from the drop-down. When you see your application in the list, click **deploy**. Give your application a few minutes to deploy.

When your deployment is complete, we can test the new functionality. Register a new user by making a POST request to http://www.[*yourdomain*].com/users/register. Make sure to include the following parameters: username, email, and password. Use whatever username and password you like, and be sure to use an SES-verified e-mail as the e-mail. Send the request, and you should see the following response:

```
{  message: "Registration successful!" }
```

Well that's a good sign. Go ahead and check your e-mail. You should have a message that looks something like that in Figure 6-15.

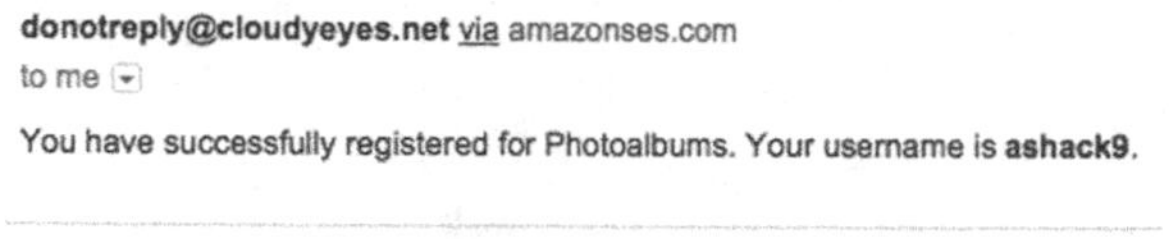

donotreply@cloudyeyes.net via amazonses.com
to me ▾

You have successfully registered for Photoalbums. Your username is **ashack9**.

Figure 6-15. *E-mail sent by SES*

Let's head back over to SES to look at our metrics. In the AWS menu, choose **SES**. In the dashboard, you should now see the results of your test, as shown in Figure 6-16. As you can see, you've sent 1 of 200, and your e-mails have a 100% delivery rate.

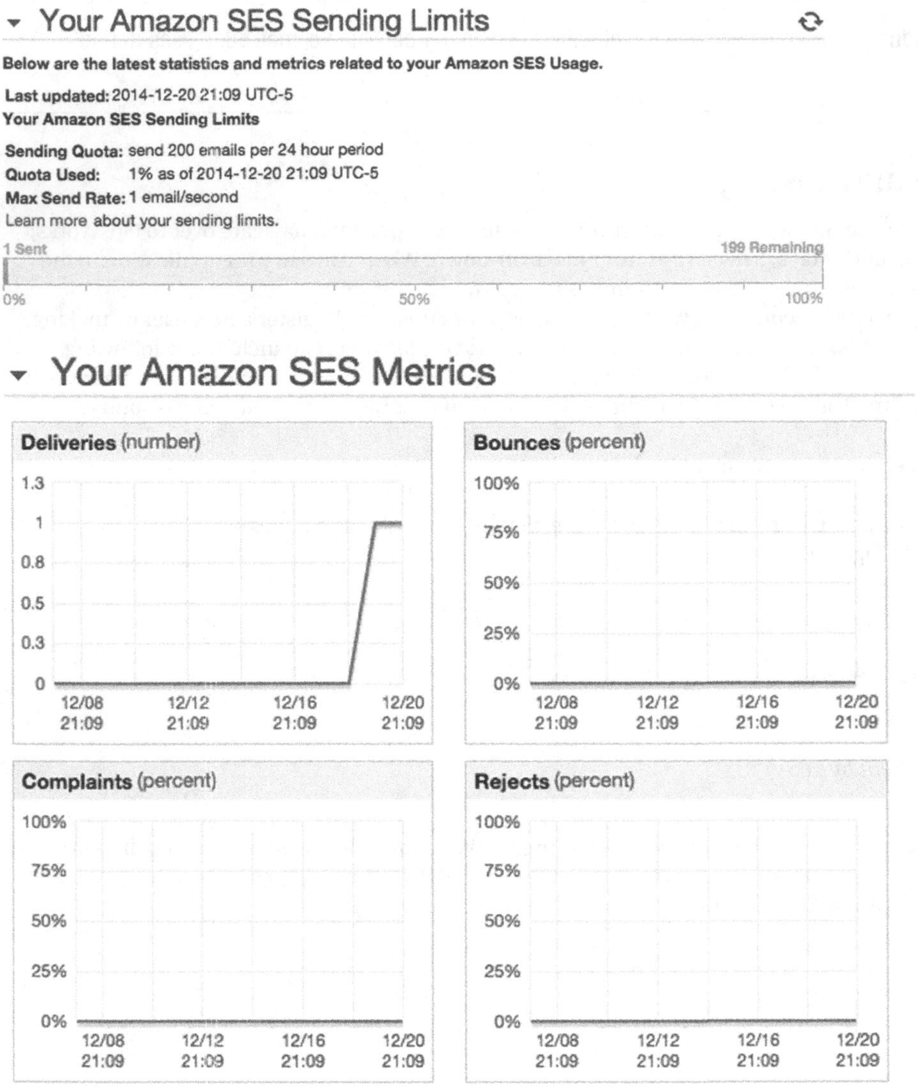

▼ Your Amazon SES Sending Limits   ⟲

Below are the latest statistics and metrics related to your Amazon SES Usage.

Last updated: 2014-12-20 21:09 UTC-5
Your Amazon SES Sending Limits

Sending Quota: send 200 emails per 24 hour period
Quota Used: 1% as of 2014-12-20 21:09 UTC-5
Max Send Rate: 1 email/second
Learn more about your sending limits.

1 Sent   199 Remaining

0%   50%   100%

▼ Your Amazon SES Metrics

Figure 6-16. SES sending limits and metrics

And that's all there is to it! You've integrated SES into your application and should be able to extrapolate on this lesson to generate e-mail from your application in other use cases. But before we conclude this chapter, we will run through a quick lesson on organizing AWS resources.

AWS Resource Groups

By the sixth chapter, you're already utilizing a number of services in your application. As your infrastructure grows, it can be difficult to keep track. There are a few ways we can organize our resources to make them easier to find. We will quickly revisit some of our AWS services and tag them with our application name and create a resource group from these tags.

As I discussed in Chapter 3, tags have no technical use; they exist purely for our own convenience. While they can help us organize our resources, they can be especially useful for analyzing your AWS billing, a subject that is beyond the scope of this book.

We can give the resources for Photoalbums a common set of tags for organizational purposes. Then, we'll create a resource group based on these common tags, which will make it easier to consolidate the moving parts of our system.

Tagging Resources

Let's begin by tagging our database. From the AWS Console, navigate to **RDS**. Click **Instances** in the left-hand navigation, which will reveal your instance in the right-hand view. At the bottom of the view, click the **Tags** button. The view will reload as the detail page for your instance. At the bottom, you'll see a table underneath the Tags header, as in Figure 6-17.

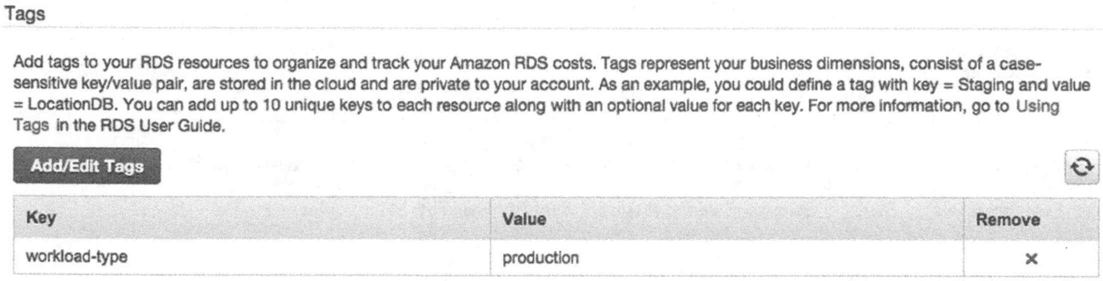

Tags

Add tags to your RDS resources to organize and track your Amazon RDS costs. Tags represent your business dimensions, consist of a case-sensitive key/value pair, are stored in the cloud and are private to your account. As an example, you could define a tag with key = Staging and value = LocationDB. You can add up to 10 unique keys to each resource along with an optional value for each key. For more information, go to Using Tags in the RDS User Guide.

Add/Edit Tags		⟳
Key	**Value**	**Remove**
workload-type	production	✕

Figure 6-17. *RDS instance tags*

The only tag currently assigned to the RDS instance is *workload-type: production*. Let's add a tag to indicate that this database is a part of the Photoalbums project. Click **Add/Edit Tags**. In the Tag DB Instance view (see Figure 6-18), click **Add another Tag**. Enter **project** as the *Key*, and **photoalbums** as the *Value*. Click **Save Tags**.

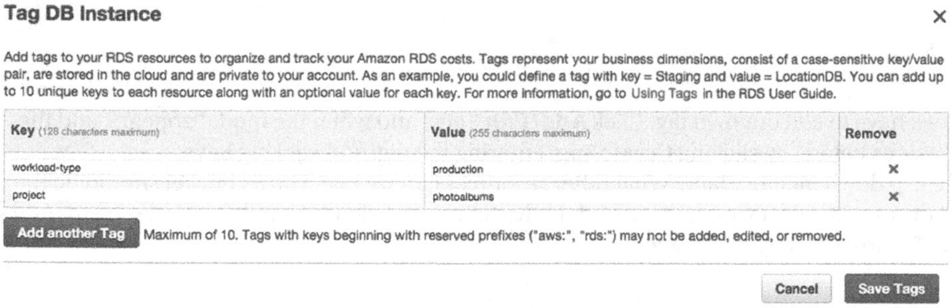

Tag DB Instance   ✕

Add tags to your RDS resources to organize and track your Amazon RDS costs. Tags represent your business dimensions, consist of a case-sensitive key/value pair, are stored in the cloud and are private to your account. As an example, you could define a tag with key = Staging and value = LocationDB. You can add up to 10 unique keys to each resource along with an optional value for each key. For more information, go to Using Tags in the RDS User Guide.

Key (128 characters maximum)	**Value** (255 characters maximum)	**Remove**
workload-type	production	✕
project	photoalbums	✕

Add another Tag	Maximum of 10. Tags with keys beginning with reserved prefixes ("aws:", "rds:") may not be added, edited, or removed.

Cancel   Save Tags

Figure 6-18. *Adding tags to the database*

This one was easy enough. Unfortunately, we cannot tag the instances in our application stack as we would like by default (but we could with a Chef script). For now, let's manually tag our EC2 instances. Head over to the EC2 dashboard. Click **Tags** in the left-hand navigation, which will display a list of EC2 tags (see Figure 6-19). You'll notice that some tags were auto-generated for your instances.

Manage Tag	opsworks:instance	nodejs-app3	1	1	0	0
Manage Tag	opsworks:instance	nodejs-app1	1	1	0	0
Manage Tag	opsworks:layer:nodejs-app	Node.js App Server	2	2	0	0
Manage Tag	opsworks:stack	Photoalbums	2	2	0	0

Figure 6-19. *EC2 tags*

Click **Manage Tags** at the top of the page. You'll now see a view in which you can multi-select instances and add new tags. Select your instance(s) and add the **project: photoalbums** tag to your instance, then click **Add Tag**. Your instances have now been tagged.

Remember: Your load balancer is in here too! Select **Load Balancers** from the left-hand menu. Select your load balancer and click the **Tags** tab. As you can see in Figure 6-20, it already has some tags (we created them in Chapter 3)! Wouldn't it be lovely if the same tag were automatically applied to all the resources we've created in OpsWorks? We can dream....

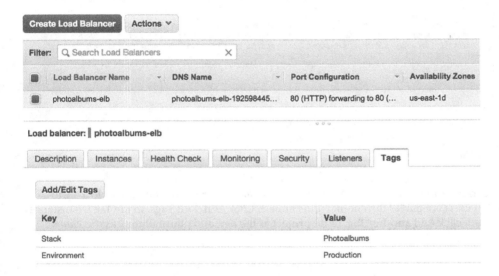

Figure 6-20. *ELB tags*

Unfortunately, we have to add our own tag. Click **Add/Edit Tags**, and when the modal appears, add the same tag key/value pair as before, by clicking **Create Tag**, entering the tag, and clicking **Save**.

This is quite the trip down memory lane. What other resources can we tag? The S3 bucket should be the last one so far. Head over to S3; select your bucket; and, in the right-hand view, expand the Tags section. Add your tag, as shown in Figure 6-21, and click **Save**.

Figure 6-21. *S3 tags*

Creating and Viewing Resource Groups

Next, let's create a resource group with our new tag. You'll notice a menu in the navigation bar titled *AWS*, which we've never used. Expand the menu, as in Figure 6-22, and click **Create a Resource Group**.

Figure 6-22. *AWS menu*

In the Create a resource group view, we can configure our resource group. In this view, we will filter our resources by tag. First, name the resource group **Photoalbums Resources**. To start, we will add two tags to our resource group. In the *Tags* drop-down, select **projects**, then, in the accompanying text field, select **photoalbums**.

In the *Regions* field, you can select which geographic regions are included in this group. All of our resources are in US East, so you can select only **US East**. Leave the *Resource types* field blank to include all resource types (see Figure 6-23). When you're finished, click **Save**.

Edit a resource group

Group name*	Photoalbums Resources
Tags*	opsworks:stack ▾ Photoalbums ✕
	⊕ Add a tag key
Regions*	US East (Northern Virginia) ✕
Resource types	All supported resource types

*Required   Cancel   Delete   Preview   Save

Figure 6-23. *Editing a resource group*

Now we have a new way of quickly accessing our resources. The Resource Group view, accessible at any time from the primary navigation in AWS, links you quickly to all of the resources in your project (see Figure 6-24).

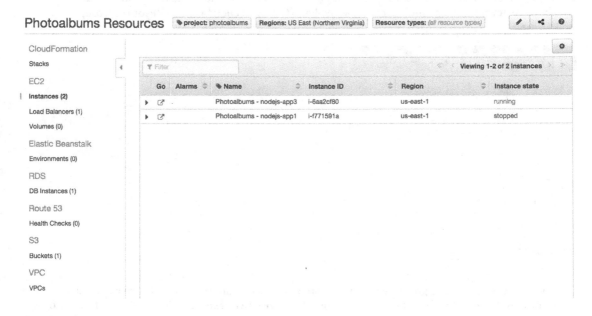

Figure 6-24. *Viewing the Resource Group*

In truth, you may never have to use this. We've gotten into the habit of navigating from service to service fairly quickly, which has its benefits. But now you know you can tag resources and, indeed, that AWS is automatically tagging some resources for you. You can use these tags to get a detailed view of your connected resources, and you can also use these tags for managing your billing.

If you wanted to maintain multiple app environments/application stacks, you could add another tag value for photoalbums dev, and you could create a tag that all stacks have in common, effectively creating different resource views across all AWS services.

Summary

Our application can now send e-mails to our users! It was a quick lesson, which should open a lot of doors. We also took a quick detour to organize our growing number of AWS resources, which can be quite helpful when you're building a complicated system in AWS. In the next chapter, we will finally make our application scale and respond to demand, as we originally set out to do.

CHAPTER 7

■ ■ ■

Monitoring the Application

We've talked a lot about the main principles by which we've been designing our system—scalability and elasticity—and in the process, you've learned about the concepts. Thus far, we have barely been able to put these principles into practice. While you have seen that you can rapidly increase your resource allocation with a variety of AWS services, we have not done so intelligently yet. Sure, you could always run your application on the largest servers possible, but that misses the point. Elasticity, once again, means being able to scale our infrastructure in response to demand or other events, which we will collectively refer to as *incidents*. In this chapter, you will learn how to apply this principle by first identifying incidents and then responding to them.

How do we know we need to scale? The first and most important obstacle in responding to incidents is assessing the health of our infrastructure. While we don't have to know specifically how many users are logged in currently, we do need to be able to assess specific metrics that have some consequence for our application. For example, if we want to know if the size of our EC2 instances is sufficient, we have to measure things such as CPU utilization and memory in order to determine the status of the current instances. If our application is running on a single instance, and its CPU utilization is 100%, there are going to be serious performance issues, and we can call this an incident.

Once we have detected an incident, we have to formulate a response. In the preceding scenario, the most obvious response would be to add another instance to our application stack. In this chapter, we will plan for this and other eventualities and automate the response to the incident. You will learn how to use load-based and time-based EC2 instances to deploy extra resources in response to, and in anticipation of, high demand. There are, of course, some incidents that will require manual intervention to fix or whose resolution is outside the scope of a beginner book. In these cases, we will set up notifications when a critical incident has occurred.

CloudWatch

Amazon has consolidated all of their monitoring metrics under an umbrella service called CloudWatch (http://aws.amazon.com/cloudwatch/). Any metric you can view in any other AWS service can also be collected and tracked in CloudWatch. Typically, the metrics will be easier to view in detail in CloudWatch. It's important to note that AWS metrics are only available for two weeks.

Let's begin by taking a look at the metrics in OpsWorks and comparing them to CloudWatch. Log in to the AWS Console and navigate to OpsWorks. Select the Photoalbums stack. Then open the Navigation drop-down and click **Monitoring**. By default, you will see the monitoring view for the layers of your application that have EC2 instances assigned (see Figure 7-1). In this view, the RDS and ELB layers do not appear.

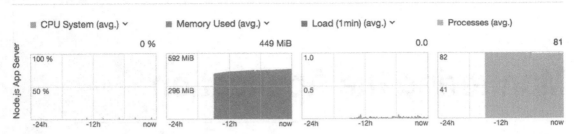

Figure 7-1. *The OpsWorks Monitoring view*

The four categories of layer metrics are displayed, each with its own graph: CPU System, Memory Used, Load, and Processes. By default, the metrics are loaded for the last 24 hours. You can quickly see whether there are any major incidents wherein the CPU system (utilization), memory use, or load were maxed or if there is a spike in active processes. Each of the first three graph headers is actually a drop-down that can be used to select another metric from that category. Figure 7-2 shows the Memory Used drop-down.

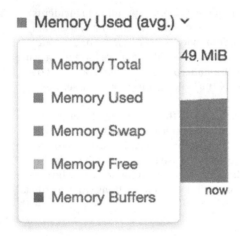

Figure 7-2. *An OpsWorks Monitoring metric drop-down*

You can also change the date range from 24 hours to another range. These seem like pretty useful metrics, but there is no way to view them in greater detail. You might think that clicking one of the graphs will expand it, but it will take you elsewhere: to the Monitoring view for the instances in the layer. Take note of the Memory Used metric, as we will be viewing this in CloudWatch. Now let's go to the CloudWatch dashboard to view this metrics there.

Open the **Services** drop-down, and select **CloudWatch**. At the top of the console, you'll see a heading titled "Metric Summary" (see Figure 7-3). Under this header, click the **Browse Metrics** button.

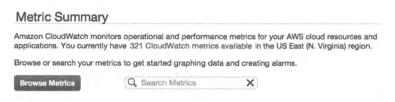

Figure 7-3. *CloudWatch Metric Summary*

In the Metrics view, you can see all the metrics for your AWS account, broken down by service and then by category within that service (see Figure 7-4). The number of metrics you see here will depend on what resources have already been created on your account.

Browse Metrics ▼	Q Search Metrics	✕

CloudWatch Metrics by Category

Your CloudWatch metric summary has loaded. Total metrics: **321**

Billing Metrics: 12	CloudFront Metrics: 6	EBS Metrics: 38
Total Estimated Charge: 1 By Service: 11	Per-Distribution Metrics: 6	Per-Volume Metrics: 38

ELB Metrics: 86	OpsWorks Metrics: 48	RDS Metrics: 60
Per-LB Metrics: 12 Per LB, per AZ Metrics: 19 By Availability Zone: 19 Across All LBs: 12 Namespace: 12 Service: 12	Instance Metrics: 16 Layer Metrics: 16 Stack Metrics: 16	Per-Database Metrics: 15 By Database Class: 15 By Database Engine: 15 Across All Databases: 15

Figure 7-4. *CloudWatch Metrics by Category*

Let's take a look at the metrics for our application. Imagine that we want to see how much memory has been used by our application layer. Under the OpsWorks Metrics header, click **Layer Metrics**. You should see a list of metrics alphabetized by name and their corresponding LayerId, as shown in Figure 7-5. Since we only have one OpsWorks layer with EC2 instances assigned to it, each metric appears once and corresponds to the Node.js application layer.

OpsWorks > Layer Metrics	
LayerId ▾	**Metric Name**
◻ e18f0595-e621-4949-a50a-b939d73da2b2	cpu_idle
◻ e18f0595-e621-4949-a50a-b939d73da2b2	cpu_nice
◻ e18f0595-e621-4949-a50a-b939d73da2b2	cpu_steal
◻ e18f0595-e621-4949-a50a-b939d73da2b2	cpu_system
◻ e18f0595-e621-4949-a50a-b939d73da2b2	cpu_user
◻ e18f0595-e621-4949-a50a-b939d73da2b2	cpu_waitio
◻ e18f0595-e621-4949-a50a-b939d73da2b2	load_1
◻ e18f0595-e621-4949-a50a-b939d73da2b2	load_15
◻ e18f0595-e621-4949-a50a-b939d73da2b2	load_5
◻ e18f0595-e621-4949-a50a-b939d73da2b2	memory_buffers
◻ e18f0595-e621-4949-a50a-b939d73da2b2	memory_cached

Figure 7-5. *OpsWorks Layer Metrics*

Scroll down to the metric named memory_used. Click the check box next to it. Underneath the metric list, a graph will magically appear, displaying the metric at 5-minute intervals over the past 12 hours (see Figure 7-6).

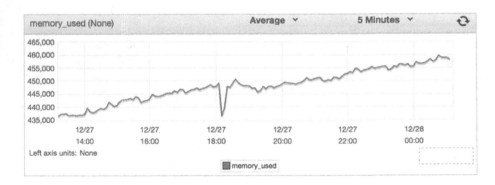

Figure 7-6. *OpsWorks Layer Metrics in CloudWatch*

This is the same metric we were just looking at in OpsWorks, only with greater detail. By default, the span and interval of the data points is different, but we can easily change the graph to 24 hours and 1-minute averages to match the graph in OpsWorks. Click **5 Minutes** to expand the interval drop-down and change to **1 Minute**. Using the *Time Range* filter to the right of the graph (not shown in the figure), change the *From* field to **24**. Then click **Update Graph**. You should now see the same data set as you saw in OpsWorks. You can also mouse over the line in the graph to view more details about each point.

Another useful feature in CloudWatch is that you can view multiple metrics. In our case, the amount of memory used is a more valuable metric when compared to the total available memory. In the metrics list, select the **memory_total** metric. Your memory_used plot should turn orange, and the memory_total metric will appear in blue. This doesn't look right, does it? If your memory_used line is above the memory_total line, you must flip your axes. Mouse over one of the lines and find the *Y-Axis* property. Then, click **switch** to change the axes. Now you should have a view of both metrics, showing you how much of your available memory has been used in the past 24 hours (see Figure 7-7).

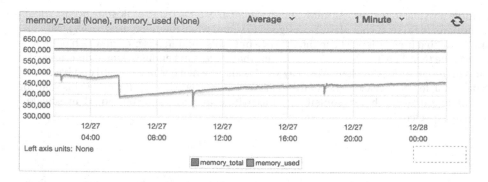

Figure 7-7. *Memory used vs. memory total*

As you can see in Figure 7-7, I have 600MB in total available memory, and my usage in the past 24 hours has hovered between 400MB and 500MB for the most part. Keep in mind that this isn't just the memory usage of the Node.js application; it includes all software, including the operating system, running on the instances. The next question is what to do with this information.

CloudWatch Alarms

When your metrics cross certain thresholds, you can configure a CloudWatch alarm to send a notification to you or your team. You can create up to 5,000 alarms on your account, using any of the metrics that are accessible in CloudWatch, and at the time of this writing, these alarms cost $.10 per month per alarm. The main purpose of creating these alarms is to quantify an incident that is occurring in your application stack, leading to either a manual or automated response.

Creating useful alarms may not be as easy as it sounds. It is entirely possible to create alarms that you would expect to go off if there was a problem with your application and then completely miss an incident occurring. For example, let's say you were creating alarms to monitor the output of your application over HTTP (more on this later). You might create an alarm that fires when an HTTP response code of 500 is returned to a user, but instead, your application just hangs, and the request times out, due to some unforeseen error in the code. Your application would be unresponsive, and you would never know it!

When you create an alarm, you choose a metric and a comparison operator (greater than, less than, greater than or equal to, etc.). You cannot create an alarm directly comparing two metrics. For example, you could not create an alarm that goes off when memory_used >= memory_total. You would have to configure the alarm to go off when memory_used >= 600,000. Unfortunately, this alarm would not be that useful, unless you intended to keep your instances at a particular scale.

At first glance, you might think, couldn't the alarm go off when we use all 600MB? Then, couldn't we add new instances and turn them back off when the alarm stops going off? When you add another instance to your layer, there will also be significant memory overhead associated with that instance, so this may not be the most practical alarm to use. As long as you have more instances (and thus more memory) online, the memory footprint may inaccurately keep the alarm state active, when in actuality the incident is no longer occurring.

An alarm has three possible states: OK, ALARM, and INSUFFICIENT_DATA. The OK state occurs when the condition for the alarm is false. If your alarm is designed to sound when memory_used == 600,000 (which as we know, is not that useful), it will be in the OK state until this condition is met, at which point it will switch to ALARM. The INSUFFICIENT_DATA state means that there is not enough data to determine whether the alarm is in the OK or ALARM state. You may see this alarm when it is first created and has not collected enough data or if, for some reason, the metric data is not currently available. If you see this state for an extended period of time, it means there is something wrong with your alarm, and you should investigate why it is not working as expected.

Alarm Periods

Of course, both AWS infrastructure and your application are prone to hiccups, just like any other technology. You don't necessarily want all of your alarms going off if your application is slow for a couple seconds, or if a single user experiences a delay. To account for this, you must define both the intervals at which your alarm state is checked and the number of consecutive periods that constitute an alarm state.

Suppose we were to set an alarm based on the CPU utilization of our application layer. We want to be notified if the CPU utilization is greater than 50%. This is a fairly important metric—if our CPU utilization is too high, it means our instances are overworked and our application is going to become unresponsive. We, therefore, should set the interval, or *period*, of the alarm to one minute, a fairly regular health check. That being said, we don't necessarily want the alarm to go off if there's an isolated spike in the CPU utilization.

The CPU utilization is one good indicator that your application is experiencing an incident of excessive demand, so it would make sense to respond to it by adding more instances to the application stack. However, we know by now that EC2 instances don't start instantaneously. If your alarm were going off one minute, then ceased the next, then went off again, you might have your extra instances stuck constantly booting and shutting down. This would constitute a tremendous waste of resources, and it would be irritating to constantly get false alarms. Therefore, let's say that three consecutive alarm periods constitute an incident, so we would configure our alarm to fire if our CPU utilization is greater than 50% for three minutes.

Simple Notification Service (SNS)

Before we begin creating CloudWatch alarms, we have to take a quick detour to the Simple Notification Service. This service allows you to tie CloudWatch alarms to a variety of notification methods, including HTTP, e-mail, mobile push notifications, and SMS. Like many other services, this one warrants a book in its own right. We will only be using SNS for its most simple utility: e-mailing a group of users when a CloudWatch alarm goes off.

From the AWS Services menu, select **Simple Notification Service**. You'll notice a few key terms here, primarily *topics* and *subscriptions*. Just as with other AWS services, a topic has a unique ARN (Amazon Resource Name—the global ID in the AWS ecosystem) and is in itself a resource—the target of a notification event. We will create a topic for all alarms pertaining to the Photoalbums infrastructure. Then, we will create subscriptions for each administrator who should be e-mailed when a notification is generated under this topic. While a subscription could also be a URL, SMS recipient, or other end point, in our simple case, you can think of a subscription as a user's e-mail address.

Let's begin by creating a topic for Photoalbums administrators. In the center of the SNS dashboard, you should see a button labeled "Create New Topic" (see Figure 7-8).

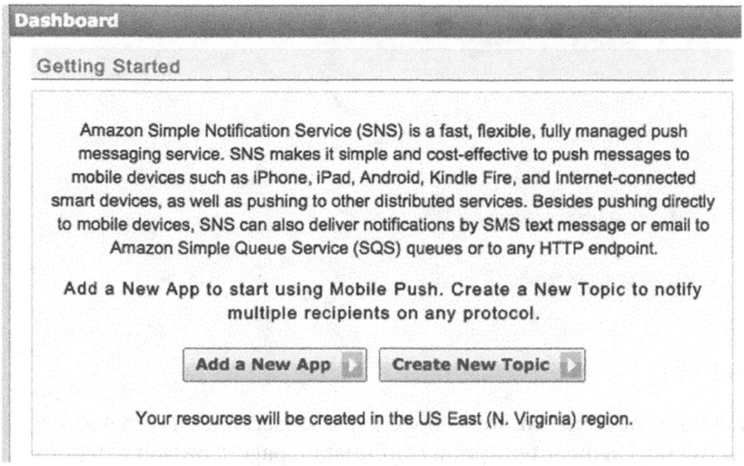

Figure 7-8. *SNS dashboard*

A modal pop-up will appear, prompting you for a *Topic Name* and optional *Display Name*. In both fields, enter **PhotoalbumsAlarms**, as this topic will solely be triggered by CloudWatch alarms for our application stack (see Figure 7-9). Click **Create Topic**.

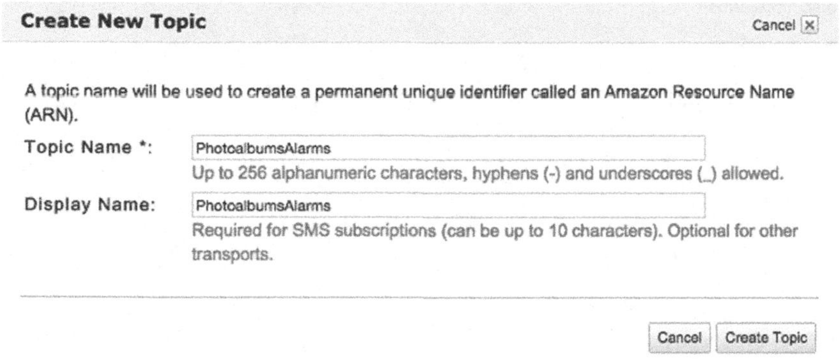

Figure 7-9. *Create SNS topic*

You will be directed immediately to the topic detail view, where you can view basic information about the topic, as well as the subscriptions to the topic. At this point, we only have to create a single subscription to this topic: an e-mail to you, the only administrator for the application. Go ahead and click the **Create Subscription** button. Another modal will appear. Expand the *Topic* drop-down and select **Email**. Enter your e-mail address in the *Endpoint* field and click **Subscribe**.

The window will display a message notifying you that the e-mail address must be confirmed. Click **Close** to return to the topic detail view. You should receive an e-mail with the subject *AWS Notification—Subscription Confirmation*. In the e-mail body, there should be a link to the subscription confirmation URL. Clicking it should direct you to a page similar to that shown in Figure 7-10.

Figure 7-10. *An SNS subscription confirmed*

If you return to the topic detail view and click **Refresh**, you will see that a subscription ID (an ARN) has been generated for your e-mail, just as you saw on the subscription confirmation page. Now you're ready to use this SNS topic! We can go ahead and run a simple test by manually publishing to this topic. At the top of the topic detail view, you'll see a **Publish** button. Click this and another modal will appear. Fill out a *Subject* and *Message* with some test content, as in Figure 7-11, and click the **Publish Message** button. Then, check your e-mail again. You should see a message with your subject from "PhotoalbumsAlarms" <no-reply@sns.amazonaws.com>.

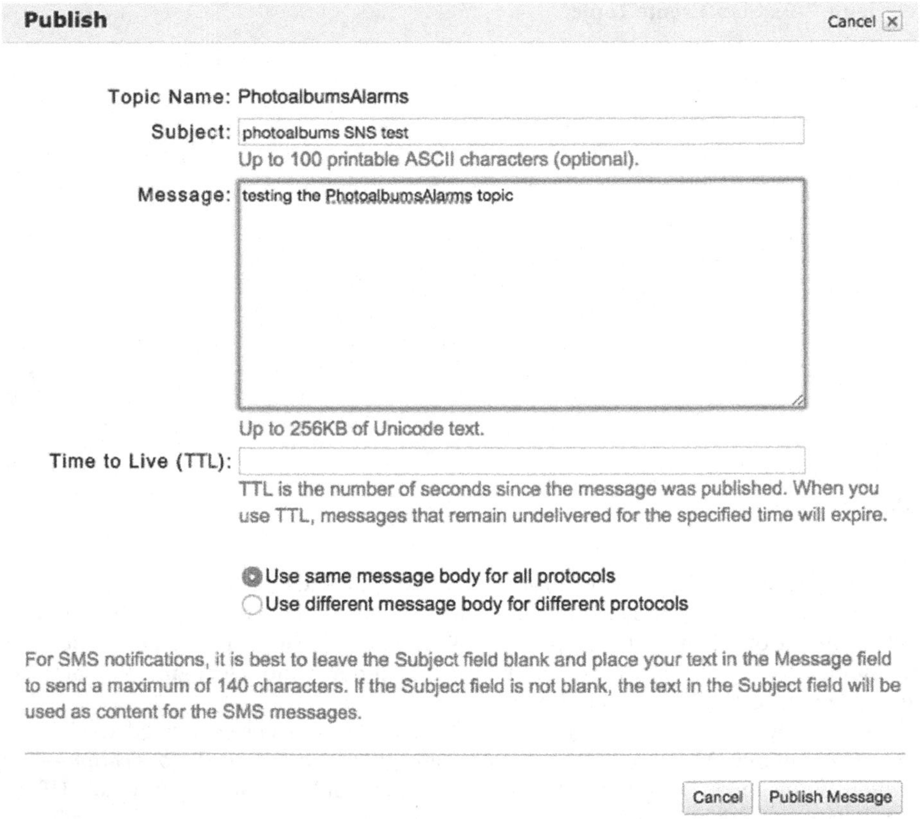

Publish   Cancel ✕

Topic Name: PhotoalbumsAlarms

Subject: photoalbums SNS test
Up to 100 printable ASCII characters (optional).

Message: testing the PhotoalbumsAlarms topic

Up to 256KB of Unicode text.

Time to Live (TTL):

TTL is the number of seconds since the message was published. When you use TTL, messages that remain undelivered for the specified time will expire.

◉ Use same message body for all protocols
◯ Use different message body for different protocols

For SMS notifications, it is best to leave the Subject field blank and place your text in the Message field to send a maximum of 140 characters. If the Subject field is not blank, the text in the Subject field will be used as content for the SMS messages.

Cancel   Publish Message

Figure 7-11. *Publishing an SNS topic*

Creating a CloudWatch Alarm

Now that we've created an SNS topic for our alarms, we are ready to create our first CloudWatch alarm. Unfortunately for the reader, each CloudWatch metric is its own topic of discussion and requires some exposition on the subject. This time, let's use a metric for our CloudFront to create an alarm. If you recall, all requests over the Web to our application will be passing through our CloudFront distribution. It might be useful to know, for example, if a lot of requests are being made.

Using the Services menu, return to the CloudWatch dashboard. This time, take a look at the left-hand navigation. Under the Metrics header, you will see a list of all services for which you have CloudWatch metrics. Click **CloudFront**, which will populate the main view with metrics for the CloudFront distribution (see Figure 7-12).

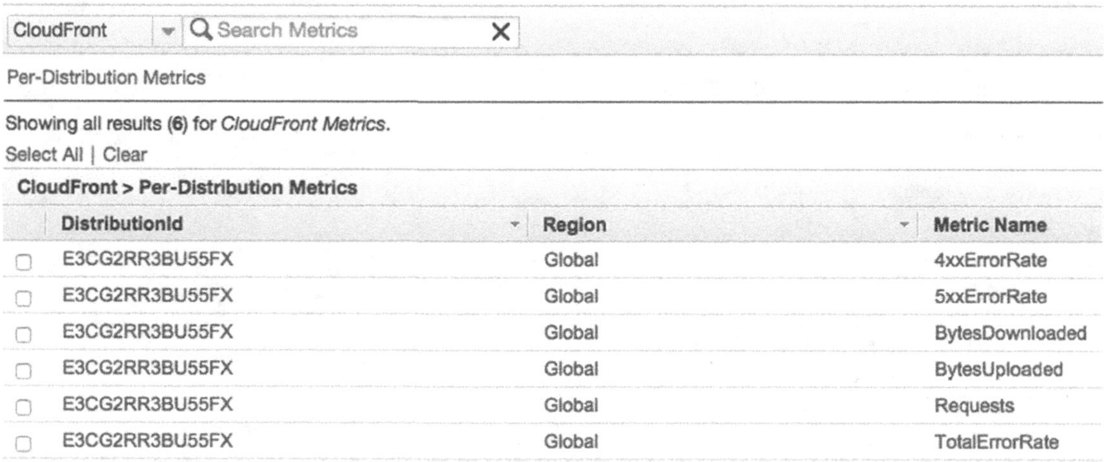

CloudFront ▾	Q Search Metrics	✕

Per-Distribution Metrics

Showing all results (6) for *CloudFront Metrics*.
Select All | Clear

CloudFront > Per-Distribution Metrics

	DistributionId ▾	Region ▾	Metric Name
☐	E3CG2RR3BU55FX	Global	4xxErrorRate
☐	E3CG2RR3BU55FX	Global	5xxErrorRate
☐	E3CG2RR3BU55FX	Global	BytesDownloaded
☐	E3CG2RR3BU55FX	Global	BytesUploaded
☐	E3CG2RR3BU55FX	Global	Requests
☐	E3CG2RR3BU55FX	Global	TotalErrorRate

Figure 7-12. *ELB metrics in CloudWatch*

Some of these metrics could be pretty useful. The first two in the list, 4xxErrorRate and 5xxErrorRate, are especially interesting. These metrics track the percentage of HTTP requests that are responded to with 400–500 error codes. The 4xxErrorRate is commonly associated with 404, or Resource Not Found, errors. A small number of 404 responses is to be expected, due to user error—people entering the wrong URL or an issue on the client side whereby requests are not formatted correctly. But if 4xx errors became a large percentage of the responses we're sending, then there's a problem worth investigating. While there isn't a magic number, we could agree that 25% of requests resulting in 4XX errors would constitute an incident.

Similarly, 5XX errors constitute internal server errors. A user may be able to induce a 404 with a badly constructed request, but a user should never be able to induce a 500 error in our application. We should tolerate a much lower threshold of 500 error codes than we do of 400s. If we were going to create a CloudWatch alarm for this metric, we might trip the alarm on a rate greater than 0%.

■ **Note** *TotalErrorRate* is the percentage rate of requests that receive any non-200 HTTP response and constitutes the combined percentage of the previous two metrics.

The Requests metric counts the raw number of requests made to your CloudFront distribution. You could theoretically use this to identify a distributed denial of service attack,[1] or to track surges in traffic.

On the latter point, this is not the best way to detect a surge of non-malicious traffic. You would be better off looking at something such as CPU and memory of your instances to identify a surge in traffic. First, not all requests are created equal. One thousand users uploading photos should not be interpreted as equivalent to one thousand users requesting images—the impact on the system is completely different. Further, many requests that reach CloudFront, such as requests for images, will not reach the application stack—and therefore affect performance—at all.

Let's start by creating a simple alarm that will go off under the conditions I discussed a moment ago—when the 4XX error rate is greater than 25%. Select the **4xxErrorRate** row for your distribution. The graph view will appear below, and there may or may not be points on the graph, depending on how you've been using your application. At the bottom-right corner, you should see a button that reads "Create Alarm" (see Figure 7-13). Click that to begin the process.

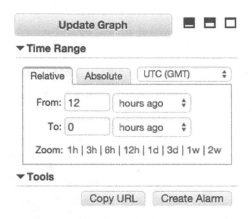

Figure 7-13. *Graph view tools and Create Alarm button (cropped to show time-range interface)*

Defining an Alarm

You should now find yourself in the second step of the alarm creation process, having already selected the metric for your alarm. There are three headers in this view: Alarm Threshold, Alarm Preview, and Actions (refer to Figure 7-14 to see the completed view). Under Alarm Threshold, we name and define the alarm. In the *Name* field, enter **Photoalbums CloudFront HTTP400 > 25%**. The name of the alarm is going to appear in your e-mail notifications, so you want it to be descriptive. The *Description* field allows you to enter a more long-form description of the alarm, so you can enter something such as **Average percentage of requests to Photoalbums CloudFront distribution has exceeded 25%**. If you wanted, you could even take the description further.

---

[1]For a study of types of DDoS attacks and countermeasures, see "A Survey of Defense Mechanisms Against Distributed Denial of Service (DDoS) Flooding Attacks," http://d-scholarship.pitt.edu/19225/1/FinalVersion.pdf.

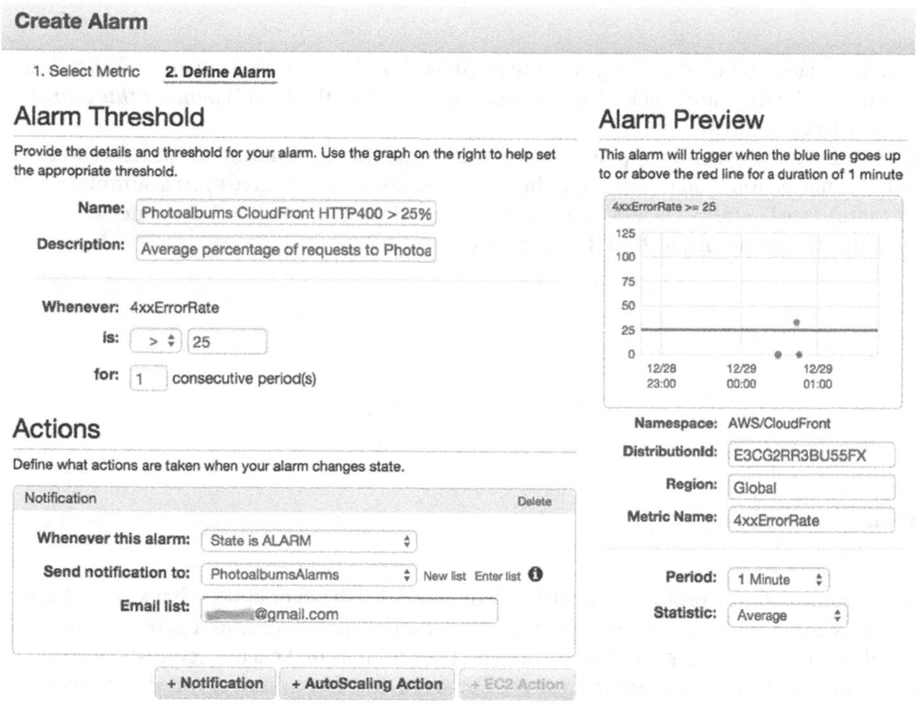

Figure 7-14. *Defining an alarm*

Below the description, you'll find the actual parameters for the alarm. The *Whenever* field is already set to the metric you've selected. In the *is:* row, set your comparison operator to >, and in the neighboring field, enter **25**.

Looking at the right-hand column, the Alarm Preview gives you the current state of your alarm, if it were enabled now. As you can see from the graph, the alarm will go off when the red line is crossed. Currently, there are no requests being made, so there isn't even a blue line on my graph. This would cause the alarm to be in a state of INSUFFICIENT_DATA. You'll notice at the bottom of this column that there are fields for *Period* and *Statistic*. Set the period to **5 Minutes**, which will be the frequency with which the metric is evaluated against the alarm threshold. The statistic is the value we measure. In this case, **Average** is fine. In some cases, you may want to measure the Maximum or Minimum of a metric instead.

Back on the left side, the Actions header indicates CloudWatch's automated response to the alarm going off. You'll see that your choices are to add a *Notification* or *AutoScaling Action*. Autoscaling Actions are not a viable option with our setup. With a more micromanaged application stack, you could configure additional EC2 instances to automatically boot up or shut down in response to an alarm. Because we are using OpsWorks to manage our instances, we will be configuring our auto-scaling there. With this CloudWatch alarm, all we will do is generate a notification. Click **+Notification** to create your first notification. Configure the notification to set *Whenever this alarm:* to **State is ALARM**, and *Send notification to:* **PhotoalbumsAlarms**. Figure 7-14 shows the completed view.

Alarm State

Now you will receive a notification when the alarm is in the ALARM state. You can also create a notification to go off when the alarm is in the OK state. Click **+Notification** again and set the field *Whenever this alarm:* to **State is OK**. Then, click **Create Alarm**.

You should see a success message at the top of the page, indicating that your alarm has been created. If you look at the left-hand navigation, you will see that the Alarms header actually gives you a summary of your current alarm states (see Figure 7-15). Because you just created your alarm, it has the state INSUFFICIENT_DATA. In a few moments, it should change to OK.

Alarms

ALARM   0

INSUFFICIENT   1

OK   0

Figure 7-15. *CloudWatch alarm states*

In a moment, we're going to find a problem with this alarm, because we never know what kind of bots, scripts, or random traffic is going to run across your domain. Nonetheless, it will serve as a good reminder of the tools at our disposal. If you want to trigger the alarm, all you have to do is make a few requests to paths that do not exist, such as `http://www.[yourdomain].com/helloworld`. In a few minutes, you should receive an e-mail indicating that the alarm is in the ALARM state.

If you wait a while longer, the alarm will probably go off pretty soon. So what do we do with this information? One of the challenges with having such an elaborate infrastructure is getting familiarized with the various points of failure.

This alarm in particular is based on a CloudFront metric, so the first thing we should do is check CloudFront and see what the problem is. Go ahead and navigate to the CloudFront dashboard. In the CloudFront navigation, click **Popular Objects**. You may recall that this provides a report on popular URL requests made to your CloudFront distribution (see Figure 7-16).

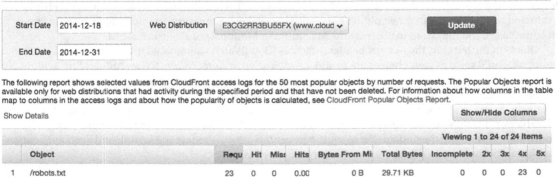

Figure 7-16. *CloudFront Popular Objects*

As you can see in Figure 7-16, the most popular object in my distribution is the /robots.txt file, which is missing. Search engines! They're looking for a robots.txt file on this domain and getting a 404 in response. You will run into the same problem, which you can fix by adding a static path to a robots.txt file in your Express application. The point is that you know how to create an alarm, investigate the problem, and can determine a response.

■ **Note** Similar metrics are available at the Elastic Load Balancing level. Instead of counting 400s and 500s from CloudFront, you could monitor the load balancer in your application stack for the same responses.

Using OpsWorks with CloudWatch

If you recall, there are three types of instances when you're adding them to your OpsWorks application layer: 24/7, load-based, and time-based. Currently, we have one 24/7 instance running. Next, let's add some load-based instances to our application. In doing this, we will design our application to handle increased demand efficiently. Later in this section, we also will look at time-based instances.

Fluctuations in traffic are normal for a web application, and we don't want to manually respond to the ebb and flow of traffic. We would prefer to use our resources elastically, so they automatically scale in response to demand. But this strategy just leads to more questions.

Suppose your application stack can normally handle 500 users running on a t1.micro EC2 instance. You routinely expect the traffic to increase to 1,000 users, so you want the resources available for when that happens (these are completely made-up numbers). More often than not, however, you probably have a budget for infrastructure, so you have to manage your resources efficiently. We can't just throw 100 servers at the problem.

Within these constraints, we will configure OpsWorks to automatically detect an incident in the application layer instances and continue adding new servers until the incident has been resolved, at which point our extra instances will automatically shut down.

NOTES ON DETERMINING SCALING BEHAVIOR

In a moment, we're going to start using metrics and scheduling to scale our infrastructure. In a perfect world, you could come away from this lesson with exact numbers to plug in. Unfortunately, it's a bit more abstract than that. You will have to use your own methods to determine the best strategy. You can test your application performance with a certain number of users, check the metrics, and extrapolate the resources you'll need from there, although this method is likely to be inaccurate. For example, if normal application use by five users brings your instance to 5% CPU utilization and twenty users brings it to 10% CPU utilization, you could test in this way to predict a curve.

Nothing beats real-world operating history in informing your decisions. Some prefer to soft launch or run a closed beta with their applications. Others deploy excess resources at launch and carefully scale back to a more conservative deployment. All of this is an art of its own. In my experience, two different applications can experience slowdown at entirely different metrics. We will also be looking at time-based scaling, which is based on the unique traffic patterns for your application. So, I cannot tell you exactly when to trigger a scaling action but, rather, can show you the tools you will be using. We're going to use a few instances in this scenario, which represent what you could actually do with large numbers of powerful instances.

Load-Based Instances

Let's face it, one t1.micro instance is not going to be enough! We need to add a few instances to scale up in response to demand. Head over to OpsWorks and select your application stack. Open the Navigation drop-down and under the Instances header, you will see a link to **Load-based** instances (see Figure 7-17). Click that, which will bring you to the blank-slate view of load-based instances.

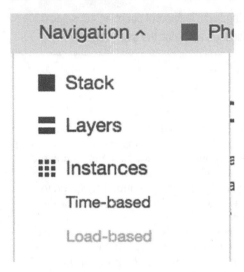

Figure 7-17. *Load-based instances in the Navigation menu*

In the middle of the screen, you should see the following message: *No load-based instances. Add a load-based instance.*

Click **Add a load-based instance**. You'll recognize the view that appears from when we added our first instance in Chapter 2. The default *Hostname* should be fine. To be thrifty, change the *Size* to **t1.micro**. You should select a different *Availability Zone*, such as **us-east-1b** (see Figure 7-18). If you recall, it is best practice to spread your instances across different availability zones, in case of an outage at AWS. This means we should be spreading 24/7 instances across availability zones, but we'll make do for now.

New	Existing

Hostname	nodejs-app2
Size NEW DEFAULT	t1.micro
Availability Zone	us-east-1b
Advanced »	

Cancel   **Add Instance**

Figure 7-18. *Adding a new instance to the application layer*

So far though, there's no difference from creating a 24/7 instance. Next, click **Advanced** to review additional settings before we create the instance. The advanced settings should look similar to those in Figure 7-19. Because we created the instance from the Load-based Instances view, the load-based scaling type was preselected. We don't have to change any of these values, but if you create load-based instances from the general instances view, you would have to make sure to change the scaling type in the advanced view. Go ahead and click **Add Instance** to proceed.

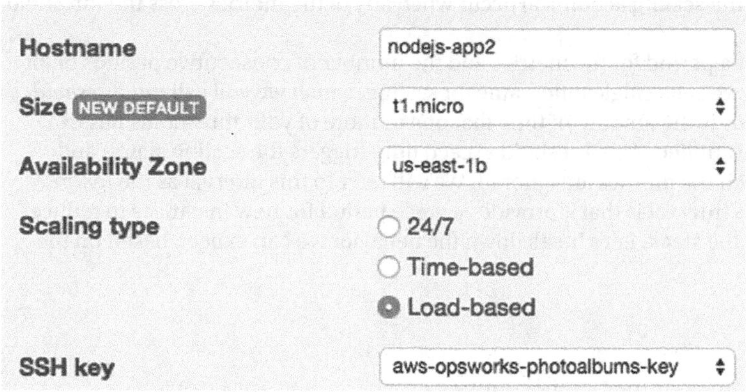

Hostname	nodejs-app2
Size (NEW DEFAULT)	t1.micro
Availability Zone	us-east-1b
Scaling type	○ 24/7 ○ Time-based ● Load-based
SSH key	aws-opsworks-photoalbums-key

Figure 7-19. Load-based instance advanced configuration

OpsWorks Auto-scaling Rules

When you return to the instances view, you should see the following message in a yellow warning box: *Load-based auto scaling is disabled—edit.*

You're seeing this warning because, while we have created a load-based instance, we have not enabled load-based scaling, nor defined the rules by which the instances are brought online. Click the **Edit** button to do that now.

First thing's first: toggle the *Load-based auto scaling enabled* switch to **Yes**. Next, let's define some auto-scaling rules. Remember, these values are essentially arbitrary as far as your application is concerned, and you would be wise to determine your own scaling thresholds based on testing and operating history. For now, we'll devise a simple rule set, as shown in Figure 7-20, and I'll discuss the behavior thereafter.

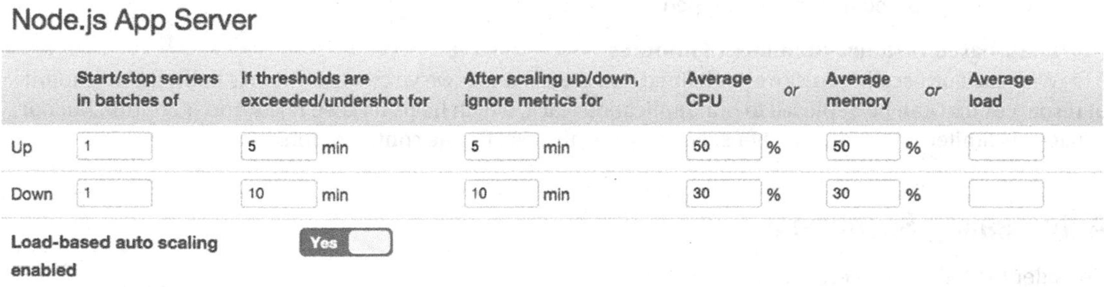

Node.js App Server

	Start/stop servers in batches of	If thresholds are exceeded/undershot for	After scaling up/down, ignore metrics for	Average CPU	or	Average memory	or	Average load
Up	1	5 min	5 min	50 %		50 %		
Down	1	10 min	10 min	30 %		30 %		

Load-based auto scaling enabled **Yes** ◯

Figure 7-20. Load-based auto-scaling rules

When you use OpsWorks auto-scaling, you work with a simplified interface that uses the underlying CloudWatch metrics we were working with earlier. There are, however, a few differences between using OpsWorks and using CloudWatch for scaling. When you set auto-scaling rules in OpsWorks, you define rules for scaling up and scaling down separately, in one distinct rule set each. When scaling up or down, you set the number of instances to add/remove per-scaling action. Instead of creating an alarm and auto-scaling action for each metric, your scaling actions are based on evaluation of up to three metrics at each interval: Average CPU (%), Average memory (%), or Average load. You do not have to use all three in your scaling rules. If you do use all three metrics, the scaling action will occur when any of the metrics cross the threshold you define.

With CloudWatch alarms, we set a period for the metrics and the number of consecutive periods before we triggered an alarm. In OpsWorks, we set a single time frame for scaling, which we will call the *threshold exceed time*, for the sake of clarity. This is the amount of time that one or more of your thresholds has to be exceeded for the scaling rule to be applied. The threshold exceed time triggers the scaling action and is followed by an interval during which the metrics are ignored. We will refer to this interval as the *ignore metric interval*. The reasoning for this interval is that it provides a grace period for new instances to reduce the workload of existing instances in the stack. Let's break down the behavior we can expect, based on the values shown in Figure 7-20.

Auto-scaling Scenario 1

Consider the following scenario:

1. A single 24/7 instance is online.
2. Average CPU utilization reaches 51% and remains there for five minutes.
3. Threshold exceed time for *Up* rule is met.
4. A single load-based instance is started.
5. Metrics are ignored for five minutes.
6. Metrics are checked again. Average CPU utilization is now reduced to 23%.
7. Ten minutes pass.
8. Average CPU utilization is still below 30%.
9. Threshold exceed time for *Down* rule is met.
10. Load-based instance is stopped.

Load-based Instance Runtime: 15 minutes

With the auto-scaling rules we've defined and the instances we've created, there is still a finite amount of resources that can be deployed to our application stack, which helps us keep costs under control, but our capacity is limited. Consider another scenario using the exact same configuration.

Auto-scaling Scenario 2

Consider the following scenario:

1. A single 24/7 instance is online.
2. Average CPU utilization reaches 75% and remains there for five minutes.
3. Threshold exceed time for *Up* rule is met.

4.　A single load-based instance is started.

5.　Metrics are ignored for five minutes.

6.　Metric checks are resumed. Average CPU utilization is at 63% and remains there for five minutes.

7.　*No additional load-based instances are available.*

8.　Average CPU utilization remains at 63% for an additional five minutes.

9.　*No additional load-based instances are available.*

10.　And so on and so on...

Load-based Instance Runtime: Indefinite

As you can see, even though we have both 24/7 and load-based resources, we are not set up to handle the demand for our application. In this scenario, our load-based instance may as well be a 24/7 instance, if it's always online to meet our baseline traffic requirements. Additionally, our lack of resources will probably begin to impact the performance of the application.

There are a few possible solutions to this problem. The simplest solution is to add additional 24/7 instances. If we believe this is a temporary surge in demand, it would be more cost-effective to add an additional load-based instance. Let's go ahead and do that, then review the behavior in another scenario.

Remember to click **Save** to create your scaling rules. The scaling rules should no longer be editable. Then, click the **+ Instance** button below the table. Once again, choose a **t1.micro** instance size. Choose a different Availability Zone, such as **us-east-1c** (see Figure 7-21). Click **Add Instance** to create your second load-based instance.

Node.js App Server　　　　　　　　　　　　　　　　　　　　　Edit

	Start/stop servers in batches of	If thresholds are exceeded/undershot for	After scaling up/down, ignore metrics for	Average CPU	*or*	Average memory	*or*	Average load
Up	1	5 min	5 min	50 %		50 %		
Down	1	10 min	10 min	30 %		30 %		

0 of 1 instances are running - Show »

✚ Instance

New	Existing

Hostname　　　　　　　nodejs-app4

Size NEW DEFAULT　　　t1.micro　　　　　　　　♦

Availability Zone　　　us-east-1b　　　　　　　♦　　Select the Availability Zone. We recommend spreading your
　　　　　　　　　　　　　　　　　　　　　　　　　　instances over multiple AZs for higher redundancy. This value
Advanced »　　　　　　　　　　　　　　　　　　　defaults to the zone specified at stack creation.

　　　　　　　　　　　　　　　　　　　　　　　　Cancel　　**Add Instance**

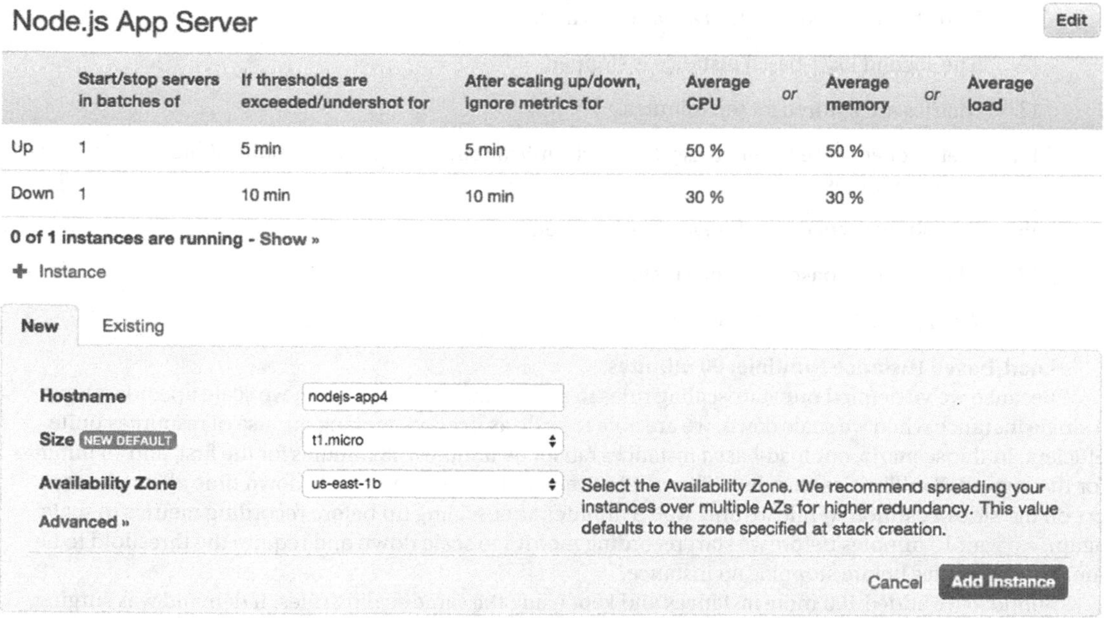

Figure 7-21. *Adding a second load-based instance*

You'll see a summary below the scaling rules that reads as follows: *0 of 2 instances are running – Show >>*.

Using our current scaling rules, let's revisit how our instances will scale differently with a second load-based instance available.

Auto-scaling Scenario 3

Consider a third scenario:

1. A single 24/7 instance is online.

2. Average CPU utilization reaches 75% and remains there for five minutes.

3. Threshold exceed time for *Up* rule is met.

4. A single load-based instance is started.

5. Metrics are ignored for five minutes.

6. Metric checks are resumed. Average CPU utilization is at 63% and remains there for five minutes.

7. Threshold exceed time for *Up* rule is met.

8. A second load-based instance is started.

9. Metrics are ignored for five minutes.

10. Metric checks are resumed. Average CPU utilization is at 25% and remains there for ten minutes.

11. Threshold exceed time for *Down* rule is met.

12. The second load-based instance is stopped.

13. Metrics are ignored for ten minutes.

14. Metric checks are resumed. Average CPU utilization is at 23% and remains there for ten minutes.

15. Threshold exceed time for *Down* rule is met.

16. The first load-based instance is stopped.

17. A single 24/7 instance is online.

Load-based Instance Runtime: 60 minutes

Because we've defined our auto-scaling rules to add a single instance when we scale up and remove a single instance when we scale down, we are able to scale as needed, making our use of resources quite efficient. In this scenario, our load-based instances ran for 60 minutes: 45 minutes for the first, and 15 minutes for the second. You'll notice that the difference between our scale up and scale down time allowed us to err on the side of caution. While we only wait 5 minutes after scaling up before recording metrics to scale again, we wait 10 minutes before we start recording metrics to scale down and require the threshold to be met for 10 minutes before stopping an instance.

Suppose we added 100 more instances and kept using the same scaling rules. If demand was surging, our application stack would automatically bring a new instance online every 10 minutes, while our instances surpassed the scale-up threshold, and instances would be taken offline every 15–20 minutes. In the face of extreme demand, this might not be rapid enough of a response. You could reduce the *threshold exceed time* for scaling up to 1 minute and reduce the *ignore metric interval* to 1 minute.

Auto-scaling Scenario 4

Lastly, consider this scenario:

1. A single 24/7 instance is online.

2. Average CPU utilization reaches 75% and remains there for one minute.

3. Threshold exceed time for *Up* rule is met.

4. A single load-based instance is started.

5. Metrics are ignored for one minute.

6. Metric checks are resumed. Average CPU utilization is at 63% and remains there for one minute.

7. Threshold exceed time for *Up* rule is met.

8. A second load-based instance is started.

9. And so on...

With a more aggressive scale-up rule, an instance can be brought online every two minutes. You could leave the scale-down rule as it is, so once an instance is online, we wait for a while to make sure the incident is over before reducing resources.

Time-Based Instances

There is one last type of instance you can create in OpsWorks: the time-based instance. If you know that most of the time your application will have higher traffic at certain times, you can create instances that automatically start and stop for the high traffic window. By the same token, if you know of times when there is usually very little traffic, you can use time-based instances where you might otherwise use a 24/7 instance.

Using all three instance types in conjunction is the most efficient way to run your application and is a much easier strategy to implement in OpsWorks than manually. You use 24/7 instances for your baseline resources, time-based instances for your higher traffic times, and load-based instances to respond to any increases in demand in the meantime. If you experience a surge in traffic when your time-based instances are scheduled to be offline, your load-based instances will still be available to respond.

Let's go ahead and start adding time-based instances to the application. Using the Navigation menu in OpsWorks, select **Time-based Instances** under the Instances header. You'll see a message just like that we saw in the load-based instances view: *No time-based instances. Add a time-based instance.*

Click **Add a time-based instance** to create a single time-based instance. Just as before, select a **t1.micro** instance in any availability zone you like. When you click **Advanced**, you will see that the *Scaling Type* is set to **Time-based** (see Figure 7-22). Click **Add Instance** to proceed to the Schedule Creation view.

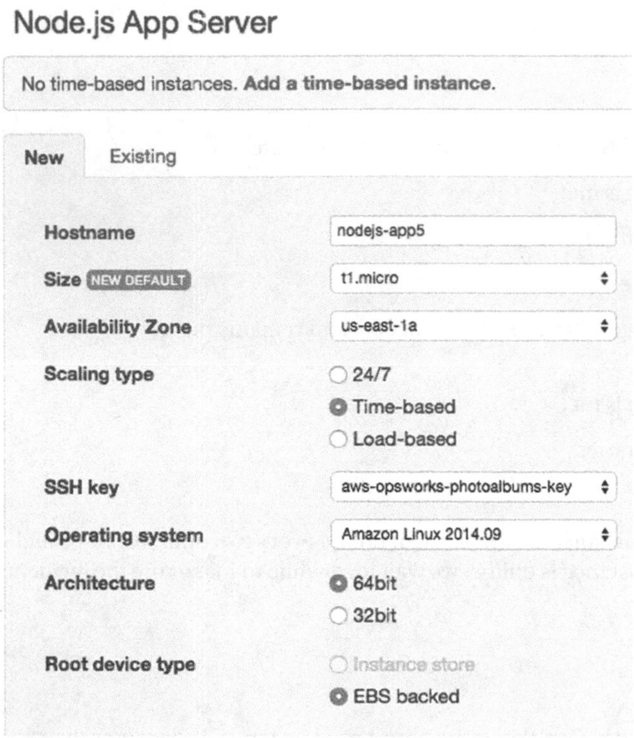

Node.js App Server

No time-based instances. **Add a time-based instance.**

New   Existing

Hostname	nodejs-app5
Size NEW DEFAULT	t1.micro ⬦
Availability Zone	us-east-1a ⬦
Scaling type	○ 24/7
	● Time-based
	○ Load-based
SSH key	aws-opsworks-photoalbums-key ⬦
Operating system	Amazon Linux 2014.09 ⬦
Architecture	● 64bit
	○ 32bit
Root device type	○ Instance store
	● EBS backed

Figure 7-22. *Adding a time-based instance*

In the Schedule Creation view, you can manually set the schedule for each time-based instance in your application layer. The interface is fairly straightforward: you select one-hour time blocks (UTC), during which your instance will be online.

Go ahead and click the box between 12 and 13, as in Figure 7-23. You'll see a brief activity indicator as your change is saved.

Node.js App Server

Figure 7-23. *Time-based instance scheduling*

Your instance will now run from 12–1 p.m. UTC on a daily basis. Let's say you also want it to run on Friday evenings from 6–8 p.m. UTC. Click the **Fri** tab to select the schedule for Fridays only. You'll see that your daily hours are automatically selected, and you simply select the additional hours you want to run on Friday. Select the 18–19 and 19–20 blocks to add Friday evening to your selection (see Figure 7-24).

Node.js App Server

Figure 7-24. Time-based instance scheduling—single-day view

Using Alarms with OpsWorks

You should be able to let your application scale up and down automatically, but you may want to be informed when this happens. You especially want to be informed when all of your instances are online. As I've discussed, if all of your load-based instances are online, this does not guarantee that the current incident has been resolved. We want an alarm to go off, notifying us when we're at or near capacity. From there, you can monitor the situation and manually add new instances.

Unfortunately, there is currently no CloudWatch metric that tracks your current OpsWorks instances count. There are, however, two very useful metrics at the ELB level: *Healthy Hosts* and *Unhealthy Hosts*. These metrics tell us the number of instances connected to the load balancer that are in the healthy state as well as the unhealthy state. You'll recall that we defined *healthy* and *unhealthy* quite a while ago!

We can use these metrics creatively to notify us of problems. For instance, an alarm that went off when *Healthy Hosts* == maximum number of instances would be sounded whenever all our instances are online. Another alarm could go off when *Unhealthy Hosts* > 1. This way, we'll be alerted when either all of our instances are online or when one of our instances is in an error state.

This approach may not work in every situation. For example, if you have 100 instances running, you may not have to respond to a single instance being unhealthy. Additionally, you will want to take into account the number of time-based instances you're using, as this will affect the number of healthy hosts that should raise the alarm.

ELB Monitoring

To create your ELB alarm, you don't have to go through the CloudWatch dashboard, you can also do so from the ELB view itself. ELB instances are accessible via the EC2 dashboard. Select **EC2** from the Services menu. In the left-hand navigation, select **Load Balancers** under the Network & Security header.

If you only have one load balancer, it will be selected automatically. If not, select it now. Then, navigate to the **Monitoring** tab. In this tab, you can see many of your CloudWatch metrics plotted on graphs, as shown in Figure 7-25.

Figure 7-25. *ELB Monitoring view*

You'll notice a Create Alarm button on the right-hand side. As you may have guessed, this lets you create a CloudWatch alarm for the selected load balancer.

When you click the button, you'll see a modal view that is simply a pared-down version of the interface in CloudWatch. Send a notification to your SNS topic. In the *Whenever* fields, select **Average** and **Healthy Hosts**. *Is* should be >= **3**, which is the sum of your 24/7 instances and your load-based instances. *For at least* could be set to **1** consecutive periods of **1 Minute** (see Figure 7-26).

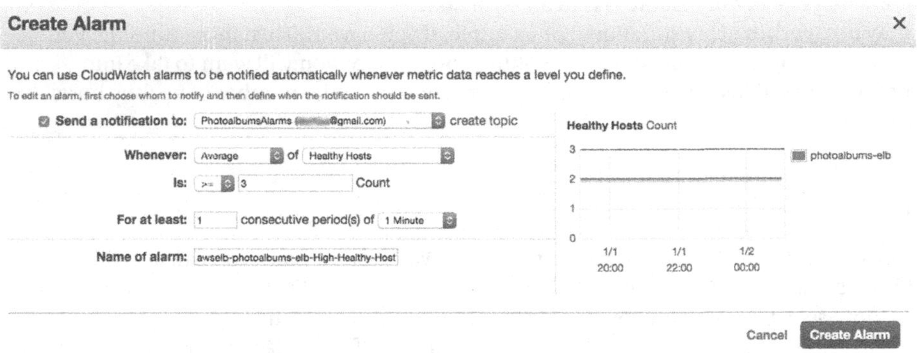

Figure 7-26. *Create ELB alarm*

When you create your alarm in this view, you can name your alarm but not set a description. The auto-generated name may not be clear enough for an e-mail notification. If you like, change the **Name of alarm** to something such as **Photoalbums - All instances online**. If everything looks correct, click **Create Alarm**.

Once again, this is an imperfect method. This alarm will go off when you have one load-based, one time-based, and one 24/7 instance online. After you've created the alarm, a modal window will confirm the action was successful (see Figure 7-27). In this modal, there is a link to the alarm in the CloudWatch dashboard, from which you can access the full view of the alarm details.

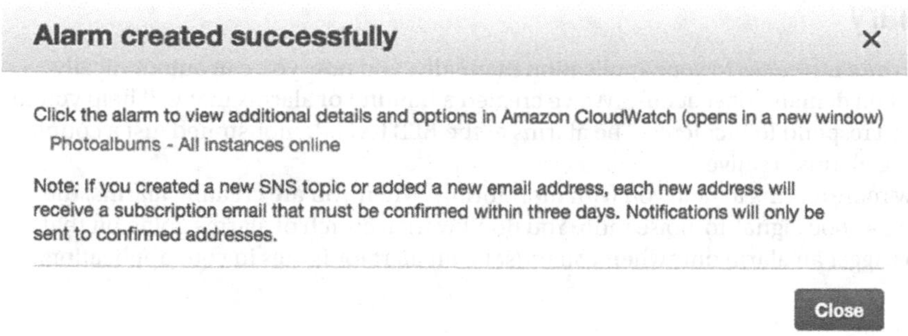

Alarm created successfully   ✕

Click the alarm to view additional details and options in Amazon CloudWatch (opens in a new window)
  Photoalbums - All instances online

Note: If you created a new SNS topic or added a new email address, each new address will
receive a subscription email that must be confirmed within three days. Notifications will only be
sent to confirmed addresses.

[Close]

Figure 7-27. ELB alarm confirmation

Next, let's create the alarm for unhealthy hosts. Note that if your application crashes due to an exception in the code, it will automatically restart. A single unhealthy instance may not warrant a response. Click the **Create Alarm** button again, and send the notification to the same SNS topic. This time, the alarm should go off whenever the average of *Unhealthy Hosts* is >= 1. To make the alarm less sensitive, you could set it to trigger when two consecutive periods of one minute elapse. As you can see in the graph on the right, you should have zero unhealthy hosts right now. Name your alarm something such as **Photoalbums - 1 or more unhealthy hosts**, as in Figure 7-28, and click **Create Alarm** again.

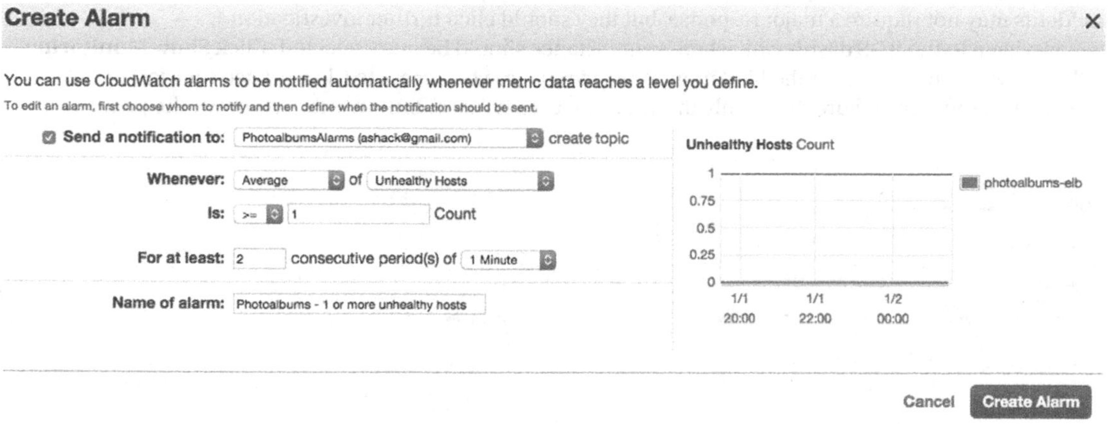

Create Alarm   ✕

You can use CloudWatch alarms to be notified automatically whenever metric data reaches a level you define.
To edit an alarm, first choose whom to notify and then define when the notification should be sent.

☑ **Send a notification to:** [PhotoalbumsAlarms (ashack@gmail.com)] create topic

Whenever: [Average] of [Unhealthy Hosts]

Is: [>=] [1] Count

For at least: [2] consecutive period(s) of [1 Minute]

Name of alarm: [Photoalbums - 1 or more unhealthy hosts]

Unhealthy Hosts Count

■ photoalbums-elb

Cancel [Create Alarm]

Figure 7-28. Creating a second ELB alarm

If you look through the other ELB metrics, you'll see that they're mostly compelling. You may want to set up additional notifications to keep an eye on the health of your application. For example, the *Average Latency* metric tracks how long it takes for instances to return a response to a request. You could set up alarms for this metric to monitor slowdowns in your application performance.

■ **Note** Remember that when you create alarms inline without the full CloudWatch UI, you will not receive a notification when the alarm returns to the OK state.

193

Auto-scaling Summary

You've seen how easy it is to add instances to your application manually, and now you can automatically scale your application based on demand or schedule. We've created a handful of alarms that will help you to monitor your application and respond to incidents. The alarms at the ELB level demonstrated just a couple of the many ways you can use alarms creatively.

Feel free to create a few more alarms to help you with monitoring. When you are creating alarms, the challenge lies in maintaining a good signal-to-noise ratio. You don't want a bunch of alarms going off that will be ignored—it's best to trigger an alarm only when you must be on alert for issues in your application.

RDS Alarms

If you recall the RDS lesson in Chapter 3, you know that we have a lot of redundancy and fail-safes built into our RDS database. We are using Provisioned IOPS to reserve increased I/O capacity for our instance, and Multi-AZ deployment to reroute requests to a backup instance when necessary. We are also taking routine automated snapshots of our database for backup purposes.

With all these tools, the RDS instance should maintain itself for the most part. Nonetheless, we don't want to be caught off guard by any problems. We can easily increase the disk space of the database or create a new instance from a snapshot with a greater capacity. We can easily swap out database credentials in OpsWorks, so if we need to roll out a backup database in a hurry, we have already learned how to do so. In short, we have a means of responding to major crises.

Let's go ahead and create some alarms to inform us of any incidents with our RDS instance. These incidents may not require a major response, but they should elicit further investigation.

Navigate to the RDS dashboard, where your instance should be auto-selected. Click **Show Monitoring** at the top. As with ELB, the embedded monitoring view gives you access to CloudWatch metrics for the selected instance (see Figure 7-29), only this time, the Create Alarm button is farther down the page.

Figure 7-29. *RDS monitoring*

You'll see a number of useful metrics here, mostly in raw numbers instead of percentages. This means that if you scale your database, you may have to adjust alarms accordingly, as in the case of the metrics we looked at in the beginning of the chapter.

Depending on how long it's taken you to get this far into the book, you probably already have some operating history for your database. Take a look at the CPU utilization in Figure 7-30, which you can access by clicking the miniature **CPU Utilization** graph.

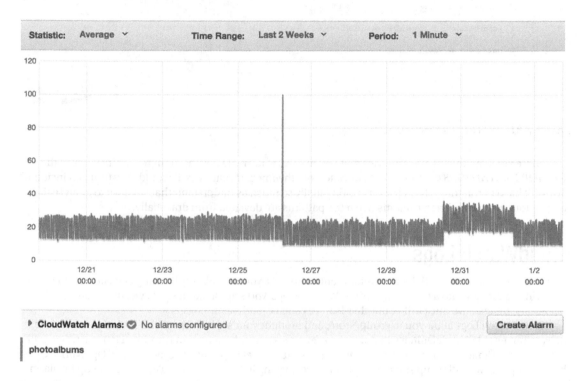

Figure 7-30. *RDS instance CPU utilization*

As you can see, for an overwhelming majority of the time, my CPU utilization stays below 40%. There is a single incident for which it suddenly spiked to 100%. While the incident was resolved automatically by AWS, we should be notified of its occurrence in the future. Click the **Create Alarm** button.

For this alarm, we'll want to be informed of CPU utilization > 60% for a single one-minute period (see Figure 7-31). Once again, we're walking the line between alarms that are too sensitive to be useful and alarms that are too permissive to detect an incident. Sixty percent of CPU utilization is well outside the normal range, and we will be informed immediately. Click **Create Alarm** to finish your alarm and return to RDS.

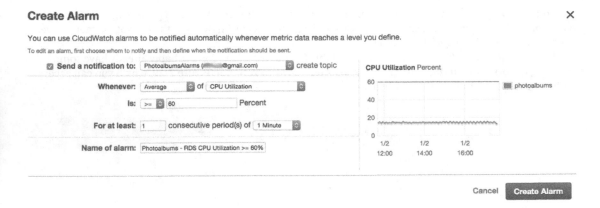

Figure 7-31. RDS CPU utilization alarm

There are a number of other metrics that you may want to create alarms for here. For instance, if the *Read IOPS* or *Write IOPS* metrics were to deviate from their normal patterns, it would constitute an incident. We don't have to run through each metric individually so much as understand that we have to analyze the metrics for patterns and create alarms when the patterns are deviated from drastically.

CloudWatch Logs

After getting comfortable with local development in Node.js, you've probably become accustomed to having logs printing directly into a terminal window. With our OpsWorks application stack, we, unfortunately, lose that ability. Instead, we must utilize another feature called CloudWatch Logs.

CloudWatch Logs allow you to group, store, and monitor your system logs in the AWS Console. While they are not enabled by default, it will only take a few steps to get them up and running. First, we will install and configure CloudWatch logs to store some of the system-level logs that are generated by OpsWorks. Once this is complete, we will set up some application-level logging in CloudWatch. Last, we will set up an alarm based on these logs.

EC2 Instance Roles

Before we dive into this further, the instances in our application stack are going to require full permissions for CloudWatch Logs. As you know, we'll have to make another stop to Identity and Access Management. Select **IAM** from the Services menu. Click **Roles** in the left-hand navigation and select **aws-opsworks-photoalbums-ec2-role** from the list. Once again, this is the role assigned to each instance in your application stack. In the role detail view, you should see the policies you've created to allow the instances to access S3 and SES (see Figure 7-32). Click **Attach Policy** to create another policy for CloudWatch Logs.

Figure 7-32. *Instance Role Policies*

Select the *CloudWatchLogsFullAccess* managed policy and click **Attach Policy**. If you view the policy document, it will look something like Listing 7-1.

Listing 7-1. CloudWatch Logs Full-Access Policy

```
{
  "Version": "2012-10-17",
  "Statement": [
    {
      "Action": [
        "logs:*"
      ],
      "Effect": "Allow",
      "Resource": "*"
    }
  ]
}
```

Your role has been updated, but the changes won't take effect on your instances until they are restarted. Now let's head back to OpsWorks and set up the logging!

Using Chef in OpsWorks

We've made a few allusions to the power of Chef, the core technology behind OpsWorks. Now we're finally going to put it to use! Don't worry, we aren't going to write any recipes, we're just going to put them to work for us.

To write our system logs to CloudWatch Logs, we must install a Chef cookbook to each instance in our application stack. Within each cookbook are one or more configuration scripts, referred to as a Chef recipe. If we had to manually install the scripts on each instance, we would be facing an enormous task. Especially now that we use time- and load-based instances, manually installing scripts on each instance would be highly inconvenient, time-consuming, and difficult to maintain.

When you start a new instance in your OpsWorks layer, there are a number of phases in the process and commands that are automatically executed during each phase. In fact, the installation of the server-side packages and AWS software is managed in Chef. After the AWS recipes are run for each phase, there is an opportunity to run custom recipes.

Writing our own recipes is an entirely separate topic. Fortunately, Amazon has been gracious enough to provide us with a sample cookbook for sending OpsWorks logs to CloudWatch. We will implement the sample cookbook in our stack and execute specific recipes in the cookbook during the *Setup* phase on our instances.

Installing Cookbooks and Recipes

To install the cookbook, we must make changes at the stack level in OpsWorks. By default, custom cookbooks are disabled, so when instances are created, there is no opportunity to add our own customization.

Navigate to OpsWorks and select **Stack** from the Navigation menu. Then, click **Stack Settings** at the top-right corner. Halfway down the page, you'll see a header that reads Configuration Management. The first thing we have to do is change the global configuration to allow custom Chef cookbooks to be installed. Toggle the *Use custom Chef cookbooks* to the **Yes** position. Immediately, you are prompted to choose the location of your cookbooks. While you are free to add as many recipes as you want, they should all be bundled into a single cookbook, stored either in a repository or zip.

The custom cookbook we will use is available at a public URL here: `https://s3.amazonaws.com/aws-cloudwatch/downloads/CloudWatchLogs-Cookbooks.zip`. Select **Http Archive** as your *Repository type* (see Figure 7-33). Even though it's stored in S3, because it's a public file, you can access it over HTTP, like any other zip on the Web.

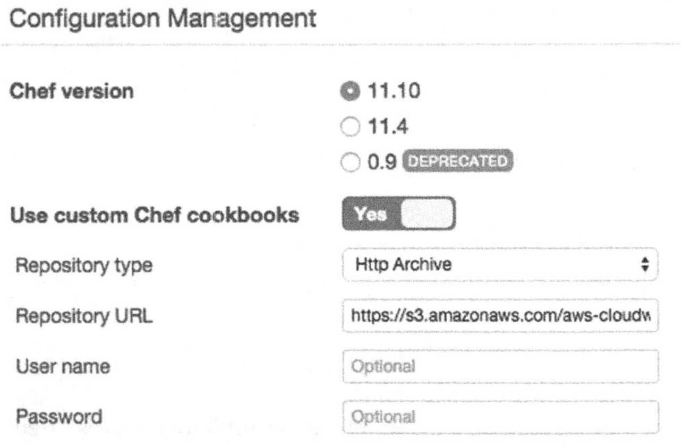

Configuration Management

Chef version	● 11.10
	○ 11.4
	○ 0.9 `DEPRECATED`
Use custom Chef cookbooks	`Yes`
Repository type	Http Archive ⇕
Repository URL	https://s3.amazonaws.com/aws-cloudw
User name	Optional
Password	Optional

Figure 7-33. Enabling custom cookbooks in OpsWorks

Click **Save** at the bottom-right corner. Next, we have to configure our instances to run certain recipes at specific points in their startup process. We do *not* do this at the instance level! Instead, we must head over to **Layers**, where the configuration is done for all instances attached to the Node.js application layer. In the Layers view, you will notice a link to edit recipes under Node.js App Server, as shown in Figure 7-34. Click this to view and edit the recipes for the application layer.

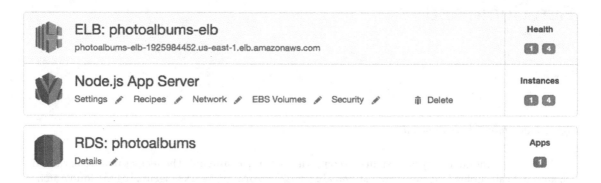

Figure 7-34. *Layers view revisited*

At the top of the recipes view, you'll see the *Built-in Chef Recipes* that are automatically installed in your instances. Each recipe is listed in the format cookbook::recipe and displayed in the phase during which it is executed. These are not editable, as they are controlled by AWS. Under the Custom Chef Recipes header, you can add custom recipes to be executed *after* the built-in recipes for each phase. We must add two recipes to the setup phase. In the text box to the right of *Setup*, input the following:

```
logs::config, logs::install
```

Then click the + button to the right. Your view should look similar to Figure 7-35. Once you've confirmed this, click **Save** at the bottom right.

Custom Chef Recipes ⓘ

Repository URL	https://s3.amazonaws.com/aws-cloudwatch/downloads/CloudWatchLogs-Cookbooks.zip (change)	
2 **Setup**	mycookbook::myrecipe, mycook ➕	Add recipes to the Setup lifecycle event.
	logs::config ✖ logs::install ✖	
Configure	mycookbook::myrecipe, mycook ➕	
Deploy	mycookbook::myrecipe, mycook ➕	
Undeploy	mycookbook::myrecipe, mycook ➕	
Shutdown	mycookbook::myrecipe, mycook ➕	

Figure 7-35. *Custom chef recipes*

Because the recipes are run during the setup phase, we have to trigger this on our running instances. Setup will be automatically run on any instances that are started in the future. If you only have one instance running right now, we can easily run the Setup command on it. Navigate to the Instances view and click the name of your running instance. In the top right, click **Run Command**. Under the Settings header, choose **Setup** from the *Command* drop-down (see Figure 7-36). Then click **Setup** at the bottom right.

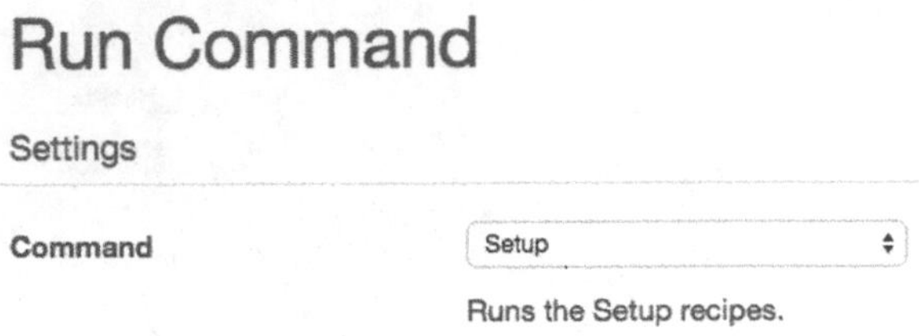

Run Command

Settings

Command   Setup   ⬍

                             Runs the Setup recipes.

Figure 7-36. *Run Setup command*

It will take a moment for your instance to complete the Setup command. The recipes that we're running will automatically upload the logs stored at `/var/log/aws/opsworks/opsworks-agent.log` to CloudWatch Logs when the instance is set up.

CHANGING THE RECIPE

If you're feeling adventurous, you could try and upload a different system log to CloudWatch, instead of the logs selected by default. There is no master list of logs available on your instances. You could try connecting to your instances with SSH and poking around for logs that are interesting to you, then alter the recipe to choose a different log file to upload and deploy the cookbook from your S3 bucket or repository.

CloudWatch Logs

In a minute, your logs will appear in CloudWatch. Let's go check it out. Go to the CloudWatch dashboard and select **Logs** from the left-hand navigation. You should soon see a single log group titled "Photoalbums," as you can see in Figure 7-37.

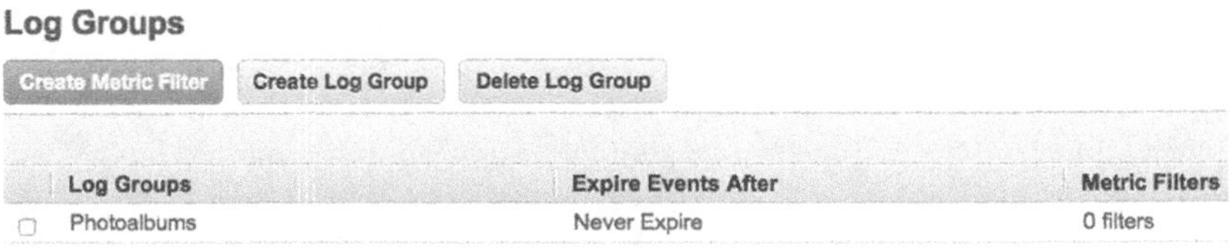

Log Groups

Create Metric Filter	Create Log Group	Delete Log Group

Log Groups	Expire Events After	Metric Filters
☐ Photoalbums	Never Expire	0 filters

Figure 7-37. *CloudWatch log groups*

CloudWatch Logs have their own hierarchy. A single log statement is referred to as an *event*. Log events are stored in a series of *streams*, which are organized into *groups* at the top level. At the group level, you can control your log retention policy, setting the time period after which log events should expire. In most cases, you are probably not going to want to keep the entire log history for your stack. If you click **Never Expire** in the log group view, you can change your retention to a period from one day to ten years.

For the time being, let's reduce our log retention to three days. Click **Never Expire**, and the Edit Retention modal view will appear. Select **3 days** from the drop-down. You'll see a message, shown in Figure 7-38, confirming that old data will be erased. Click **OK** to confirm.

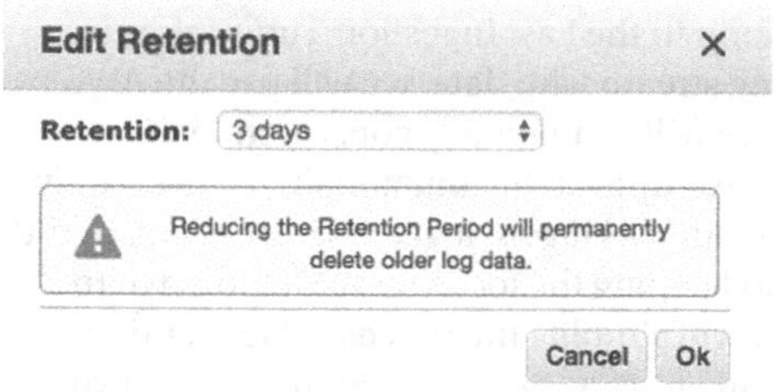

Figure 7-38. Changing CloudWatch log retention

Another interesting feature is called Metric Filters. You can create Metric Filters to automatically scan your logs for specific terms or patterns and use them to create a custom CloudWatch metric. Once your logs are generating quantifiable metrics, you can create a CloudWatch alarm to notify you when the metric has passed a certain threshold.

This is a powerful, if underappreciated, feature. We can automatically scan our logs for specific types of errors and trigger an alarm when the error is detected. This feature could be very useful for application-level logging: we can be notified when an error occurs and quickly respond to it.

Before we set up application-level logging, click the **Photoalbums** log group. Within the group, you should see a log stream for each EC2 instance in your application layer: nodejs-app1, nodejs-app2, etc. You will only see the instances which have run the Setup command after you enabled the custom recipes. If you have load-based and time-based instances in your stack, they will automatically create log streams when they are started.

Storing system-level logs in instance-specific log streams makes sense. If there are problems starting an instance, you would want to review logs specific to that instance. The same cannot be said for application logs. When your application is running on multiple instances, your load balancer will determine which instance handles requests from your users. If one of these users encounters an error, you can't be certain on which instance the error occurred. The simplest solution is to create a separate log stream for our application-level logging, which will consolidate all log events generated in our application.

Application Log Stream

While we could fairly easily create timestamped log streams, we will just keep one master log stream for this example. We will use the three-day log retention policy to keep our logs from becoming bloated with too much historical data.

While you're in the Log Streams view, click the **Create Log Stream** button at the top. A modal window will appear, asking you to name your log stream. Enter the name **application**, as in Figure 7-39, and click **Create Log Stream**.

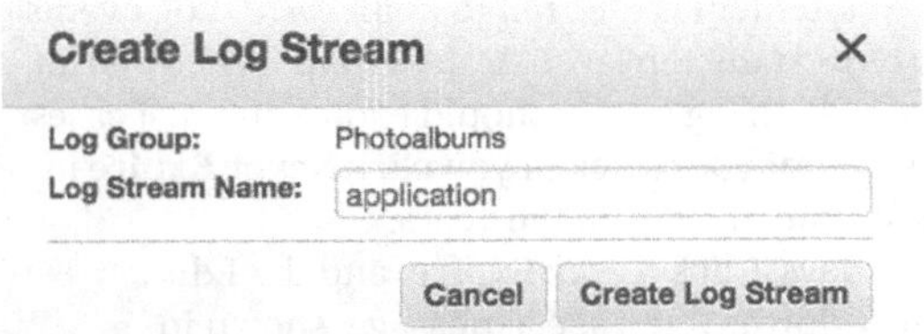

Create Log Stream ✕

Log Group: Photoalbums

Log Stream Name: application

Cancel   Create Log Stream

Figure 7-39. Creating an application log stream

You'll notice that while the other log stream(s) have a timestamp in the Last Ingestion Time column, there is not one for our new log stream. In order to populate our log stream with data, we will use the AWS SDK to post events programmatically. In the following examples, we will be manually constructing the strings that we send to the logs. That being said, this is merely one example of the functionality. It is entirely possible to integrate CloudWatch Logs with other logging libraries, such as log4js, logger, winston, etc. In the interest of minimizing dependency on third-party modules, and in keeping the focus on AWS tools, we're taking the simpler path. However, using an existing logging library will simplify the process of formatting and standardizing your log data. If and when you've chosen a logging library, I highly recommend that you integrate it with CloudWatch Logs based on the following example.

Custom CloudWatch Logging Class (cwlogs)

First, let's create a new class to abstract our use of the AWS SDK. In the /lib directory, create a new file called cwlogs.js. At the top of the file, we have to add the AWS SDK. We'll also store a single object, which we will use to store log events. See Listing 7-2.

Listing 7-2. /lib/cwlogs.js

```
var aws= require('aws-sdk');
var cloudwatchlogs = new aws.CloudWatchLogs({region:'us-east-1'});

var logParams = {
  logGroupName: 'Photoalbums',
  logStreamName: 'application',
  logEvents: []
};
```

The logParams object is hard-coded to the "Photoalbums" log group as well as the "application" log stream. You could easily make these dynamic and post to multiple different log streams or even log groups, if you wanted to keep elaborate and well-organized logs. For example, you could keep one log stream for normal application activity and another for critical errors.

Next, we'll add a public method for creating a log event from a simple string. The function simply creates an object with properties message and timestamp and adds them to the logParams.logEvents array. Add the code in Listing 7-3 to /lib/cwlogs.js.

Listing 7-3. logEvent Function

```
// store event in logs to be sent to CloudWatch Logs
function logEvent(message){
  var eventTimestamp = Math.floor(new Date());
    var newEvent = {
      message: message,
      timestamp: eventTimestamp
  }

  logParams.logEvents.push(newEvent);
}
```

It would be a waste of resources to upload every single log message to CloudWatch at the moment of creation. Instead, we will aggregate the logs as the application is running and upload the logs periodically. How often you upload the logs is entirely up to you. Because we are separating logging events and uploading them, we have a separate publish method for putting the logs. Add Listing 7-4 to the file.

Listing 7-4. putLogs Function

```
function putLogs(){
  if(logParams.logEvents.length > 0){
    getSequenceToken(function(err, token){
      if(token){
        logParams.sequenceToken = token;
      }
      cloudwatchlogs.putLogEvents(logParams, function(err, data) {
        if (err){
        } else {
          logParams.sequenceToken = data.nextSequenceToken;
          logParams.logEvents = [];
        }
      });
    });
  }
}
```

When you use the AWS API, existing log streams have a sequence token. In order to post a log event to the stream, you must first retrieve the next sequence token for that stream. This process is carried out in a private function that we will review shortly. If the token exists, cloudwatchlogs.putLogEvents() uploads the logs to the stream using the logParams object. If this is successful, the logParams.logEvents array is emptied, and the log events in memory are destroyed. If no log events have been uploaded to the stream yet, there will not be a sequence token for that stream, and you don't have to include one when you use putLogEvents.

In order to get the next sequence token, we have to use the method describeLogStreams to retrieve all the log streams for a particular log group. Listing 7-5 shows this in action, in the getNextSequenceToken function. Add this function, and the exports declarations, to make logEvent and putlogs public.

Listing 7-5. getNextSequenceToken Function

```
function getSequenceToken(callback) {
  cloudwatchlogs.describeLogStreams({logGroupName:logParams.logGroupName}, function(err,
data){
    if (err){
      callback(err);
    } else {
      for(var i = 0; i < data.logStreams.length; i++){
        var logStream = data.logStreams[i];
        if(logStream.logStreamName == logParams.logStreamName){
          callback(null, logStream.uploadSequenceToken);
          break;
        }
      }
    }
  });
}

exports.logEvent = logEvent;
exports.putLogs = putLogs;
```

Integrating cwlogs

Now it's time to start adding some basic logging to the code base! We'll just run through a simple example. Suppose that you want to log the workflow for a specific route in your web service, printing a few values to the console. Open /routes/users.js, where we will add some logging to the GET /users/user/:user route. First, include the cwlogs class at the top of your file, as follows:

```
var cwlogs  = require('./../lib/cwlogs');
```

Locate the router.get(/user/:user) function, where we will add a couple of log statements. Replace the function with Listing 7-6.

Listing 7-6. getUser with Logging Enabled

```
router.get('/user/:user', function(req, res) {
  var params= {
    username: req.param('user')
  }
  var eventMessage = 'GET /users/user/' + params.username;
  cwlogs.logEvent(eventMessage);
  model.getUser(params, function(err, obj){
    if(err){
      res.status(500).send({error: 'An unknown server error has occurred!'});
    } else {
      var eventMessage = 'getUser ' + params.username + ' ' + JSON.stringify(obj);
      cwlogs.logEvent(eventMessage);
      res.send(obj);
    }
  });
  cwlogs.putLogs();
});
```

We're only logging a couple of things here: the method and path of the request and the object retrieved from `model.getUser()`. Because you can pass any string to `cwlogs`, it's flexible enough for you to decide what works. At the end of the route, `cwlogs.putLogs()` uploads the logs to CloudWatch. There should be only two entries, but you could easily add more, including a few in the users model.

Time to fire it up! Commit these changes to your repository, then head back to OpsWorks and select your stack. Choose **Deployments** from the Navigation menu and click **Deploy an App** at the top-right corner. Add some deployment notes, if you wish, and click **Deploy** at the bottom-right corner. Once your deployment has finished, go ahead and make a GET request to /users/user/[*your username*].

You should get the same JSON response you were getting before, but this time, some data was added to your CloudWatch Logs. Return to CloudWatch and select **Logs** from the navigation. When you click the **Photoalbums** log group, you should see that the *application* log stream now has a value in the Last Ingestion Time column. That's a good sign! Click **application** to view the log stream. You should see something like Figure 7-40.

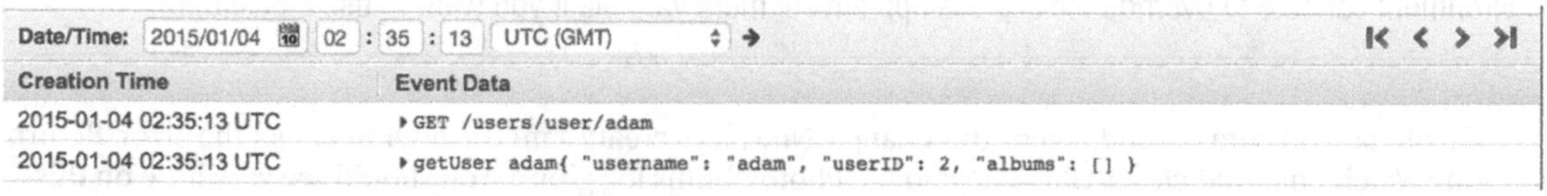

Date/Time: 2015/01/04 📅 02 : 35 : 13 UTC (GMT) ⬦ ➜		K ‹ › ›I
Creation Time	**Event Data**	
2015-01-04 02:35:13 UTC	▸ GET /users/user/adam	
2015-01-04 02:35:13 UTC	▸ getUser adam{ "username": "adam", "userID": 2, "albums": [] }	

Figure 7-40. *Viewing the CloudWatch Log Stream*

Hooray! Have application logs ever been so exciting?

Exception Handling

Let's take this to the next logical step, which is to upload exceptions to CloudWatch Logs. Once we do this, we can create a metric filter and generate an alarm, informing us that an exception has occurred in the application.

Instead of trying to break the app, let's just force an error to occur. Add the following code to /routes/users.js:

```
router.get('/error', function(req, res) {
  throw new Error("[ERROR] This is an intentional error");
});
```

This is purely for testing purposes, and you should remove it as soon as we're done. Next, we will add `cwlogs` to the Express middleware. Open /server.js and, once again, include `cwlogs` at the top.

```
var cwlogs = require('./lib/cwlogs');
```

Then, locate the middleware function that looks like the following:

```
app.use(function(err, req, res, next) {
});
```

For any error that makes it to this function, we will send the error message to CloudWatch. Change the function to be like Listing 7-7.

Listing 7-7. `server.js` error-handling Middleware

```
app.use(function(err, req, res, next) {
  cwlogs.logEvent(err.message);
  cwlogs.putLogs();
  res.status(err.status || 500);
  res.send({
    message: err.message,
    error: {}
  });
});
```

■ **Note**   You may have development and production versions of this middleware. You can use the OpsWorks environment variable to override the Express app environment variable if you want to use this feature.

Go ahead and commit and deploy this change. Now, let's create a metric filter to detect the error. Return to CloudWatch Logs and click **0 filters** next to the Photoalbums log group. You should see very little on this page aside from a button to Add Metric Filter. Click this.

In the Define Logs Metric Filter view, you can create a text pattern to match your metric filter. We'll create a simple one, which counts any log event with the text "[ERROR]." In the *Filter Pattern* field, enter the text **"[ERROR]"** (including the double quotes), as in Figure 7-41. If you are trying to create a filter that catches existing log data, there's a handy tool on the page for testing your filter patterns. Click **Assign Metric** to proceed.

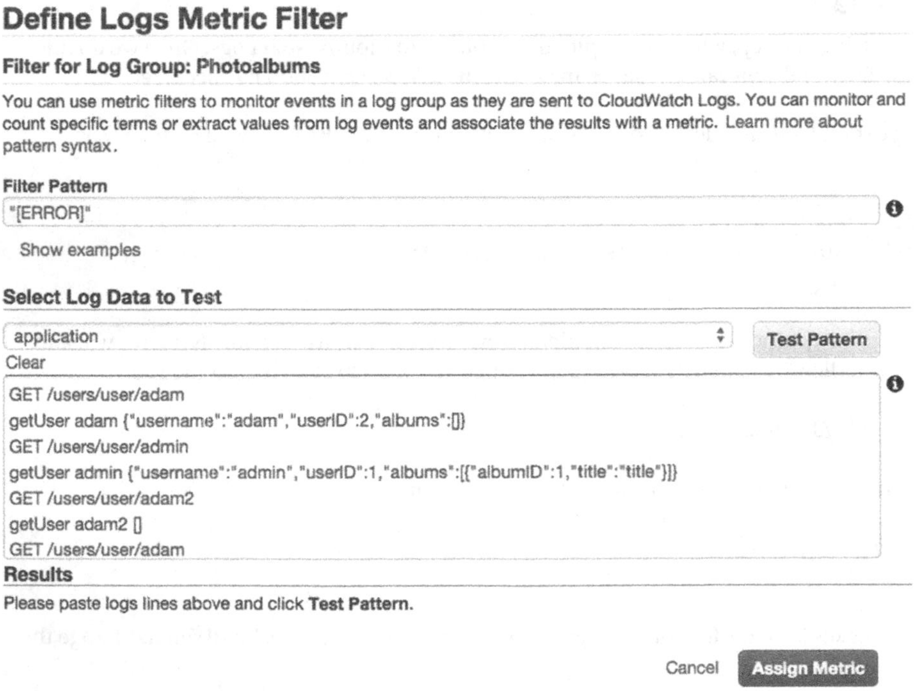

Define Logs Metric Filter

Filter for Log Group: Photoalbums

You can use metric filters to monitor events in a log group as they are sent to CloudWatch Logs. You can monitor and count specific terms or extract values from log events and associate the results with a metric. Learn more about pattern syntax.

Filter Pattern

| "[ERROR]" | ❶ |

Show examples

Select Log Data to Test

| application | ⬍ | **Test Pattern** |

Clear

```
GET /users/user/adam
getUser adam {"username":"adam","userID":2,"albums":[]}
GET /users/user/admin
getUser admin {"username":"admin","userID":1,"albums":[{"albumID":1,"title":"title"}]}
GET /users/user/adam2
getUser adam2 []
GET /users/user/adam
```
❶

Results

Please paste logs lines above and click **Test Pattern**.

Cancel   **Assign Metric**

Figure 7-41. *Create metric filter*

In the next view, you can name your filter as well as the metric which it filters. The filter name is useful for managing metric filters if you have a lot of them, whereas the metric name is the name of the value actually being counted in CloudWatch. You can leave the *Filter Name* as is, but be sure to set the *Metric Name* to something such as **UncaughtErrors**, as in Figure 7-42. Then, click **Create Filter**.

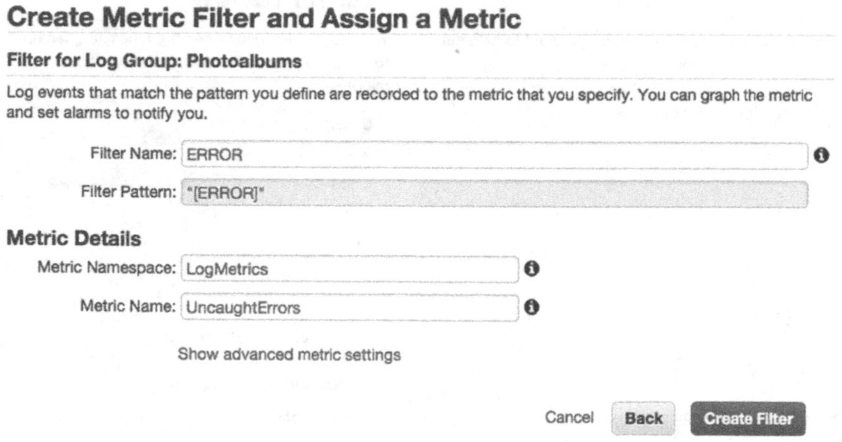

Create Metric Filter and Assign a Metric

Filter for Log Group: Photoalbums

Log events that match the pattern you define are recorded to the metric that you specify. You can graph the metric and set alarms to notify you.

Filter Name: `ERROR` ⓘ

Filter Pattern: `"[ERROR]"`

Metric Details

Metric Namespace: `LogMetrics` ⓘ

Metric Name: `UncaughtErrors` ⓘ

Show advanced metric settings

Cancel   **Back**   **Create Filter**

Figure 7-42. Filter and metric names

You will see only your new filter in the Filters view, along with a success message (see Figure 7-43). From here, you can edit or delete the filter or, more important, create an alarm based on the metric.

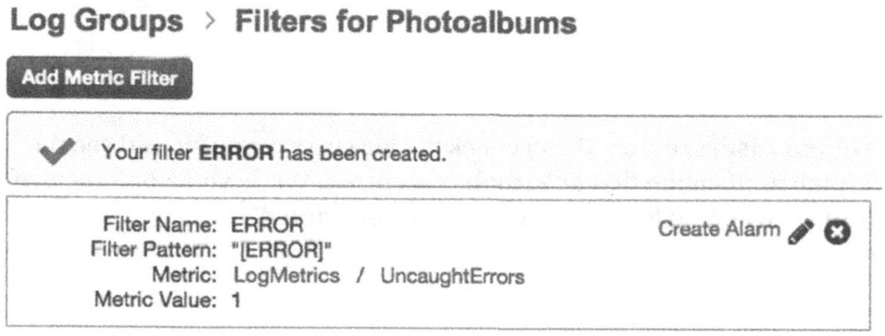

Log Groups > Filters for Photoalbums

Add Metric Filter

✔ Your filter **ERROR** has been created.

Filter Name: ERROR   Create Alarm ✏ ✖
Filter Pattern: "[ERROR]"
Metric: LogMetrics / UncaughtErrors
Metric Value: 1

Figure 7-43. Photoalbums filters

Click **Create Alarm** to create a new CloudWatch alarm for this metric. The idea for this alarm is that anytime an exception is thrown, the alarm will go off. As such, we want the alarm to go off whenever **UncaughtErrors >= 1**. Name the alarm **Photoalbums - Uncaught Error Occurred** and make the alarm send a notification to the **PhotoalbumsAlarm** list, as shown in Figure 7-44.

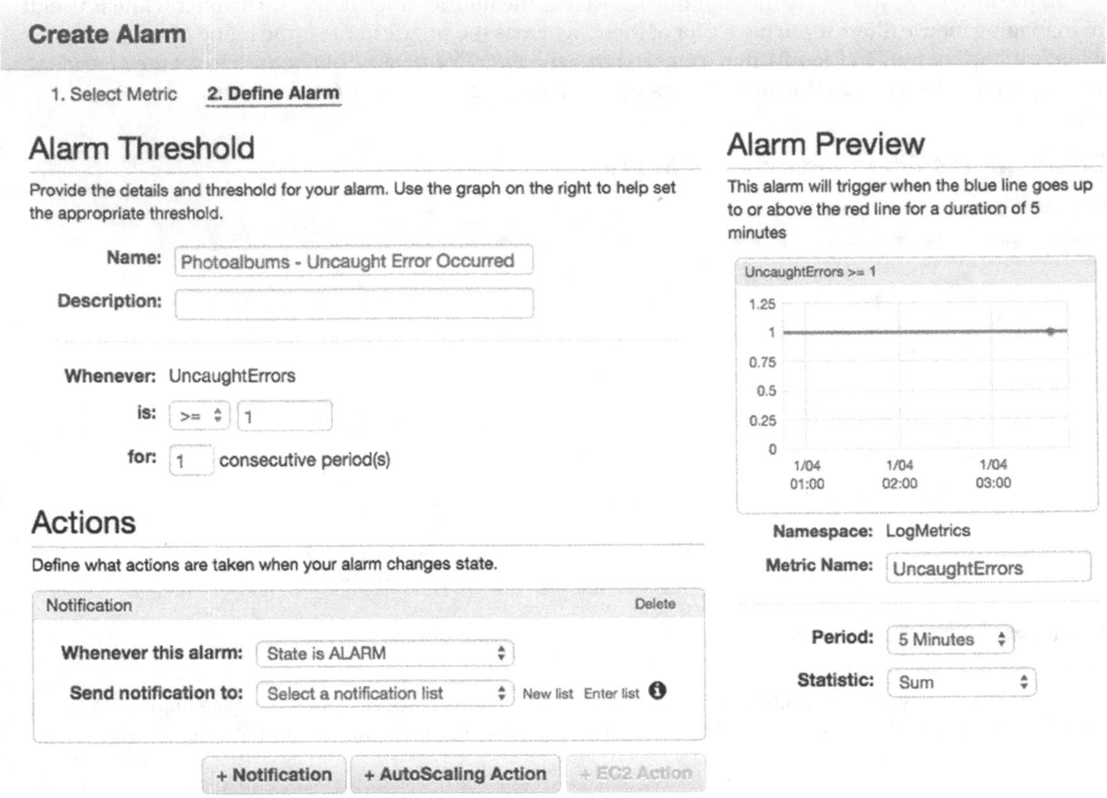

Figure 7-44. *Metric filter alarm*

Click **Create Alarm**, then make a GET to /users/error. If you check the log stream, you should see the error, and you should also receive an e-mail notification that an error has occurred. While you won't receive an e-mail copy of the error, you know exactly where to look to see what the error printed!

Summary

From here, there are a *lot* of different ways you can go. You could change the error logging to record the error stack (hint: *err.stack* instead of *err.message*), or you can rework cwlogs to use your favorite logging library. You could also create multiple log streams for different types of information, depending on how organized you want to be.

At the beginning of this chapter, you had very little insight into how to monitor, maintain, and scale our application stack. By the end, you have servers auto-scaling according to our rules, alarms monitoring a variety of points of failure, and multi-instance application logs saving in CloudWatch. One of the challenges in presenting this chapter has been staying on the rails with the core lessons when there are so many possibilities!

In the next and final chapter, I will be focusing on security and, finally, adding authentication to the application. You probably noticed that anyone can just walk right in and start uploading content. Like the other lessons, our security measures will be a combination of coding and putting AWS services to work.

■ ■ ■

CHAPTER 8

Securing the Application

In the final chapter, we will be implementing a number of security measures in our application. There are, in fact, a number of disparate tasks we will carry out under the "security" blanket. First, we will provision an SSL certificate for our domain, then we can restrict sensitive interactions between the user and application to HTTPS. We can subsequently implement secure login for our application's users and store passwords in encrypted fields in the database.

While this may seem like a lot of tasks to carry out, there is some good news. So far, we've been diligent about security. Let's quickly review some of the security measures we've already taken.

- Access credentials are stored only in OpsWorks, and not in the source code.

- The various roles and users in our application only have permission to use the services they need, although you could take this a step further and restrict IAM permissions to specific ARN IDs (a suggestion alluded to earlier).

- Our database only accepts connections from the OpsWorks instances and our local IP address.

We've already been pretty diligent about best practices, and it really wasn't that difficult. Now we just have to ensure that users can connect to our application securely and make sure their credentials are properly encrypted.

Using HTTPS

You may have noticed the tiny padlock icon in the corner of your browser, next to the address bar (see Figure 8-1), and wondered what it meant. This padlock has become a universal sign that your connection to the host occurs over HTTPS instead of the unencrypted HTTP.

Figure 8-1. *The padlock in the address bar indicates an HTTPS connection*

You can even click the padlock to see more details about the SSL certificate used to verify the connection to the host. We will be adding this layer of security to our application, allowing users to connect over HTTPS and signing the connection with a trusted certificate.

When we use the HTTPS protocol for communication with our application, we are using a method of encrypted transport that is verified by trusted third parties known as *certificate authorities*. Encrypting communication with HTTPS is a science unto itself.

We are going to use HTTPS to encrypt traffic between the user (client) and CloudFront and between CloudFront and the load balancer. This means that data is safely encrypted between the client and the load balancer. The application will begin using session cookies, connecting the user's session to a specific instance through the load balancer. We will also restrict HTTP requests to the instances, so that they are only accepted from the ELB. Because the user can only create a session by connecting through the load balancer, the odds of a user's session being hijacked are at best theoretical.

SECURITY IS A SHARED RESPONSIBILITY

Occasionally, a vulnerability will be discovered in the SSL protocol, and AWS quickly deploys the required patches and notifies its customers via e-mail. So, you can rest assured that as vulnerabilities are discovered, AWS will take immediate action to neutralize the threat.

As an AWS customer, your responsibility lies largely in adhering to its recommended best practices for security. We have done so thus far, by restricting IAM roles and users only to the permissions they need, and by minimizing the risk of access keys and credentials being exposed.

Put another way, AWS is responsible for security *of the cloud*, and you're responsible for security *in the cloud*. Of course, SSL is one of many moving parts that AWS maintains on your behalf. For more information, you should review the *AWS Shared Security Model* at `http://aws.amazon.com/compliance/shared-responsibility-model/`.

It's worth noting that communication between the EC2 instances and the load balancer is *not* gaining an extra layer of encryption. Adding this extra layer of encryption is known as back-end authentication, and it is beyond the scope of a book for beginners. The lessons in this book will give you a secure application, but if you have specific security compliance standards to adhere to, you should review those protocols thoroughly.

From the time we've spent in the AWS Console, it should be clear that HTTPS is a supported transport method for a variety of AWS services. However, we've put this feature to the side until the very end, so we can implement the protocol across the board. Because we are serving content from our own domain, we must upload a valid SSL certificate for that domain to AWS. Remember that requests to our application first pass through CloudFront and our ELB and are altered by these services. Supporting SSL will require that we reconfigure both services.

Of course, storing and validating SSL certificates falls under the jurisdiction of Identity and Access Management. Don't bother looking for an SSL certificate tab in IAM, however, as there isn't one! Once we have a valid certificate, we will have to use the AWS command-line interface (CLI) to upload it to IAM.

SSL Certificate Generation

First and foremost, we have to generate and sign an SSL certificate for our domain. This is a multistep process, during some of which you will be on your own. I've done my best to keep the lessons in the AWS Console, where it's easy to see what's being done, and to avoid reliance on third-party tools. Unfortunately, to complete this section, we must use a number of command-line tools. Let us now go on a journey of installing software.

During the process, you will have to obtain a signed certificate from a Certificate Authority. You will have to walk through the steps required by the Certificate Authority, and I can provide a general description of the steps you'll have to take. We'll assume that you have the ability to verify the domain you're using for your application, as this will be required in some capacity when you get your certificate signed. For the next few steps, you'll have to use both a web browser and command-line interface. Open Terminal or its equivalent to begin.

Installing OpenSSL

The first step is to install OpenSSL on your machine. OpenSSL is an open-source cryptographic tool that we will use for generating a private key and certificate signing request (CSR). Your machine may already have it installed. Find out by typing **openssl** on the command line. If this opens an OpenSSL prompt instead of throwing an error, you're ready to begin.

If you don't have OpenSSL installed, you can download it for Mac/Linux here: www.openssl.org/source. On Windows, you can download a binary here: www.openssl.org/related/binaries.html.

■ **Note**   If you have trouble installing OpenSSL, try the wiki:
http://wiki.openssl.org/index.php/Compilation_and_Installation.

Creating a Key and CSR

Once you've completed the installation, you must generate a private key and corresponding certificate signing request, or CSR. In the command-line interface, input the following command:

```
openssl req -new -newkey rsa:2048 -nodes -keyout photoalbums.key -out photoalbums.csr
```

Instead of photoalbums.key and photoalbums.csr, you can use a file name that pertains to the domain we're obtaining a certificate for. In the CLI, you're going to be prompted to fill out a number of questions. You'll fill each one out and press **Return** to continue.

```
Country Name (2 letter code) [AU]:
State or Province Name (full name) [Some-State]:
Locality Name (e.g., city) []:
Organization Name (e.g., company) [Internet Widgits Pty Ltd]:
Organizational Unit Name (e.g., section) []:
Common Name (e.g., server FQDN or YOUR name) []:
Email Address []:
```

Most of those fields are self-explanatory. Go ahead and input your country, state/province, locality, and organization info. In the *Common Name* field, input your domain name without the www. And definitely use your e-mail address.

After you've completed these, you'll be prompted to enter optional fields. You should press **Return** for each of these, without entering any information.

```
Please enter the following 'extra' attributes to be sent with your certificate request
A challenge password []:
An optional company name []:
```

You should now have a .key and .csr in the directory in which you're working. Next, we have to request a certificate from a Certificate Authority.

Request Certificate

We have to submit our key and certificate signing request to a Certificate Authority. Which provider you use is entirely up to you. Amazon makes no recommendations, instead directing users to a partial list here: www.dmoz.org/Computers/Security/Public_Key_Infrastructure/PKIX/Tools_and_Services/Third_Party_Certificate_Authorities/.

It's often easier to use a vendor that sells certificates signed by a Certificate Authority. Depending on the company you used to register your domain, it may also offer certificate services. Alternatively, NameCheap is a reputable vendor, and you can get a certificate signed by Comodo through them for about $9/year. Using NameCheap takes about ten minutes. If you just want a valid certificate for development, this may be the path of least resistance.

At the SSL certificate vendor, you will first select a certificate package/price. Once you've paid for it, you begin the process of requesting the certificate and validating the domain. You will be asked to provide a CSR. To do this, you'll have to open the .csr in a plain-text editor. The contents should look something like the following:

```
-----BEGIN CERTIFICATE REQUEST-----
FYvKlArPvGZYWNmCMeNDjwa3pxtHWVu6CeXsXUsU4Axwaqtc60VMofEoQCqfwCi+
CDLLoSnwMQIDAQABoAAwDQYJKoZIhvcNAQEFBQADggEBAAzFDJs+FNdUgvNmdsBO
5qeETlUtIHyw9rDLSwF/wvMWS/86uSyuq3wR7GiDPIYSjs5dIWqmAleyroKRaMZd
FzAVBgNVBAMTDmNsb3VkeWV5ZXMubmVOMRwwGgYJKoZIhvcNAQkBFg1hZGFtQGNy
5qeETlUtIHyw9rDLSwF/wvMWS/86uSyuq3wR7GiDPIYSjs5dIWqmAleyroKRaMZd
PyrafU/eidGboCv83NYMSUUyJOxDVCbIe4EoJUnpOmzu7eO7vZDbB5cZDCaJWpuo
15tf9361gLcJrKxwiHuPffipf9vv4qoM1jwdNgKtUNGSq11FdiYqlfXR87iSTMEI
nNuScyAUWgX3yXjeGhCszUIfNMbGEHL3oOKsWvpYP/Kj+ESr5DDrNujHol9n3CQz
CDLLoSnwMQIDAQABoAAwDQYJKoZIhvcNAQEFBQADggEBAAzFDJs+FNdUgvNmdsBO
5qeETlUtIHyw9rDLSwF/wvMWS/86uSyuq3wR7GiDPIYSjs5dIWqmAleyroKRaMZd
PyrafU/eidGboCv83NYMSUUyJOxDVCbIe4EoJUnpOmzu7eO7vZDbB5cZDCaJWpuo
15tf9361gLcJrKxwiHuPffipf9vv4qoM1jwdNgKtUNGSq11FdiYqlfXR87iSTMEI
5qeETlUtIHyw9rDLSwF/wvMWS/86uSyuq3wR7GiDPIYSjs5dIWqmAleyroKRaMZd
PyrafU/eidGboCv83NYMSUUyJOxDVCbIe4EoJUnpOmzu7eO7vZDbB5cZDCaJWpuo
15tf9361gLcJrKxwiHuPffipf9vv4qoM1jwdNgKtUNGSq11FdiYqlfXR87iSTMEI
SevmFhb6EkqLe1sEeDODqKj/FcDZYYjISNEe6ftwPGdBEivRXJpHIH/11wQRQuSw
7ws=
-----END CERTIFICATE REQUEST-----
```

Select the entire contents of the file and copy-paste into the field where prompted. You may also be asked to select a *Webserver Type*. If you have the option, choose **Apache+OpenSSL**. If the certificate is valid, the domain name will be automatically extracted from the Common Name you entered when you generated the CSR. The Certificate Authority will then attempt to validate the domain. To do so, it may send an e-mail with a verification code to the e-mail address registered as the admin of the domain. For reference, you can find this by typing **whois yourdomain.com** on the command line and finding the Admin Email in the response. You may also be able to select an e-mail address at the domain for which you're requesting a certificate. In any case, expect a verification process to occur, most likely over e-mail.

When your certificate request is approved, you will receive from the Certificate Authority a few files with the extension .crt. They should be named logically and otherwise labeled for you. One of these files is the Root CA certificate; another is your SSL certificate, which should be named something such as *yourdomain*_com.crt. In addition to these, you will have one or more intermediate CA certificates.

Before we can use these with AWS services, we have to address a compatibility problem. AWS only accepts certificates in the X.509 PEM format. We can use OpenSSL to convert our certificates to PEM. Execute the following command in the CLI and press **Return**:

openssl rsa -in photoalbums.key -text > aws-private.pem

This is the private key, generated on your machine, which will be uploaded to AWS. Next, let's convert the public key, which was provided by the Certificate Authority. Input the following command, replacing yourdomain_com with the actual file name of your certificate:

```
openssl x509 -inform PEM -in yourdomain_com.crt > aws-public.pem
```

Now you have your public and private key. The last file that we need is the certificate *chain*. Without getting too much into the details (on which I am not an authority), there are two types of certificate authorities: *root* and *intermediate*. Each certificate is issued to an authority by a trusted authority, forming a trust chain from our domain, through the intermediate CAs, to the root Certificate Authority. The certificate chain is generated by stitching together certificates from intermediate certificate authorities in order, reflecting this trust chain. We have to create the certificate chain in X.509 PEM format, just like the public and private keys.

When you received your certificates, they should have been accompanied by an ordered listing, similar to the following, but with naming conventions dependent on the Certificate Authority you used:

- Root CA Certificate—AddTrustExternalCARoot.crt

- Intermediate CA Certificate—CANameAddTrustCA.crt

- Intermediate CA Certificate—CANameDomainValidationSecureServerCA.crt

- Your PositiveSSL Certificate—yourdomain_com.crt

When we create the certificate chain, we will be taking note of the order of the intermediate CA Certificates and *reversing them*. On the command line, input the following:

(openssl x509 -inform PEM -in CANameDomainValidationSecureServerCA.crt; openssl x509 -inform PEM -in CANameAddTrustCA.crt) >> aws-certchain.pem

To be clear, the second intermediate CA certificate is first, and the first one is second. They are being combined into a single .pem file named aws-certchain.pem. If you open the file, it will look something like the following (only much longer):

```
-----BEGIN CERTIFICATE-----
MIIGCDCCA/CgAwIBAgIQKy5u6tl1NmwUim7bo3yMBzANBgkqhkiG9w0BAQwFADCB
hTELMAkGA1UEBhMCR0IxGzAZBgNVBAgTEkdyZWF0ZXIgTWFuY2hlc3RlcjEQMA4G
A1UEBxMHU2FsZm9yZDEaMBgGA1UEChMRQO09NTORPIENBIExpbWl0ZWQxKzApBgNV
bS9DT01PRE9SU0FEZXJ0aWZpY2F0aW9uQXV0aG9yaXR5LmNybDBxBggrBgEFBQcB
0fxQ8ANAe4hZ7Q7drNJ3gjTcBpUC2JD5Leo31RpgOGcg19hCC0Wvgmje3WYkN5Ap
lBlGGSW4gNfL1IYoakRwJiNiqZ+Gb7+6kHDSVneFeO/qJakXzlByjAA6quPbYzSf
+AZxAeKCINT+b72x
-----END CERTIFICATE-----
```

```
-----BEGIN CERTIFICATE-----
MIIFdDCCBFygAwIBAgIQJ2buVutJ846r13Ci/ITeIjANBgkqhkiG9w0BAQwFADBv
MQswCQYDVQQGEwJTRTEUMBIGA1UEChMLQWRkVHJ1c3QgQUIxJjAkBgNVBAsTHUFk
ZFRydXN0IEV4dGVybmFsIFRUUUCBOZXR3b3JrMSIwIAYDVQQDExlBZGRUcnVzdCBF
VQQDEyJDTO1PRE8gUlNBIENlcnRpZmljYXRpb24gQXV0aG9yaXR5MIICIjANBgkq
hkiG9w0BAQEFAAOCAg8AMIICCgKCAgEAkehUktIKVrGsDSTdxc9EZ3SZKzejfSNw
B5a6SE2Q8pTIqXOi6wZ7I53eovNNVZ96YUWYGGjHXkBrI/V5eu+MtWuLt29G9Hvx
PUsE2JOAWVrgQSQdso8VYFhH2+9uRvOV9dlfmrPb2LjkQLPNlzmuhbsdjrzch5vR
pu/xO28QOG8=
-----END CERTIFICATE-----
```

Now we're ready to use the certificates!

The AWS Command-Line Interface (CLI)

As mentioned previously, there is no SSL view in the IAM dashboard. Instead, we have to use the AWS command-line interface to upload our certificates to AWS. To do this, we must install and configure the AWS CLI tool on your machine. Instructions for installing AWS CLI on your operating system are available here: http://docs.aws.amazon.com/cli/latest/userguide/installing.html.

Follow the steps provided by Amazon, and you should have no problems. You now have the capability to execute any of the commands we've carried out in the console, with a command-line interface. Before we begin using it, we have to be sure we have permissions configured properly.

Configuring Permissions

We can use our **photoadmin** IAM user and generate an access key for use with the command-line interface. Navigate to IAM in the AWS Console and select **Users** from the left-hand navigation.

In Chapter 1, we made the photoadmin user a member of the *PhotoAdmins* group. The user does not have any unique policies but, rather, inherits permissions from the IAM group. We want to use this user to upload the SSL certificate to IAM, but giving the entire group full IAM access seems a bit extreme. We can temporarily grant this user additional permissions at the User level.

Select **photoadmin** from the users list. In the user detail view, click **Attach Policy**. Once again, you will be selecting a managed policy. Scroll down (or filter the list by typing **iam** in the **Policy Type** filter field) until you find *IAMFullAccess* and click the checkbox (see Figure 8-2).

Attach Policy

You can have up to two managed policies attached.

Filter:	Policy Type ▾	iam			Showing 2 results
		Policy Name ⬍	Attached Entities ⬍	Creation Time ⬍	Edited Time ⬍
☑	📖	IAMFullAccess	0	2015-02-06 13:40 EST	2015-02-06 13:40 EST
☐	📖	IAMReadOnlyAccess	0	2015-02-06 13:40 EST	2015-02-06 13:40 EST

Figure 8-2. IAM Full Access policy

Click **Attach Policy to attach it and return to the user detail view.** When you return to the user detail view, you will see that our user now has policies at both the User and Group levels, as in Figure 8-3. While you cannot edit the group policy from here, you can easily edit or remove the user policy.

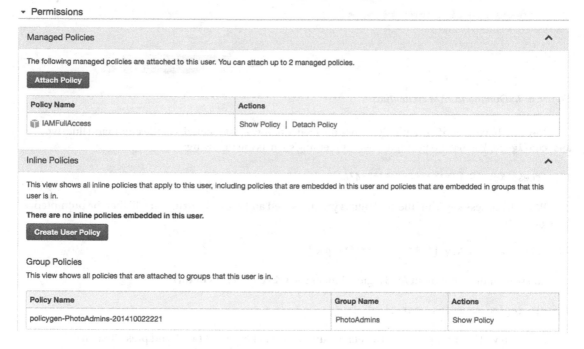

Figure 8-3. *IAM user and group policies*

If you're curious, you can click **Show Policy** to review the policy statement. It should look something like the following code.

```
{
  "Version": "2012-10-17",
  "Statement": [
    {
      "Effect": "Allow",
      "Action": "iam:*",
      "Resource": "*"
    }
  ]
}
```

Now that the user has the correct policy, we must generate an access key. Under the Security Credentials header, click **Manage Access Keys**. A modal window will appear with a Create Access Key button. Click it, and the modal will update, prompting you to download a copy of the credentials. This will be your only chance to do so (see Figure 8-4). Click **Download Credentials** to store a local copy.

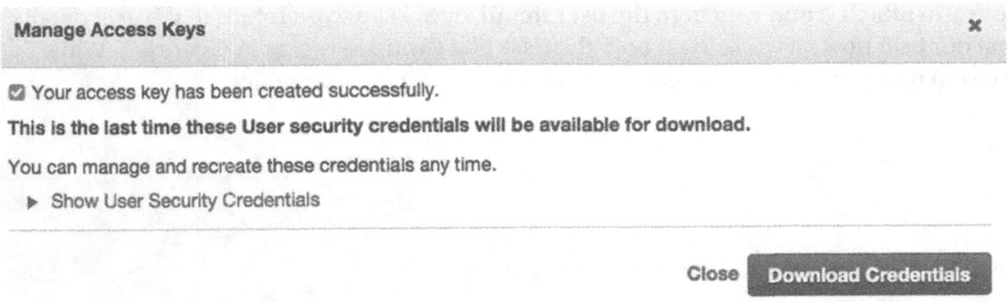

Manage Access Keys ✖

☑ Your access key has been created successfully.

This is the last time these User security credentials will be available for download.

You can manage and recreate these credentials any time.

▶ Show User Security Credentials

Close   **Download Credentials**

Figure 8-4. Download IAM credentials

Next, we have to configure the CLI to use the credentials we just created. On the command line, type **aws configure**. You will be prompted with something such as the following:

```
AWS Access Key ID [***************4ZAA]:
```

Paste the access key from the credentials you just saved and press **Return**. You will then be prompted for your secret.

```
AWS Secret Access Key [***************FpdG]:
```

You will input your default AWS region. Enter **us-east-1** and press **Return**.

```
Default region name [us-east-1]:
```

Last, you will be prompted to set a default output format. Leave this blank and press **Return**.

```
Default output format [None]:
```

Uploading the SSL Certificates

All of this configuration has been leading up to the execution of a single command. In one line, we will upload the certificates and make them accessible in CloudFront. It's important that the certificate path is set to CloudFront, as at this stage, all requests to our application go through CloudFront. It is the gatekeeper of our application. Make sure your .pem files are in the same directory as you're working, and enter the following command:

aws iam upload-server-certificate --certificate-body file://aws-public.pem --private-key file://aws-private.pem --certificate-chain file://aws-certchain.pem --server-certificate-name *yourdomain*_com --path /cloudfront/www.*yourdomain*.com/

There are some nuances to this. It's important that your –path parameter is set to /cloudfront/www.*yourdomain*.com/, using your domain, and *including* the trailing slash at the end. The –server-certificate-name value (shown as yourdomain_com in the command) should simply be your domain. The file:// paths are relative, but if you have to use an absolute path, use file:///.

When you press **Return**, you will either get an error or a JSON response like the following:

```
{
    "ServerCertificateMetadata": {
        "ServerCertificateId": "ASCAJLNQBYPFYEYN5BQNU",
        "ServerCertificateName": "yourdomain_com",
        "Expiration": "2016-01-05T00:03:54Z",
        "Path": "/cloudfront/www.yourdomain.com/",
        "Arn": "arn:aws:iam::061246224738:server-certificate/cloudfront/
        www.yourdomain.com/yourdomain_com",
        "UploadDate": "2015-01-05T01:04:36.593Z"
    }
}
```

Enabling HTTPS in CloudFront

Congratulations are in order—that was not a simple task. Now that we have a valid SSL certificate, we have to go through our infrastructure and enable it. The first place we must do this is in CloudFront. You're done with the command line. Navigate to CloudFront in the AWS Console and select your distribution. In the General tab, click **Edit**.

We will have to enable a custom SSL certificate at the distribution level. Next to the SSL Certificate header, you'll see that the Default CloudFront Certificate is selected. Switch to **Custom SSL Certificate** and select yours from the drop-down (see Figure 8-5).

Figure 8-5. *CloudFront custom SSL certificate*

When you select a custom SSL certificate, you have to determine whether you will support all clients or only those that support Server Name Indication. To support all clients, you will have to request access, and you will pay substantially more than for SNI-enabled clients only. Unless your application has specific reasons for supporting all clients, it's unlikely you would need to incur this extra expense. This topic is a bit outside the scope of this book, so go with the latter option, unless you have a specific reason for supporting All Clients.

Click **Yes, Edit** at the bottom right. As we know, it takes several minutes for changes to CloudFront distribution settings to propagate. You can keep an eye on your distribution's status field, waiting for it to change from *InProgress* to *Deployed*. When that's complete, visit your Hello World page in the browser, making sure to add **https://** before the URL. You should now see that comforting little padlock icon (refer to Figure 8-1) next to the address!

While it is now possible to connect to our domain via HTTPS, it is optional at this point. You can see this in action by entering your URL in the address bar of your browser with just http instead of https. The padlock will disappear! For the time being, this may be OK for some parts of our application. However, there are some paths for which we will require a secure session, if the user is to interact with our application. If you think back to the lessons on CloudFront, you'll remember that our distribution is not forwarding cookies to the load balancer.

In your distribution, select the **Behaviors** tab. You will see, as in Figure 8-6, that the *Viewer Protocol Policy* for all behaviors is set to *HTTP and HTTPS*.

	Precedence	Path Pattern	Origin	Viewer Protocol Policy
☐	1	/users/*	ELB-photoalbums-elb-1925984452	HTTP and HTTPS
☐	2	/albums/*	ELB-photoalbums-elb-1925984452	HTTP and HTTPS
☐	3	/photos/search	ELB-photoalbums-elb-1925984452	HTTP and HTTPS
☐	4	/photos/*	ELB-photoalbums-elb-1925984452	HTTP and HTTPS
☐	5	/uploads/*	S3-photoalbums-cdn	HTTP and HTTPS
☐	6	Default (*)	ELB-photoalbums-elb-1925984452	HTTP and HTTPS

Figure 8-6. *CloudFront behaviors—Viewer Protocol Policy*

We're going to have to support some additional behaviors for requests that require an HTTPS connection and session cookie. These are the routes that we need to restrict:

- /users/login
- /users/register
- /users/logout
- /albums/upload
- /albums/delete
- /photos/upload
- /photos/delete

It would be nice if we didn't have to create seven new behaviors. See any patterns? I think we can accomplish our goals with the following five paths:

- /users/login
- /users/register
- /users/logout
- /*/upload
- /*/delete

Create all five behaviors with the same rules. The *Origin* should be the **ELB**, and *Viewer Protocol Policy* should be set to **HTTPS Only**. *Allowed HTTP Methods* should be **GET, HEAD, OPTIONS, PUT, POST, PATCH, DELETE**. *Forward Headers* and *Forward Cookies* should be set to **All** (see Figure 8-7).

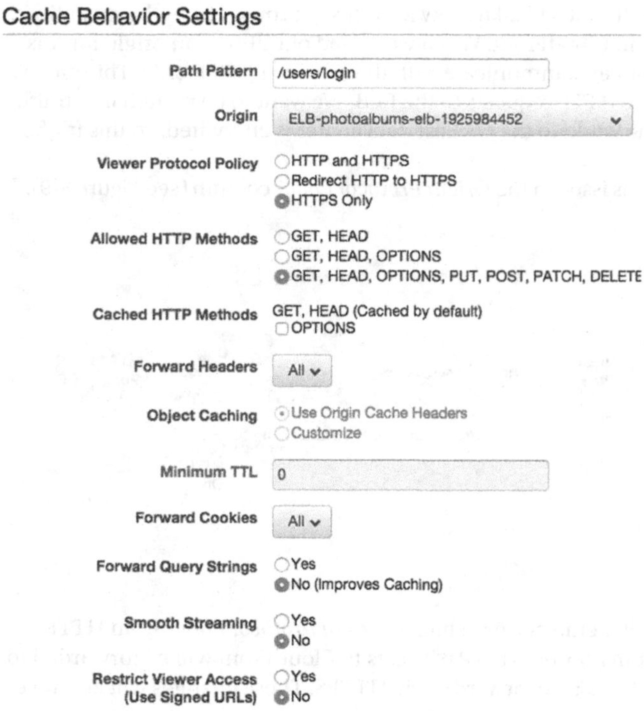

Cache Behavior Settings

Path Pattern	/users/login
Origin	ELB-photoalbums-elb-1925984452 ⌄
Viewer Protocol Policy	○ HTTP and HTTPS ○ Redirect HTTP to HTTPS ● HTTPS Only
Allowed HTTP Methods	○ GET, HEAD ○ GET, HEAD, OPTIONS ● GET, HEAD, OPTIONS, PUT, POST, PATCH, DELETE
Cached HTTP Methods	GET, HEAD (Cached by default) ☐ OPTIONS
Forward Headers	All ⌄
Object Caching	⦿ Use Origin Cache Headers ○ Customize
Minimum TTL	0
Forward Cookies	All ⌄
Forward Query Strings	○ Yes ● No (Improves Caching)
Smooth Streaming	○ Yes ● No
Restrict Viewer Access (Use Signed URLs)	○ Yes ● No

Figure 8-7. *Origin behavior settings*

Repeat this process for all of the routes. When you've finished, remember that the order of origins is important. Rearrange them so that the session-based behaviors are at the top, as in Figure 8-8.

Precedence	Path Pattern	Origin	Viewer Protocol Policy	Forwarded Query Strings
1	/users/login	ELB-photoalbums-elb-1925984452	HTTPS Only	No
2	/users/register	ELB-photoalbums-elb-1925984452	HTTPS Only	No
3	/users/logout	ELB-photoalbums-elb-1925984452	HTTPS Only	No
4	/*/upload	ELB-photoalbums-elb-1925984452	HTTPS Only	No
5	/*/delete	ELB-photoalbums-elb-1925984452	HTTPS Only	No
6	/users/*	ELB-photoalbums-elb-1925984452	HTTP and HTTPS	No
7	/albums/*	ELB-photoalbums-elb-1925984452	HTTP and HTTPS	No
8	/photos/search	ELB-photoalbums-elb-1925984452	HTTP and HTTPS	Yes
9	/photos/*	ELB-photoalbums-elb-1925984452	HTTP and HTTPS	No
10	/uploads/*	S3-photoalbums-cdn	HTTP and HTTPS	No
11	Default (*)	ELB-photoalbums-elb-1925984452	HTTP and HTTPS	No

Figure 8-8. *Beahviors ordered*

As usual, the changes we've made in CloudFront will take a few minutes to propagate. In the meantime, we must change an even more obscure setting in CloudFront. When we added our ELB as an origin for this CloudFront distribution, we allowed CloudFront to communicate with the ELB over HTTP only. This means that HTTPS requests to CloudFront will become HTTP requests to the ELB. We want to be certain that traffic from our CloudFront edge locations around the world to the US East data center is encrypted, so this traffic should be over HTTPS.

Select the **Origins** tab, where you will see this issue in the *Origin Protocol Policy* column (see Figure 8-9).

	General	Origins	Behaviors	Error Pages	Restrictions	Invalidations	

	Create Origin	Edit	Delete						

	Origin Domain Name and Path	Origin ID	Origin Type	Origin Access Identity	Origin Protocol Policy	HTTPS Port	HTTP Port
☐	photoalbums-cdn.s3.amazonaws.com	S3-photoalbums-cdn	S3 Origin	origin-access-identity/cloudfront/E3IN5GOSBQTWNF	-	-	-
☐	photoalbums-elb-1925984452.us-east-1.elb.amazonaws.com	ELB-photoalbums-elb-1925984452	Custom Origin	-	HTTP Only	443	80

Figure 8-9. *CloudFront Origins*

Select your ELB and click **Edit**. In the Origin Settings view, change *Origin Protocol Policy* from HTTP Only to **Match Viewer**, then click **Yes, Edit**. From now on, HTTP requests to CloudFront will be forwarded to the ELB over HTTP, and HTTPS requests will likewise be forwarded via HTTPS. These changes will also take a few minutes to propagate.

Enabling HTTPS in ELB

Remember that CloudFront Edge Locations are scattered around the globe, and data has to travel from CloudFront to the ELB in a different region. In order to properly secure our traffic, we must make sure that HTTPS requests that reach CloudFront can be securely forwarded to the ELB. This means that our SSL certificate must also be installed on the ELB, and it needs to be configured to accept requests over HTTPS.

As you just saw, HTTPS requests are listened for on port 443. CloudFront is now forwarding the requests to the ELB on this port. When CloudFront attempts to reach the origin (the ELB) on port 443, it finds a closed port. CloudFront believes it cannot reach the origin at all.

Listening for HTTPS Connections

We have to open the port on our ELB if the request is going to go through. In AWS parlance, our ELB has to have a listener added to port 443. By default, the ELB is configured to listen on port 80 for unencrypted HTTP requests only.

Navigate to EC2 and select **Load Balancers** from the left-hand navigation. With your ELB instance selected, open the **Listeners** tab. You'll see that only port 80 is open. Click **Edit** to add HTTPS to your ELB's listeners. A modal window will appear in which you can configure your listeners.

Add a *Load Balancer Protocol* for **HTTPS (Secure HTTP)** using **Load Balancer Port 443**. The *Instance Protocol* should be **HTTP** and the *Instance Port* should be **80**. In the *SSL Certificate* column, click **Change**. Select **Choose an existing certificate** and choose your certificate. Figure 8-10 shows the completed settings.

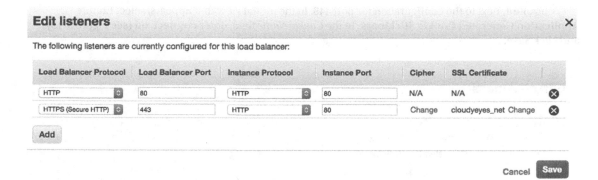

Figure 8-10. *Adding an HTTPS ELB listener*

Click **Save** to return to the previous view. Click **Save**, and you will see confirmation that the port has been opened, as in Figure 8-11.

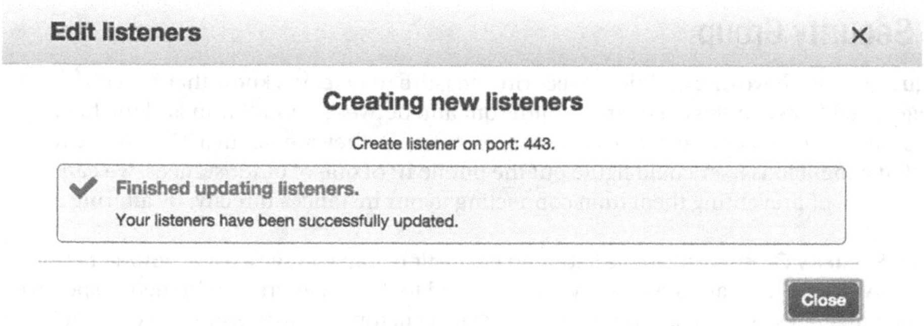

Edit listeners   ×

Creating new listeners

Create listener on port: 443.

✓ **Finished updating listeners.**
   Your listeners have been successfully updated.

Close

Figure 8-11. *Confirmation that HTTPS listener was created*

Enabling Cookie Stickiness

There's *one more* setting that we have to change on the ELB. We know that our application is going to start using session-based cookies. But with our application running on several instances, there's no guarantee that once a user logs in, he or she will be directed to the same instance twice. This will effectively prevent sessions from being usable at all. Fortunately, there's an ELB feature called *Stickiness* that allows us to bind a user's session to a specific instance and forward the relevant cookie. This means that once a user has started a session on an instance, all future requests in that session will be tied to that instance.

Return to the Description tab for your load balancer and locate the *Port Configuration* settings (see Figure 8-12).

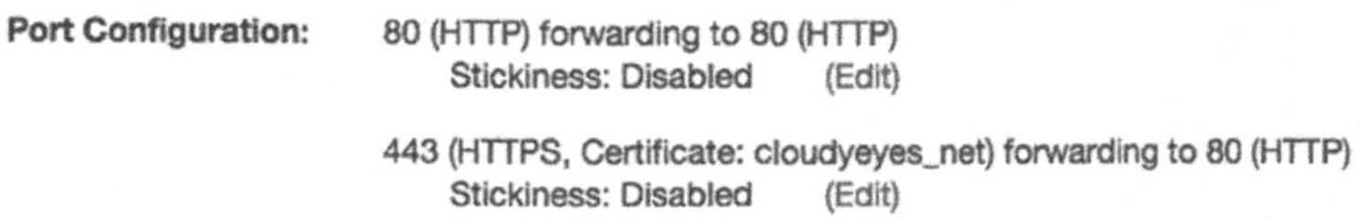

Port Configuration: 80 (HTTP) forwarding to 80 (HTTP)
                                    Stickiness: Disabled   (Edit)

                           443 (HTTPS, Certificate: cloudyeyes_net) forwarding to 80 (HTTP)
                                    Stickiness: Disabled   (Edit)

Figure 8-12. *ELB Port Configuration*

Click **Edit**, next to the configuration for port 443. In the modal view that appears, select **Enable Application Generated Cookie Stickiness**. In the *Cookie Name* field, enter **connect.sid** (see Figure 8-13) and click **Save**.

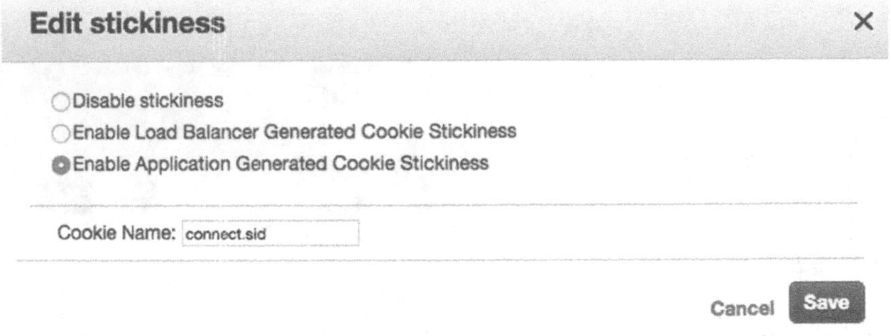

Figure 8-13. Enabling cookie stickiness

Modifying the Security Group

To finish our configuration, we have one additional security measure to take. We know that HTTPS connections are negotiated between the client and CloudFront and between CloudFront and the load balancer. It is still possible to connect directly to the instances, because they are not in a VPC. While it seems improbable that a malicious user could figure out the public IP of one of our instances, we can still take the extra measure of preventing them from connecting to our instances directly, by altering our security group.

In EC2, select the **Security Groups** link in the left-hand navigation. You will see a list of auto-generated security groups for OpsWorks. These are the security rules applied to instances created in their respective OpsWorks layers. To change these settings, you can either assign a custom security group to your stack or alter the auto-generated security group. Though it takes additional effort, we will create our own custom security group.

In the list of security groups, locate *AWS-OpsWorks-nodejsApp*. Open the **Actions** menu above and click **Copy to new**. Name your security group **Photoalbums-nodejs-App** and give it a useful *Description*, such as **Security Group for Photoalbums App, restricting HTTP and HTTPS connections**. You don't need to select a VPC.

Next, you must change the security rules for Inbound HTTP and HTTPS connections. Locate the *HTTP* row and change the *Source* to **Custom IP**. In the *IP* field, enter **amazon-elb/amazon-elb-sg**. Locate *HTTPS* and make the same change. When you're finished (see Figure 8-14), click **Create**.

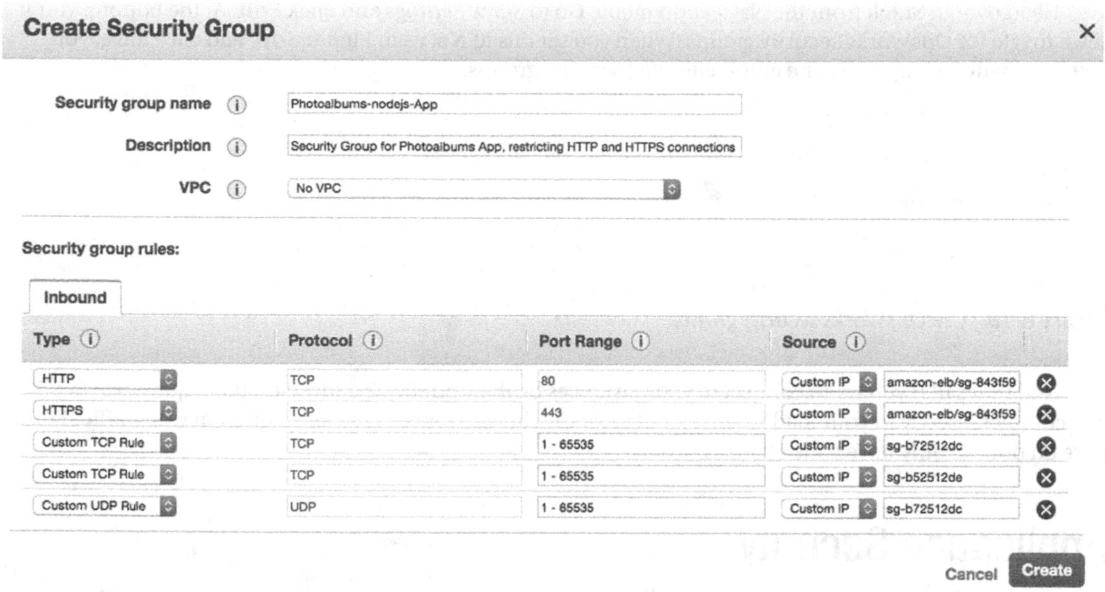

Create Security Group   ✕

Security group name	ⓘ	Photoalbums-nodejs-App
Description	ⓘ	Security Group for Photoalbums App, restricting HTTP and HTTPS connections
VPC	ⓘ	No VPC ◇

Security group rules:

Inbound

Type ⓘ	Protocol ⓘ	Port Range ⓘ	Source ⓘ	
HTTP ◇	TCP	80	Custom IP ◇ amazon-elb/sg-843f59	✕
HTTPS ◇	TCP	443	Custom IP ◇ amazon-elb/sg-843f59	✕
Custom TCP Rule ◇	TCP	1 - 65535	Custom IP ◇ sg-b72512dc	✕
Custom TCP Rule ◇	TCP	1 - 65535	Custom IP ◇ sg-b52512de	✕
Custom UDP Rule ◇	UDP	1 - 65535	Custom IP ◇ sg-b72512dc	✕

Cancel   **Create**

Figure 8-14. *New security group*

Next, we must make our application stack use this new security group. Navigate to OpsWorks and select your application stack. We can't leave our application layer without any security groups, so first, we have to add the custom security group, then remove the default one. Select **Layers** from the Navigation menu and click **Security** next to the application layer. Click the **Edit** button at the top right. Select your custom security group from the drop-down (see Figure 8-15) and click **Save**.

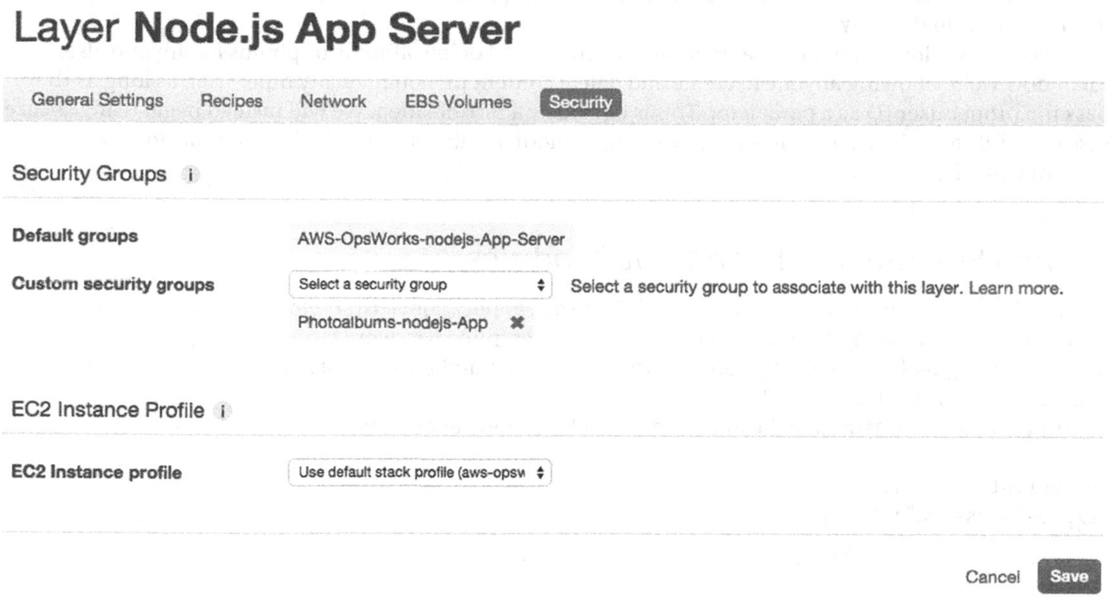

Layer **Node.js App Server**

| General Settings | Recipes | Network | EBS Volumes | Security |

Security Groups ⓘ

Default groups	AWS-OpsWorks-nodejs-App-Server
Custom security groups	Select a security group ⬍ Select a security group to associate with this layer. Learn more.
	Photoalbums-nodejs-App ✖

EC2 Instance Profile ⓘ

| EC2 Instance profile | Use default stack profile (aws-opsw ⬍ |

Cancel   **Save**

Figure 8-15. *Custom security group*

Head over to **Stack** from the Navigation menu. Go to *Stack Settings* and click **Edit**. At the bottom, you'll see a toggle for OpsWorks security groups. When you set this to **No**, as in Figure 8-16, and click **Save**, your instances will no longer use the auto-generated security groups.

Security

Use OpsWorks security   No
groups

Figure 8-16. *Use OpsWorks security groups*

And that's it! If you try to connect to your instances by their public IP addresses, the request will fail. You can connect directly to your load balancer, but the individual instances are closed off from web traffic. From here on out, we only have code changes to make.

Application Security

It's time to build authentication into our application. As you proceed through the following steps, please consider these security techniques as *suggestions*. You may already have your own authentication strategy in mind. By all means, go with your experience. While we will be implementing one of many encryption modules, you should be able to easily swap this one for another. Likewise, you can implement more restrictive or less restrictive security in your application, depending on your needs. The goal here is to demonstrate one technique and then follow the steps to bring our application in line with the changes we made in AWS.

We have two security patterns that we need to implement in our application. First, we must start storing passwords, and they absolutely must be encrypted in our database. Every now and then you hear about a database being leaked with a bunch of passwords stored as plain text for anyone to steal. We don't want to make the news in that way.

Second, we don't want any user to be able to create and delete albums or photos for anyone else. Right now we're allowing anyone to create and delete content on behalf of any other user, as long as they pass the proper user ID as a parameter. This is obviously a terrible idea. We will instead begin using secure sessions and store the user ID in session cookies. Without a valid user ID session, attempts to delete content will be ignored.

Adding Session and Encryption Modules

We're going to have to add two additional modules to our application: *easycrypto* and *express-session*. Easycrypto is one of many libraries for encrypting and decrypting password strings. If you prefer a different library, feel free to use it. Express-session is session middleware built specifically for ExpressJS applications—so, just like it sounds.

In your `package.json`, add the following to the dependencies object:

```
"easycrypto": "0.1.1",
"express-session": "^1.7.6",
```

Make sure you don't have any trailing commas, as your dependencies should look something like the following:

```
{
  ...
  "debug": "~1.0.4",
  "easycrypto": "0.1.1",
  "express-session": "^1.7.6",
  "jade": "~1.5.0"
  }
```

On the command line, navigate to your working directory and type the command: **npm install**. Your dependencies should install automatically, as they have previously.

Adding Password Encryption

Next, we'll add our password encryption/decryption. This code will take place entirely within /lib/model/model-user.js. Open that file and add a variable named encryptionKey to the top. Set the value to any random string you like.

```
var encryptionKey   = '80smoviereferencegoeshere';
```

At the bottom of the file, we will add two private methods for generating a hashed password and for decrypting a hashed password. Add the code in Listing 8-1.

Listing 8-1. Encrypt/Decrypt Hash Password

```
function generatePasswordHash(password){
  var easycrypto - require('easycrypto').getInstance();
  var encrypted = easycrypto.encrypt(password, encryptionKey);
  return encrypted;
}

function decryptPasswordHash(passwordHash) {
  var easycrypto = require('easycrypto').getInstance();
  var decryptedPass = easycrypto.decrypt(passwordHash, encryptionKey);
  return decryptedPass;
}
```

When a user registers, he/she will pass a *password* parameter to our router. We want to take this password, hash it, and store it in the database. When a user logs in later, we will compare the password he/she provides to the password stored in the database. The first thing we have to change in our existing functionality is the password that gets saved to the database. Instead of saving the password parameter directly, we will first invoke generatePasswordHash() on the input. Replace the createUser function with Listing 8-2.

Listing 8-2. createUser

```
function createUser(params, callback){
  var newUser = {
    username: params.username,
    password: generatePasswordHash(params.password),
    email: params.email
  }
  var query = 'INSERT INTO users SET ? ';
  connection.query(query, newUser, function(err, rows, fields) {
      if (err) {
      if(err.errno == 1062){
          var error = new Error("This username has already been taken.");
          callback(error);
      } else {
        callback(err);
      }
    } else {
      callback(null, {message:'Registration successful!'});
    }
  });

}
```

Now, replace loginUser() with Listing 8-3. After you enable this, your users with plain-text passwords will no longer be able to log in.

Listing 8-3. loginUser

```
function loginUser(params, callback){
  connection.query('SELECT username, password, userID FROM users WHERE username=' +
connection.escape(params.username), function(err, rows, fields) {
      if(err){
          callback(err);
      } else if(rows.length > 0){
        var decryptedPass = decryptPasswordHash(rows[0].password);
        if(decryptedPass == params.password){
          var response = {
            username: rows[0].username,
            userID: rows[0].userID
          }
          callback(null, response);
        } else {
          var error = new Error("Invalid login");
          callback(error);
        }
      } else {
        var error = new Error("Invalid login");
        callback(error);
      }
  });
}
```

Using Secure Sessions

This is going to be a little more involved, but it really depends on the goals of your application. If there are entire sections of your app that you want to restrict to authenticated users, it can be a little simpler to implement. In our case, all routes have a mixture of restricted and unrestricted API end points. As such, we will manually secure our application at the individual route level.

We will first configure our application to use the *express-session* middleware. In `server.js`, add the express-session middleware immediately after including express.

```
var express = require('express');
var expressSession = require('express-session');
var path = require('path');
```

Then, ahead of the other `app.use` statements, add the following:

```
app.use(expressSession({secret: 'ssshhhhh'}));
```

Go ahead and replace the value of the secret with your own secret key—`ssshhhhh` is definitely not the best choice. There are a lot more settings you can modify for *express-session*, but we're going to leave them as is. This is all it takes to enable sessions; now, we have to get and set values in the sessions. First, we must set a value identifying users in their session cookies when they log in. For simplicity's sake, we'll use the user ID, though you might consider something such as e-mail or multiple values. Open `/routes/users.js` and locate the `/login` route. In the callback for `model.loginUser()`, set the session's `userID` as in Listing 8-4.

Listing 8-4. `/users/login`

```
router.post('/login', function(req, res) {
  if(req.param('username') && req.param('password') ){
    var params = {
      username: req.param('username').toLowerCase(),
      password: req.param('password')
    };

    model.loginUser(params, function(err, obj){
      if(err){
        res.status(400).send({error: 'Invalid login'});
      } else {
        req.session.userID = obj.userID;
        res.send(obj);
      }
    });
  } else {
    res.status(400).send({error: 'Invalid login'});
  }
});
```

Likewise, the /logout route can be simplified. All it has to do is destroy the current session (see Listing 8-5).

Listing 8-5. /users/logout

```
router.post('/logout', function(req, res) {
  if(req.session){
    req.session.destroy();
  }
  res.send({message: 'User logged out successfully'});
});
```

Now let's make our critical routes require session cookies instead of POST parameters. Open /routes/ photos.js. Locate the /upload route. We will be enclosing all of our functionality in a conditional checking for req.session and req.session.userID. Additionally, we will send req.session.userID to the model, instead of req.param('userID'). Replace your code with that in Listing 8-6.

Listing 8-6. /photos/upload

```
router.post('/upload', function(req, res) {
  if(req.session && req.session.userID){
    if(req.param('albumID') && req.files.photo){
      var params = {
        userID : req.session.userID,
        albumID : req.param('albumID')
      }
      if(req.param('caption')){
        params.caption = req.param('caption');
      }

      fs.exists(req.files.photo.path, function(exists) {
        if(exists) {
          params.filePath = req.files.photo.path;
          var timestamp = Date.now();
          params.newFilename = params.userID + '/' + params.filePath.replace('tmp/', timestamp);
          uploadPhoto(params, function(err, fileObject){
            if(err){
              res.status(400).send({error: 'Invalid photo data'});
            }
            params.url = fileObject.url;
            delete params.filePath;
            delete params.newFilename;
            model.createPhoto(params, function(err, obj){
              if(err){
                res.status(400).send({error: 'Invalid photo data'});
              } else {
                res.send(obj);
              }
            });
          });
```

```
        } else {
          res.status(400).send({error: 'Invalid photo data'});
        }
      });
    } else {
      res.status(400).send({error: 'Invalid photo data'});
    }
  } else {
    res.status(401).send({error: 'You must be logged in to upload photos'});
  }
});
```

We also need to wrap /photos/delete in a session check. Replace it with the code in Listing 8-7.

Listing 8-7. /photos/delete

```
router.post('/delete', function(req, res) {
  if(req.session && req.session.userID){
    if(req.param('id')){
      var params = {
        photoID : req.param('id') ,
        userID : req.session.userID
      }
      model.deletePhoto(params, function(err, obj){
        if(err){
          res.status(400).send({error: 'Photo not found'});
        } else {
          res.send(obj);
        }
      });
    } else {
      res.status(400).send({error: 'Invalid photo ID'});
    }
  } else {
    res.status(401).send({error: 'Unauthorized to create album'});
  }
});
```

We also need to make this change in /routes/albums.js. Open the file and overwrite /upload and /delete with the new functions (see Listing 8-8).

Listing 8-8. /albums routes

```
router.post('/upload', function(req, res) {
  if(req.session && req.session.userID){

    if(req.param('title')){
      var params = {
```

```
          userID : req.session.userID,
          title : req.param('title')
        }
        model.createAlbum(params, function(err, obj){
          if(err){
            res.status(400).send({error: 'Invalid album data'});
          } else {
            res.send(obj);
          }
        });
      } else {
        res.status(400).send({error: 'Invalid album data'});
      }
    } else {
      res.status(401).send({error: 'Unauthorized to create album'});
    }
});

router.post('/delete', function(req, res) {
  if(req.session && req.session.userID){
    if(req.param('albumID')){
      var params = {
        albumID : req.param('albumID') ,
        userID : req.session.userID
      }
      model.deleteAlbum(params, function(err, obj){
        if(err){
          res.status(400).send({error: 'Album not found'});
        } else {
          res.send(obj);
        }
      });
    } else {
      res.status(400).send({error: 'Invalid album ID'});
    }
  } else {
    res.status(401).send({error: 'Unauthorized to create album'});
  }
});
```

We must also make some changes to our models. Previously, any user could delete anyone's albums or photos. Chaos would ensue! We have to make sure that users are only deleting content they own.

In /lib/models/model-photos.js, replace the deletePhotobyID() method with the Listing 8-9.

Listing 8-9. Photos deletePhotoByID Method

```
function deletePhotoByID(params, callback){
  var query = 'UPDATE photos SET published=0 WHERE photoID=' + connection.escape
(params.photoID)  + ' AND userID=' + params.userID;
  connection.query(query, function(err, rows, fields){
    if(rows.length > 0){
      callback(null, rows);
    } else {
      if(rows.changedRows > 0){
        callback(null, {message: 'Photo deleted successfully'});
      } else {
        var deleteError = new Error('Unable to delete photo');
        callback(deleteError);
      }
    }
  });
}
```

You'll notice that the SQL query changed to restrict users to updating their own content. Additionally, there's a new error manually constructed and returned to the callback. If an UPDATE query does not change any rows, the rows object in the handler will have a property changedRows that equals 0. While this isn't an error in itself, our application should treat it as one. It means the user tried to delete a photo that either doesn't exist or doesn't belong to him/her.

We need to apply the same logic to albums as well. Open /lib/models/model-albums.js and replace the deleteAlbum() method with Listing 8-10.

Listing 8-10. Albums deleteAlbum Method

```
function deleteAlbum(params, callback){
  var query = 'UPDATE albums SET published=0 WHERE albumID=' + connection.escape
(params.albumID) + ' AND userID=' + params.userID;
  connection.query(query, function(err, rows, fields){
    if(err){
      callback(err);
    } else {
      if(rows.changedRows > 0){
        callback(null, {message: 'Album deleted successfully'});
      } else {
        var deleteError = new Error('Unable to delete album');
        callback(deleteError);
      }
    }
  });
}
```

That's all the code changes we have to make. Commit the changes to your code repository. Deploy to your OpsWorks instances and wait for the process to complete. When it's done, you can start testing. Your previous users will now be invalid. The application will attempt to decrypt them, resulting in a mismatch. The easiest way to test is to register a new user, log in, and then create an album. You should be able to successfully achieve these actions by making HTTPS POST requests to the domain, or to the load balancer itself. Attempts to log in to the domain over HTTP will be declined.

Conclusion

This wraps up the final lesson! We moved pretty quickly through a variety of tasks. If you look back at where we were in Chapter 1, you may be impressed with yourself.

In creating these lessons, there was a constant debate over where to draw the line, especially with the source code. Right now, we have an application that has a lot of major hallmarks of an enterprise application. It's secure, redundant, scalable, and uses powerful caching and notifications. But building a truly commercially viable web application is no simple task, and ours still has a lot of shortcomings. Just looking at users, we're missing things such as password resets, user search, and so forth. The goal wasn't so much to teach you how to write an application as much as to teach you to write an application *for AWS*. The hope is that from here, you feel confident in your ability to extrapolate on these ideas in this or any other software you write.

Another major challenge is keeping current with AWS (much less Express!). Amazon routinely unveils new features. They occasionally acquire a startup and six months later unveil their technology rolled into the AWS platform. Staying on top of new features in AWS requires constant vigilance, but it's also exciting. In fact, some features changed while this book was being written, requiring some revision.

You've seen the power of the tools we have and how quickly we built something that wouldn't have been possible for the average developer ten years ago. Indeed, the role of web developer has changed dramatically in a short time, and AWS has played no small part in these changes. If this book gives you, the reader, the confidence to grow with these changes, then you've picked up the most important lesson in the book.

Index

■ D

Get the eBook for only $10!

Now you can take the weightless companion with you anywhere, anytime. Your purchase of this book entitles you to 3 electronic versions for only $10.

This Apress title will prove so indispensible that you'll want to carry it with you everywhere, which is why we are offering the eBook in 3 formats for only $10 if you have already purchased the print book.

Convenient and fully searchable, the PDF version enables you to easily find and copy code—or perform examples by quickly toggling between instructions and applications. The MOBI format is ideal for your Kindle, while the ePUB can be utilized on a variety of mobile devices.

Go to www.apress.com/promo/tendollars to purchase your companion eBook.